Level 2

MENTORING GUIDEBOOK

Exploring Teaching Strategies

Edited by Kay Burke

SkyLight
Professional
Development

Mentoring Guidebook Level 2: Exploring Teaching Strategies

Published by SkyLight Professional Development
2626 S. Clearbrook Dr., Arlington Heights, IL 60005
800-348-4474 or 847-290-6600
Fax 847-290-6609
info@skylightedu.com
http://www.skylightedu.com

President: Carol Luitjens
Executive Vice President, Product Development: John Nolan
Executive Editor: Chris Jaeggi
Editor: Anne Kaske
Editorial Assistant: Carrie Straka
Cover Design: Herman Adler Design
Designer: Bruce Leckie
Formatter: Donna Ramirez
Production Supervisor: Bob Crump

LCCCN 2002103543
ISBN 1-57517-607-6

3078-V
ZYXWVUTSRQPONMLKJIHGFEDCBA
09 08 07 06 05 04 03 02   15 14 13 12 11 10 9 8 7 6 5 4 3 2 1

There are
one-story intellects,
   two-story intellects, and
     three-story intellects with skylights.

All fact collectors, who have no aim beyond their facts, are

           one-story minds.

         Two-story minds
     compare, reason, generalize,
      using the labors of the fact collectors
         as well as their own.

             Three-story minds
idealize, imagine, predict—their best illumination comes from above,

               through the **skylight**.

—Oliver Wendell Holmes

SkyLight
Professional
Development

Dedication

In memory of Louise Adams Moss
Her ability to make everyone she met feel special
continues to inspire her students, family, and friends.

Contents

Acknowledgments

I have always depended on the kindness of strangers.
                                            —Blanche Dubois in
                                        A Streetcar Named Desire

Near the end of Tennessee Williams' classic drama, *A Streetcar Named Desire,* the tragic heroine Blanche Dubois comments that all her life she has depended upon the kindness of strangers. In some ways Blanche's sentiments parallel those of beginning teachers. They enter a new profession, report to a new school, greet new colleagues, and meet their new students. Some will be fortunate enough to get a mentor to guide them; others will have to depend upon the "kindness" of strangers to help them survive the challenges of the first year of teaching.

Fortunately, I have been able to rely on the kindness and support of my colleagues and family members throughout the planning, writing, and editing of *Mentoring Guidebook Level 2: Exploring Teaching Strategies.* This second book in the SkyLight mentoring series has truly been a group effort beginning with the contributions of my friends and co-authors. I would like to thank Robin Fogarty, Jim Bellanca, Jan Skowron, Judy Stoehr, Julie Sausen, and Barry Sweeny for allowing me to compile their practical strategies and thoughtful insights for effective teaching from their books into this guidebook.

I would also like to thank the core members of the SkyLight mentoring task force whose mission is to develop and present a quality mentoring program that integrates the best practices in teaching and learning through books, training manuals, videos, and live and online delivery systems. Julie Sausen, Susan Gray,

Carol Luitjens, Gail Moran, Vikki Myers, and John Nolan have all committed themselves to structuring a quality mentoring program. The team has worked tirelessly to create the SkyLight Mentoring Program to meet the needs of novice teachers, mentors, and administrators throughout the country.

The publishing team of Donna Ramirez, Heidi Ray, Bruce Leckie, Carrie Straka, and Bob Crump, under the thoughtful lead of Chris Jaeggi and the expert editing and infinite patience of Anne Kaske, continue to amaze me. The professionalism and skill of my friend and colleague, Mary Jane Bloethner, and the support of my husband Frank, mother Lois, and the Brown and Burke relatives help me appreciate the importance of family and friends.

Novice teachers may walk through the school doors alone and apprehensive, but, hopefully, they will soon experience the spirit of collaboration and sense of confidence that will support them and nurture them throughout their successful teaching careers.

—KAY BURKE
May, 2002

Introduction

Educators have known or suspected all along—and research and experience have proven them to be right—that support of new teachers in the form of mentoring by seasoned peers not only contributes to the induction and retention of novices into the profession, but also provides a positive professional experience for the veteran teachers who do the mentoring.

—Portner, 2001

ne of the goals of any mentoring program is to enable both novice teachers and veteran teachers to experience a positive professional experience. If the educational climate promotes a culture of collaboration, commitment to students, and a belief in lifelong learning, both mentors and protégés grow professionally. *Mentoring Guidebook Level 1: Starting the Journey,* the first volume in SkyLight's mentoring series, introduces the basic components necessary for a positive and professional educational climate. I selected excerpts from books written by leading educational experts that define the characteristics of a mentoring program and the attributes of effective mentors and protégés. The selections describe how mentors use appropriate communication skills to help gain the trust of novice teachers in order to establish a solid mentoring relationship. One selection demonstrates tools for developing lesson plan designs and unit plans correlated to curriculum goals and learning standards that address the students' multiple intelligences. *Starting the Journey* also reviews strategies to help teachers create a positive classroom environment by setting expectations, rules, and consequences in the first few days of school so that students accept responsibility not only for their own learning, but also for their own behavior. Mentors and protégés can teach students how to develop and practice social skills related to communication, team building, and conflict resolution in order to interact appropriately with all the members of their classroom community. The final selection reviews a variety of problem-solving strategies all teachers can implement in order to deal with behavior problems that could disrupt the classroom and detract from the learning process. In summary, *Mentoring Guidebook Level 1: Starting the Journey,* outlines the basic tools mentors and protégés need to develop a successful mentoring relationship and to develop practical strategies new teachers need to organize their classrooms and plan their instruction.

This second volume of SkyLight's mentoring series, *Mentoring Guidebook Level 2: Exploring Teaching Strategies,* uses the foundation of a positive mentoring relationship based on trust to help improve beginning teachers' teaching skills and to help them grow as professionals. In order to support and guide new teachers, mentors need not only to know the best practices in teaching and learning, but also to be able to model them for their protégés. *Mentoring Guidebook Level 2: Exploring Teaching Strategies* expands the teaching strategies introduced in *Starting the Journey* and presents additional instructional strategies teachers can explore to meet the diverse needs of their students. The selections review a repertoire of instructional methodologies to implement integrated and cooperative learning, develop authentic assessment techniques, and establish a powerful learning community within the classroom. The final section defines the term *reflective practitioner* and provides opportunities for novice teachers to grow professionally by creating a philosophy of teaching and using journals to reflect on their own growth and development. Since many first-year teachers are required to develop a professional growth plan or a portfolio, mentors can help facilitate the process by taking the time to discuss and analyze progress toward meeting goals.

If the educational climate promotes a culture of collaboration, commitment to students, and a belief in lifelong learning, both mentors, and protégés grow professionally.

Section I—Designing Learning Strategies

Studies in cognitive psychology, strategic instruction, and teaching for transfer offer a new definition of how students learn. Lipton and Wellman (1998) explain how the most significant change has been the shift from the focus on the teacher-centered classroom to the learner-focused classroom. "This is not an easy shift. Like the learning process itself, this shift can be uncomfortable and fraught with uncertainty. The comfort of presenting the content and covering the material needs to be expanded so that the learners experience meaningful interactions working with concepts, skills, and ideas" (3). Mentors can help beginning teachers motivate students by discussing and modeling explicit instructional strategies that engage the students in discovering meaning for themselves. Effective teachers may use the direct instruction method to introduce concepts or content, but they also use additional teaching strategies to encourage the students to take ownership of their own learning.

Some teachers believe they "vary" their teaching whenever they introduce new subject matter. Although the subject matter may change, the instructional strategies of direct instruction, silent reading, and answering the questions at the end of the chapter remain the same. Effective teachers utilize pedagogical techniques that include learning that is cooperative, inquiry-based, brain-compatible, project-based, and performance-based in order to challenge students and escape the mindset of "one-size-fits-all" teaching. "Most teachers do not demonstrate this range, not because they don't want to, but because they have limited images of good teaching. The ways in which they were taught and the isolation in which they work have limited their range" (Wasley 1999, 7). Mentors, however, can help new teachers expand the repertoire of techniques learned during their preservice preparation and student teaching experience by supplementing their "tool box" through the modeling of a variety of instructional strategies. Often, the mentor invites the new teacher into his or her classroom to observe the mentor's use of these techniques. The conversations that follow help novices understand how an explicit instructional strategy works and how it can be modified to adapt to the needs of different students.

Section II—Assessing Student Work

In addition to helping beginning teachers expand their range of instructional techniques, mentors can also share and model ways to assess and evaluate students. With the increased emphasis on accountability, beginning teachers need practice in developing effective teacher-made tests that measure student understanding of important concepts. Too often novice teachers rely on commercially made tests that do not always meet the needs of their students. Also, new teachers may be overwhelmed by the idea of having students keep portfolios of their work, even though many districts are now requiring them. Mentors, therefore, can share their secrets and organizational tips for making a portfolio system manageable. Instruction is, of course, very important, but effective assessments provide concrete evidence that the students are learning. Moreover, assessments show new teachers how they need to change their instruction in order to make sure all students are meeting the standards and their curriculum goals.

Section III—Establishing Learning Communities

Teaching and learning extend beyond the classroom. Teachers need to work with a learning community that combines the roles of parents, paraprofessionals, community members, and other school personnel with whom teachers interact on a regular basis. Communicating with parents and collaborating with other educational professionals requires a level of interpersonal skills that may not seem important to a new teacher—until he or she makes a mistake that causes problems. An effective mentor guides the protégé through the critical and precarious steps of developing a collaborative relationship with all the stakeholders in each child's education. Dealing with administrators, counselors, substitutes, paraprofessionals, bus drivers, cafeteria staff, and others requires expert communication skills and finesse. The mentors can guide the new teachers in establishing a harmonious working relationship with members of the classroom, school, and community.

Section IV—Reflecting on Professional Growth

Along the mentoring journey, new teachers gradually begin to realize the importance of their own professional growth. Once new teachers move beyond the survival mode of only thinking about how *they* are doing, they begin to focus more on how the *whole class* is doing and, in turn, how they are changing as teachers to meet their students' needs. Mentors nurture their protégés' quests for professional growth by modeling their own search for better answers and by learning from their mistakes and building on their successes. Rowley (1999) describes a good mentor as a model of a continuous learner who is open to learning from colleagues, including beginning teachers, and willing to grow as a professional. "[Mentors] lead and attend workshops. They teach and enroll in graduate classes. They develop and experiment with new practices. They write and read articles in professional journals. Most important, they share new knowledge and perplexing questions with their beginning teachers in a collegial manner" (22).

The professional growth process relates to portfolios, growth plans, data gathering, and reflections. The new teachers become reflective practitioners who share many "metacognitive moments" with their mentors as they discuss their instructional and assessment strategies and the impact they have on their students' learning. Brookfield (1995) says, "When we take critical reflection seriously, we also begin to think differently about professional development" (42). Induction and mentoring are the first phases many beginning teachers go through in their quest to become excellent teachers. As Sweeny (2001) states, "Whether a beginner learns to teach within or without an induction and mentoring program, it is known that the habits formed during the induction years become the teacher's disposition toward professional practice throughout his or her career" (124). Mentors who communicate their own hope and optimism to their protégés help them face the challenges of each day. Good mentors "demonstrate their hope and optimism for the future by their willingness to help a new teacher discover the same joys and satisfaction that they have found in their own career" (Rowley 1999, 22).

Conclusion

The selections in this volume provide mentors and their protégés ideas for discussion, experiences to share, and strategies to implement and reflect upon during informal conversations and formal conferences. Beginning teachers and veteran teachers are always exploring new ways to engage their students in meaningful learning experiences. The challenge is to find the most effective instructional strategies that meet the needs of the novice teacher and, more importantly, meet the needs of the students he or she teaches. Successful teachers have to move beyond teaching content only and experiment with pedagogical tools that help students process information and apply skills in performances that provide evidence of transfer. As Costa (2001) states, "As we enter an era in which knowledge doubles in less than five years—the projection is that by the year 2020 it will double in every 73 days—it is no longer feasible to anticipate an individual's future information requirements" (xv).

Many of the protégés entering the profession today may still be teaching in 2020. The content they teach may change or be long forgotten. Many new instructional strategies and technological innovations will be introduced. The goal of mentors should be to help all teachers develop the flexibility to change their instruction and become lifelong learners in the quest to motivate students to learn and to achieve results. As Brookfield (1995) states, "We never have the luxury of regarding ourselves as fully finished critical products who have reached the zenith of reflective evaluation. We see our ideas and practices as needing constant investigation" (42). Mentors who share the gift of instructional strategies with their protégés empower them to become independent problem solvers who can vary their teaching and adjust their curriculum to meet the needs of their students—not only during their first year of teaching but for a *lifetime* of teaching!

The challenge is to find the most effective instructional strategies that meet the needs of the novice teacher and, more importantly, meet the needs of the students he or she teaches.

REFERENCES

Brookfield, S. D. 1995. *Becoming a critically reflective teacher.* San Francisco, CA: Jossey-Bass Publishers.

Costa, A. L. 2002. Introduction: The vision. In *Developing minds: A resource book for teaching thinking,* 3rd Ed. Edited by Arthur L. Costa. Alexandria, VA: Association for Supervision and Curriculum Development.

Lipton, L., and B. Wellman. 1999. *Pathways to understanding: Pattern and practices in the learning-focused classroom,* 2nd ed. Guilford, VT: Pathways Publishing.

Portner, H. 2001. *Training mentors is not enough: Everything else schools and districts need to do.* Thousand Oaks, CA: Corwin Press, Inc.

Rowley, J. B. 1999. The good mentor. *Educational Leadership* 56(8): 20–22.

Sweeny, B. W. 2001. *Leading the teacher induction and mentoring program.* Arlington Heights, IL: SkyLight Training and Publishing.

Wasley, P. 1999. Teaching worth celebrating. *Educational Leadership* 56(8): 7–13.

Level 2

MENTORING GUIDEBOOK

SECTION I

Designing Learning Experiences

Method is not always crucial . . . what is crucial is that teachers develop a deep knowledge about the subjects that they love because they'll then be eager to share what they've learned. And, in that eagerness, teachers will be inspired to acquire the instructional approaches that best help students learn.

—Hilliard as cited in Checkley and Kelly 1999

ven though a mentor might be described as a sage or guru who knows all the answers and imparts knowledge to the beginning teacher, the mentor's ultimate goal should be to empower the novice to become an independent problem solver who feels confident in the classroom. A beginning teacher develops the "capacity and confidence to make his or her own informed decisions, enrich his or her own knowledge, and sharpen his or her own abilities regarding teaching and learning" (Portner 1998, 7). If mentors are successful, their protégés will acquire the necessary skills and self-confidence to make hundreds of decisions each day related to their instruction and their students' learning.

In this section, ***Designing Learning Experiences***, educational experts offer ideas about creating a brain-compatible classroom, designing integrated lesson plans, developing an integrated thematic unit, and forming cooperative groups to foster collaborative learning.

In Selection 1, **Defining Brain-Compatible Classrooms**, Fogarty describes numerous innovations that fit with the brain research and are supported by educationally sound pedagogy. She demonstrates how Caine and Caine's (1991, 1993) principles of the brain and learning make the case for best practices in the K–college classroom. Best practices include activating prior knowledge, using themes to create patterns in an integrated curriculum, allowing students more time to reflect and process what they learn, using performance tasks to develop problem solving, and implementing a multiple intelligences approach to motivate all students to learn. Fogarty draws on current research to help protégés set the climate *for* thinking, teach the skills *of* thinking, structure the interaction *with* thinking, and help students think *about* their thinking. As Pelletier (2000) states: "Lesson plans work only when appropriate strategies and delivery techniques are used. Some student teachers have outstanding plans and good intentions but lack the ability to select a method that will enhance the plan and create an opportunity for student learning" (95). The same could be said about beginning teachers.

Writing a good lesson plan is essential, but what looks good on paper may not always translate into an effective lesson. In *Mentoring Guidebook Level 1: Starting the Journey*, Skowron explained how to develop a basic lesson plan model. She also provided samples and templates of a basic lesson plan correlated to curriculum goals and standards. In this volume (Selection 2, **Integrated Instructional Design**), Skowron shares a model for designing an integrated lesson. She believes that it is far more valuable for students to understand the relationships and connections among different content areas than it is for them to know isolated bits and pieces of information from one content area. Citing Caine and Caine's (1991) theory that the brain searches for patterns and connections to provide a more lasting and deeper meaning, she offers a template to design integrated instruction. Her lesson design plan integrates content, learning standards, instructional strategies, and assessments to help students achieve a deeper understanding of key concepts or big ideas. An integrated approach to learning provides continuity and order for students. Mentors can share their own integrated lesson ideas with their protégés and share Skowron's templates for new teachers to use as a framework to design an integrated lesson.

One of the most common forms of curriculum integration is the thematic learning unit. Fogarty and Stoehr (1995) believe a thematic learning unit extends the lesson design by using a theme as a *visible organizer* that helps teachers coordinate curricular content and ignite students' learning. Fogarty and Stoehr focus on themes as *organizing centers* and they provide examples of topics, concepts, events, projects, novels, films, and songs that can serve as umbrellas for curriculum and instruction. "As students immerse themselves in a thematic unit, they realize how all of the activities connect under the umbrella of the theme. Themes as catalysts have kid appeal and are relevant, purposeful, meaningful, holistic, and contextual" (Fogarty and Stoehr 1995, 87).

In Selection 3, **Themes**, Fogarty and Stoehr help teachers move beyond the single integrated lesson and develop an integrated thematic unit. The mentor can guide the novice teacher to select rich themes that lead to deeper understanding of important concepts. The theme must be worth the time spent on studying it; moreover, it must be structured to ensure the students are learning targeted curriculum goals and standards within the context of the thematic framework.

In Selection 4, **The Blueprints Approach to Cooperative Groups**, Bellanca and Fogarty introduce cooperative learning as a powerful instructional strategy. "Cooperative learning . . . uses cooperative groups as a tool for creating a more cooperative classroom in which student achievement, self-esteem, responsibility, high-level thinking, and favorable attitudes toward school increase dramatically" (Bellanca and Fogarty 2002). Mentors can help protégés understand the structure of cooperative learning by reviewing the specific strategies Bellanca and Fogarty provide, such as jigsaws, KWL, think-pair-share, business cards, and Mrs. Potter's questions. Bellanca and Fogarty also review individual, competitive, and cooperative lessons so mentors and their protégés can determine how to structure lessons and when to use cooperative learning to improve student learning.

In this section, *Designing Learning Experiences*, experts provide mentors and protégés with strategies for designing brain-compatible learning experiences through integrated lessons, thematic units, and cooperative learning experiences. Portner (1998) states that "The beginning teacher is responsible for providing the structure in which learning occurs. A consistent research finding is that when teachers appropriately structure instructional information, student achievement is increased" (90).

As Brookfield (1995) states, "One of the hardest things teachers have to learn is that the sincerity of their intentions does not guarantee the purity of their practice" (1). In the never-ending challenge of motivating students to learn, the strategies provided in this section serve as a scaffold to support new teachers.

Hopefully, the mentors can guide new teachers as they design meaningful learning experiences, decide how to deliver content effectively, and determine how students will be able to understand important concepts more clearly.

REFERENCES

Bellanca, J., and R. Fogarty. 2002. *Blueprints for achievement in the cooperative classroom,* 3rd ed. Arlington Heights, IL: SkyLight Training and Publishing.

Brookfield, S. D. 1995. *Becoming a critically reflective teacher.* San Francisco, CA: Jossey-Bass Publishers.

Caine, R. N., and G. Caine. 1991. *Making connections: Teaching and the human brain.* New York: Innovative Learning Publications/ Addison Wesley Publications.

———. 1993. *Making connections: Teaching and the human brain,* 2nd ed. New York: Innovative Learning Publications/Addison-Wesley Publications.

Checkley, K., and L. Kelly. 1999. Toward better teacher education: A conversation with Asa Hilliard. *Educational Leadership* 56(8):58.

Fogarty R., and J. Stoehr. 1995. *Integrating curricula with multiple intelligences: Teams, themes and threads.* Arlington Heights, IL: SkyLight Training and Publishing.

Pelletier, C. M. 2000. *A handbook of techniques and strategies for coaching student teachers.* Needham Heights, MA: Allyn & Bacon

Portner, H. 1998. *Mentoring new teachers.* Thousand Oaks, CA: Corwin Press, Inc. A Sage Publications Company.

Fogarty reviews Caine and Caine's twelve principles about the brain and shows how these principles make the case for best practices in the K–college classroom. She shares interactive strategies to help new teachers deliver content to motivate students to succeed.

Defining Brain-Compatible Classrooms

by **Robin Fogarty**

Implications for Schooling

Steeped in the knowledge of the brain and the workings of the brain, Caine and Caine (1991, 1993) have synthesized their information into a set of twelve principles about the brain. An overarching four-corner framework (Fogarty and Bellanca 1993) and Caine and Caine's twelve principles provide the basis that guide educators' work with children in the brain-compatible classroom.

Principles About the Brain

Caine and Caine's principles, within the four-corner framework, provide an understanding of how the numerous educational innovations fit with brain research and sound pedagogy. The twelve principles are (1) the brain is a parallel processor, (2) learning engages the entire physiology, (3) the search for meaning is innate, (4) the search for meaning occurs through patterning, (5) emotions are critical to patterning, (6) the brain processes parts and wholes simultane-ously, (7) learning involves both focused attention and periph-eral perception, (8) learning always involves conscious and unconscious processes, (9) the brain has a spatial memory sys-tem and a set of systems for rote learning, (10) understanding and remembering occur best when facts and skills are embed-ded in natural, spatial memory, (11) learning is enhanced by challenge and inhibited by threat, and (12) each brain is unique (Figure 1.1).

The Four-Corner Framework

The origin of the four-corner framework is found in an earlier publication, *Patterns for Thinking, Patterns for Transfer* (Fogarty and Bellanca 1993). Based on an editorial by Brandt that appeared in an issue of *Educational Leadership* in the early 1980s, the idea of teaching *for, of,* and *about* thinking emerged. Fogarty and Bellanca (1993) thought a fourth element was essential and added the idea of teaching *with* thinking. Thus, the four-corner framework of teaching *for, of, with,* and *about* thinking evolved (see Figure 1.2). These four elements are held to be essential to the thoughtful classroom, to the classroom that requires rigor and vigor in thinking, to the classroom that values cognitive and cooperative structures for increasing stu-dent achievement and fostering high self-esteem, and to the standards-based classroom that honors the teaching/learning process.

Four-Corner Framework

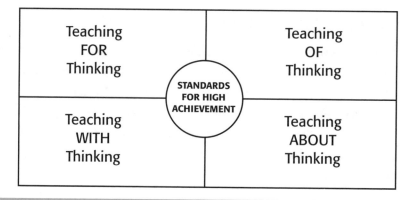

Figure 1.2

GUIDEBOOK

Principles About the Brain*

Principles of Brain and Learning	Making the Case for Best Practices in the K–College Classroom
1. The brain is a parallel processor.	Case for multimodal instruction . . .
2. Learning engages the entire physiology.	Case for nutrition, exercise, and relaxation . . .
3. The search for meaning is innate.	Case for activating prior knowledge . . .
4. The search for meaning occurs through patterning.	Case for themes and threads to create patterns in an integrated curriculum . .
5. Emotions are critical to patterning.	Case for emotional intelligence . . .
6. The brain processes parts and wholes simultaneously.	Case for skill/drill and relevant application . . .
7. Learning involves both focused attention and peripheral perception.	Case for enriched environments and time to engage in the environments . . .
8. Learning always involves conscious and unconscious processing.	Case for more reflective processing and time to think things over . . .
9. The brain has a spatial memory system and a system for rote memory.	Case for both experiential and rote kinds of learning . . .
10. Understanding and remembering occur best when facts and skills are embedded in natural, spatial memory.	Case for constructivist approach in hands-on learning environment . . .
11. Learning is enhanced by challenge and inhibited by threat.	Case for high-level, complex performance tasks . . .
12. Each brain is unique.	Case for multiple intelligences approach . . .

*Based on Caine and Caine's (1991, 1993) twelve principles.

Figure 1.1

SkyLight Professional Development

Section I: Designing Learning Experiences | 9

Defining Brain-Compatible Classrooms

The Framework of the Brain-Compatible Classroom

The four-corner framework of the brain-compatible classroom represents the many instructional innovations that comprise current understandings of pedagogy and best practice. In addition, the framework design is developed with a focus on teaching behavior. The teachers in a brain-compatible classroom set the climate *for* thinking, teach the skills and concepts *of* thinking, structure the interaction *with* thinking, and think *about* thinking (see Figure 1.3). (Please note: Figures 1.3, 1.4, 1.5, 1.6, 1.7, and 1.8 appear at the end of this discussion of the four-corner framework.)

To further understand how these four elements are critical to the learner-centered classroom and to clarify the implications for the teaching/learning process, a more thorough description of each element follows. In addition, the research base is stated (see Figure 1.4), as well as the names of the leading voices in the literature on brain research and learning theory (see Figure 1.5). The research is then bridged to the twelve brain-based principles (see Figure 1.6), enumerated by Caine and Caine (1991, 1993), in an attempt to "summarize the accumulated insights . . . [of the human brain] in a form that is of practical benefit to educators . . ." (p. 87). The principles also provide guidelines for programs and methodologies that are delineated as implications for learning (see Figure 1.7) and teaching (see Figure 1.8).

Teaching FOR Thinking: Setting the Climate

Teaching for thinking is about setting the climate for thinking (see Figure 1.3). It means creating a learning environment that offers a safe and caring place for all learners, regardless of race, color, creed, age, aptitude, or abilities, to go about the business of learning. In setting a safe climate for thinking, risk taking is the norm and learners understand that to learn is to make mistakes as well as experience successes. The ideal learning environment presents a rich and stimulating setting for learners to explore, investigate, and inquire.

 SkyLight Professional Development

GUIDEBOOK

Research Base—Physiology, Emotions, Environment

Research on brain physiology (MacLean 1969, 1978; Ornstein and Sobel 1987) and on the actual development of neural networks provides empirical evidence related to setting the climate for thinking. More specifically, two distinct lines of research relate to this critical element. One group of studies (Isaacson 1982; Hart 1983; Mayer and Salovey in Gibbs 1995; Goleman 1995) concerns the role emotions play in the teaching/learning scenario, and another set of investigations (Diamond 1988) targets the concept of enriched environments (see Figures 1.4 and 1.5).

To summarize the critical findings on emotions succinctly: emotions are the gatekeepers to the intellect. In short, emotional hooks are necessary for long-term learning; negative emotions can become blocks to learning. The findings on the benefits of an enriched environment, although convincing, invariably lead to the age-old controversy known as the nature versus nurture argument. Basically, the question is: Are people born, by nature, with an unchanging brain/mind/ intellect or does nurturing through a rich environment impact the brain and actually increase the neural pathways of intellectual activity? The jury is still out on the actual balance of natural endowments and the nurturing environment, but most researchers agree that the nurturing side of the equation is a critical component.

Principles of Brain-Compatible Learning

The following are Caine and Caine's (1991, 1993) principles that relate to setting the climate FOR thinking (see Figure 1.6):

Learning is enhanced by challenge and inhibited by threat. The brain learns optimally when appropriately challenged; thus, a safe, rich environment fosters a state of relaxed alertness for learning. The mind becomes engaged in problem solving and decision making, especially in open-ended problem scenarios. For example, in lab settings, rather than telling students what to do, teachers guide the process as students figure out what seems best.

Emotions are critical to patterning. Emotions and cognition cannot be separated; thus, positive emotional hooks, such as intriguing questions, enhance learning. Other ways to tap into emotional intelligence include role plays in which there is some emotional risk, surprise introductory sets that intrigue the students, public opinion polls that encourage safe risk taking, and relevant stories that pull at the heartstrings.

Learning involves both focused attention and peripheral perception. The brain responds to the entire sensory context; thus, in an enriched environment, peripheral information can be purposely organized to facilitate learning. For example, informative bulletin boards, instructional graphics on the board, appropriate background music, varied lighting, posters, charts, and maps are all part of the learning environment that influences learning.

Implications for Learning

Implications for learning (see Figure 1.7), based on brain research and pedagogical theory, suggest that certain methodologies are more brain-compatible or more in sync with how the brain takes in information, remembers it, and, in turn, triggers that information for relevant use. In essence, techniques that set a safe climate and challenge the brain in engaging ways are implied or hinted at by the findings about how the brain works.

Because brain functioning is enhanced by challenge and inhibited by threat and learning involves both focused and peripheral learning, certain instructional methods and climate-setting techniques are dictated for the brain-compatible classroom. For example, higher-order questions, time to think before answering, room arrangement, and enriched environmental stimuli seem more brain-compatible, or conducive to learning, in ways that are easily adapted to how the brain works.

The following are some ways to set the climate in a brain-compatible classroom:

- Be aware of verbal and nonverbal behaviors.
- Establish classroom guidelines.
- Recognize emotional and moral intelligence.
- Ask high-level questions (fat/skinny, three-story intellect).
- Probe for depth in answers (people searches, wait-time, response strategies, Socratic dialogue).
- Group students diversely (age, ability, etc.).
- Schedule blocks of time.
- Conduct a year-round school.
- Arrange room for learning.
- Create a rich environment (equipment, supplies, sensory input, language stimulation).
- Set up learning centers.

Implications for Teaching: Satisfactory

Based on the four-corner framework for the brain-compatible classroom, if the teacher sets a warm, safe, and inviting climate for thinking and authentic student learning, the teacher is doing a satisfactory job (see Figure 1.8). Immersed in a rich, secure environment, students learn. In fact, they learn naturally, in the inductive way they learn outside of the formal school setting.

Teaching OF Thinking: Skills

Teaching the skills of thinking encompasses the life skills and concepts that thread through all subject matter content in a standards-based curriculum (see Figure 1.3). These skills range from communication and social skills to the microskills of thinking and reflecting to the technological skills of the information age to the skills needed for solving algebraic equations and for computer programming and even to the skill training involved in a craft or athletics. Direct instruction of skill development moves through predictable stages: novice, advanced beginner, competent, proficient, and expert.

Defining Brain-Compatible Classrooms

Research Base—Brain, Mind, Intellect

Early research on the brain/mind/intellect focuses on understanding the relationship between the brain and the learning process (Hart 1983; Luria 1976). More current research on the brain and its implications for learning (Epstein 1978; Jensen 1996; Sousa 1995; Sylwester 1995; Wolfe 1996, 2001) is appearing at an incredible rate. In addition, emergent theories of the intellect, including the traditional general intelligence (Spearman in Gould 1981), multiple intelligences (Gardner 1983), successful intelligences (Sternberg 1986), emotional intelligence (Goleman 1995; Mayer and Salovey in Gibbs 1995), moral intelligence (Coles 1997), and intelligent behaviors or habits of mind (Costa and Kallick 2000), as well as ways of outsmarting IQ (Perkins 1995), are inextricably related to this element of the skills that thread through our lives. (See Figures 1.4 and 1.5.)

Principles of Brain-Compatible Learning

The following are Caine and Caine's (1991, 1993) principles that relate to teaching the skills OF thinking (see Figure 1.6):

The brain processes parts and wholes simultaneously. Bilateralization of the right and left hemisphere processing, though inextricably interactive, allows the brain to reduce information into parts and, at the same time, to perceive and work with it as a whole; thus, immediate application of direct instruction allows the learner to perceive the information from both perspectives. Examples include teaching adverbs through a skill/drill method and accompanying the drill with an exercise that requires students to explicitly use adverbial phrases in their writing; learning multiplication facts and then applying them to story problems; and working with punctuation and then using specific kinds of punctuation in journal writing, lab reports, and expository essays.

The brain has a spatial memory system (implicit) and a set of systems for rote learning (explicit). There is a natural, spatial memory that needs no rehearsal and affords instant memory, and there are facts and skills that are dealt with in isolation and require practice and rehearsal; thus, teaching must focus on the personal world of the learner to make the learning relevant, as well as rote memorization techniques to foster long-term learning for transfer. Rote memorization requires more conscious effort because the facts being memorized may have little meaning or relevance to the learner. When the brain senses that there is no need to remember (i.e., lack of relevance) it tends to let go of the information. Thus, rote memorization of isolated facts often needs more explicit work to learn and recall the information, whereas spatial memory has built-in cues that help in the retrieval of the information. For example, spatial memory can be used to prepare students for a big test by having them study in the same room and at the same desk—essentially the same exact location—as they will be when they take the actual test. For rote learning, students need a lot of practice and repetition in various contexts: flash cards, musical lyrics, rhyming sounds, acronyms, and repeated rehearsals.

Implications for Learning

The knowledge that the brain processes parts and wholes simultaneously and that memory is both spatial and rote implies that learning in the classroom needs to happen in ways that are compatible to brain functioning. Included in these brain-friendly methods is direct instruction in skill development, accompanied by application of the learned skills in authentic situations (see Figure 1.7).

The following are ways to teach skills in the brain-compatible classroom:

- Promote collaboration (leadership, communication, conflict resolution, team building).
- Foster critical and creative thinking.
- Develop academic content skills and concepts (math, science, social studies, language arts).
- Incorporate technology (literacy, graphics).
- Require performance tasks (athletics, visual arts, performing arts, practical arts).
- Apply problem-solving and decision-making skills.

- Support communication.
- Build a knowledge base (research, word processing).
- Use innovation skills.
- Develop production skills.
- Incorporate embedded application.
- Incorporate performance skills.
- Use direct instruction.
- Develop skills and content learning.
- Identify peak performance and FLOW.

Implications for Teaching: Good

Teaching that develops skills, concepts, and attitudes through direct instruction techniques as well as creates a risk-free climate within rich classroom environments is considered to be good teaching (see Figure 1.8). This kind of teaching moves beyond the first element of climate setting and, in fact, combines two essential elements by teaching *for* thinking and by teaching the skills *of* thinking. The reason this combination of elements is considered better or more skillful than merely setting a safe, enriched environment is because the learning is guided by the teacher explicitly. In this way, the learner is moved more directly to specific realms of learning—to areas of study that the learner may not have approached without intervention.

Teaching WITH Thinking: Structuring Interaction

Teaching with thinking is about structuring the interaction with thought-provoking activities that require intense involvement from the learner (see Figure 1.3). Learning is shaped by an internal process and by social interaction (Vygotsky 1978). Active learning permits the learner to construct meaning in the mind; thus, optimal teaching/learning situations invite the learner to become an integral part of the learning process through hands-on learning as well as dialogue with others. This includes the use of cooperative learning, graphic organizers, multiple intelligences, and authentic curriculum models such as case studies and problem-based learning.

Research Base—Active Learning/Constructivist

The research basis for the element of structuring the interaction with thinking comes from literature on experiential learning (Dewey 1938; Bruner 1973), the constructivist theory (Piaget 1970; Brooks and Brooks 1993), the active learning theory (Harmin 1994), the work of Caine and Caine (1991, 1993) in their synthesis of brain research and their subsequent call for more connected and interrelated ways of learning, as well as related work about developing a coherent curriculum (Beane 1995). (See Figures 1.4 and 1.5.)

Principles of Brain-Compatible Learning

The following are Caine and Caine's (1991, 1993) principles that relate to structuring the interaction WITH thinking (see Figure 1.6):

The brain is a parallel processor. Thoughts, emotions, imagination, and predispositions operate simultaneously; thus, optimal learning results from orchestrating the learning experience to address multiple operations in the brain. For example, complex performance tasks such as producing a dramatic play, authentic projects such as creating a brochure, or service learning that requires complex negotiations with community agencies are the types of orchestrated learning that engage the brain most fully.

Learning engages the entire physiology. Learning is as natural as breathing, yet neuron growth, nourishment, and emotional interactions are integrally related to the perception and interpretation of experiences; thus, stress management, nutrition, exercise, and relaxation become a focus of the teaching/learning process. For example, modeling nutritious snacks of nuts, fruits, and cheeses for school celebrations; incorporating frequent movement into the classroom regime; and building in opportunities for downtime to foster reflection and deeper understanding are strategies that honor this principle.

Each brain is unique. While most normal brains have a similar set of systems for sensing, feeling, and thinking, the set is integrated differently in each brain; thus, teaching that is multifaceted with inherent choices and options for the learner fosters optimal learning. For example, classroom approaches that honor students by creating freedom of choice within a given structure—choices within terms of multiple intelligences (Gardner 1983; verbal, visual, mathematical, musical, interpersonal, intrapersonal, and bodily), or within types of media to use, kinds of processes required, and end products accepted are classrooms in which students embrace diversity and uniqueness.

Understanding and remembering occur best when facts and skills are embedded in natural, spatial memory. Specific items are given meaning when embedded in ordinary experiences, such as learning grammar and punctuation and applying the learning to writing; thus, experiential learning, which affords opportunities for embedding learning, is necessary for optimal learning.

Implications for Learning

With an understanding that each brain is unique, that the brain is a parallel processor, that learning engages the entire physiology, and that learning is embedded in the natural/spatial memory, the suggestions for learning are clear (see Figure 1.7). The multiple intelligences approach taps into the uniqueness of each brain, while experiential kinds of learning are useful tools for embedding the learning into natural memory pathways and engaging the learner holistically in sensory stimuli.

The following are ways to structure interaction in a brain-compatible classroom:

- Use cooperative learning.
- Utilize graphic organizers.
- Target multiple intelligences.
- Design integrated curricula.
  - Create performance tasks.
  - Develop thematic units.
  - Do problem-based learning.
  - Design projects or service learning opportunities.
  - Use case studies.

Implications for Teaching: Excellent

Teaching that focuses on creating a safe and caring climate within an enriched environment setting; on targeting specific skills, concepts, and attitudes necessary for high achievement; and on intensely involving the learners in active and interactive experiences is considered excellent teaching (see Figure 1.8). When attention is focused on climate, skills, and interaction, students are invited into learning in irresistible ways. Complex tasks, problems to encounter, and time to dig into learning are key.

Teaching ABOUT Thinking: Metacognition

Teaching about thinking is teaching about reflection, self-regulation, and self-assessment (see Figure 1.3). Teaching about one's own thinking is called metacognitive (beyond [meta] the cognitive) reflection. It is about self-awareness and subsequent self-regulatory processing, or self-evaluation. This is the element in the brain-compatible classroom that requires student-regulated goal setting, self-monitoring, and reflective actions as well as the teacher's personal reactions to the student and her learning. It is the cornerstone of the learner-centered concept that drives personal application and transfer of learning.

Research Base—Deep Understanding/Transfer

The research basis for this element of metacognitive reflection, or the idea of thinking about how you think and learn, is grounded in literature on cognition (Luria 1976), the mind (Vygotsky 1978), transfer of learning (Hart 1983; Perkins 1986; Perkins and Salomon 1989), mediation theory (Feuerstein 1980), deep understanding (Gardner 1993; Perkins 1986), and metacognition (Flavell in Costa 1991; Brown and Palinscar in Costa 1991; and Costa 1991). (See Figures 1.4 and 1.5.)

Defining Brain-Compatible Classrooms

Principles of Brain-Based Research

The following are Caine and Caine's (1991, 1993) principles that relate to thinking ABOUT thinking (see Figure 1.6):

The search for meaning is innate. The search for meaning cannot be stopped, only channeled and focused; thus, classrooms need stability and routine as well as novelty and challenge, and the learning can be shepherded explicitly through mediation and reflection. Illustrations of how teachers might foster the search for meaning in students include encouraging students to see patterns, themes, and big idea concepts; chunking or re-arranging information in meaningful ways; or connecting the new learning to past learning or to future applications through skillful questions.

The search for meaning occurs through patterning. The brain has a natural capacity to integrate vast amounts of seemingly unrelated information; thus, when teaching invokes integrated, thematically reflective approaches, learning is more brain-compatible and learning is subsequently enhanced. For example, the use of integrated thematic instruction within or across several disciplines naturally produces patterns and themes.

Learning always involves conscious and unconscious processes. Enormous amounts of unconscious processing go on beneath the surface of awareness; thus, teaching needs to be organized experientially and reflectively to benefit maximally from the deep processing.

Implications for Learning

Based on the principles that the search for meaning is innate, occurs through patterning, and that both conscious and unconscious processes occur in learning, the call for the mediation of learning is clear (see Figure 1.7). Through reflection, metacognitive monitoring, and explicit transfer strategies, the processing becomes more brain-compatible or aligned to how the brain puts learning into long-term memory.

The following are ways to teach thinking ABOUT thinking in the brain-compatible classroom:

- Create personal relevance.
- Construct knowledge.
- Foster deep understanding.
- Make generalizations.
- Promote mindful engagement.
- Use mediation strategies.
- Embrace metacognition (plan, monitor, evaluate).
- Move to application.
- Shepherd the transfer of learning.
- Check for understanding (traditional assessment, dynamic assessment).

Implications for Teaching: Superior

When one enters a classroom in which superior teaching is clearly the norm, it is immediately and visibly evident. In the scenario of superior teaching, the climate is warm and accepting, the environment rich and inviting; appropriate skills and concepts are targeted for mastery; and students are actively engaged in experiential learning (see Figure 1.8). But one other element surfaces beyond the others, and the difference in the learning atmosphere is astoundingly obvious. The critical element is self-reflection and self-monitoring. In this classroom, the teacher believes in the innate ability of students to make meaning of their world. That is to say, there are clear and explicit expectations for high standards and high achievement for all students to not only learn but also *to be in charge* of their own learning.

Definition of Brain-Compatible Classrooms

Brain-compatible classrooms are brain-friendly places. They are classrooms in which the teaching/learning process is dictated by how the brain functions and how the mind learns. In brain-compatible classrooms (or brain-based classrooms), the

Defining Brain-Compatible Classrooms

distinguishing feature is that these classrooms link learning to what is known about the human brain.

These classrooms are set up with safe, stimuli-rich environments and a balance between direct instruction for skill development and authentic learning that immerses the learners in challenging experiences. In addition, brain-compatible classrooms tap into the uniqueness of each learner and shepherd relevant transfer for future application of the learning.

To illustrate how brain-compatible classrooms differ from other classrooms, consider the following examples:

- Since brain research suggests that *the brain learns by patterning ideas or chunking notions* that seem to go together naturally, classrooms in which themes are used frequently to connect ideas are seen to be more brain-friendly than classrooms where information is doled out in discrete and separate pieces.
- Since brain research suggests that *an emotional visceral reaction happens when the brain senses a threat,* testing situations in the brain-compatible classroom are managed explicitly by the teacher to diminish the anxiety and fear and to thus enable the learners to function at their highest cognitive levels.
- Since findings on the functioning of the brain suggests that *learning involves the entire physiology,* real or simulated experiences that tap into the many ways of learning seem to be more brain-friendly. For example, problem-based learning scenarios in which students actually take on the roles of stakeholders seem to be a curriculum model that addresses that brain finding.

In brief, not all classrooms are brain-compatible, or brain-friendly. While they may appear to be places of learning, they may not explicitly target the principles of brain research. The brain-compatible classroom is specifically designed to teach *for, of, with,* and *about* thinking based on the emergent findings about how the brain works and how the mind remembers and learns.

Brain-Compatible Classrooms
Description

Setting the Climate FOR Thinking	**Teaching the Skills OF Thinking**
Creating a rich environment and an emotionally safe climate	Teaching life skills from novice level to expert level

STANDARDS FOR HIGH ACHIEVEMENT

Structuring the Interaction WITH Thinking	**Thinking ABOUT Thinking**
Constructing meaning with intense, active involvement of the learners	Fostering application and transfer with metacognitive reflection

Figure 1.3

MENTORING

Brain-Compatible Classrooms
Research Base

Setting the Climate FOR Thinking	Teaching the Skills OF Thinking
Research on physiology, emotions, and environment	Research on mind, memory, intellect, and skill/concept development

STANDARDS FOR HIGH ACHIEVEMENT

Structuring the Interaction WITH Thinking	Thinking ABOUT Thinking
Research on experiential learning, active learning, the constructivist theory of learning, connected and coherent learning, and coherent curriculum	Research on cognition, the mind, deep understanding, transfer of learning, mediation theory, and metacognition

Figure 1.4

Brain-Compatible Classrooms
Researchers

Setting the Climate
FOR Thinking

Sousa (biology)
Wolfe (biology)
MacLean (triune brain)
Diamond (environment)
Hart (emotions)
Isaacson (limbic system)
Ornstein & Sobel (healthy brain)
Goleman (emotional intelligence)
Mayer & Salovey (emotional intelligence)
O'Keefe & Nadel (memory)
Lozanov (limbic)
Jensen (movement)

Teaching the Skills
OF Thinking

Epstein (education)
Hart (learning)
Luria (higher cortical functions)
Sylwester (learning, acquisition)
Sternberg (successful intelligence)
Gardner (multiple intelligences)
Goleman (emotional intelligence)
Coles (moral intelligence)
Perkins (intelligence)
Costa & Kallick (intelligent behavior)
Mayer & Salovey (emotional intelligence)
Jensen (learning)
Sousa (learning)
Wolfe (learning)
Spearman (in Gould) (intelligence)
   Sprenger (memory)

STANDARDS
FOR HIGH
ACHIEVEMENT

Structuring the Interaction
WITH Thinking

Ornstein & Sobel (parallel processing)
Healy (active learning)
Gardner (multiple intelligences)
Caine & Caine (connections)
Bruner (learning theory)
Dewey (experience)
Brooks & Brooks (constructivism)
Beane (coherent curriculum)
Harmin (active learning)
Piaget (constructing meaning)
Bloom (active learning)
Goodlad (active learning)
Johnson & Johnson (cooperative learning)
Vygotsky (social interaction)

Thinking
ABOUT Thinking

Luria (cognition)
Vygotsky (mind)
Feuerstein (mediation)
Perkins (transfer, deep understanding)
Perkins & Salomon (transfer)
Hart (transfer)
Palincsar & Brown (metacognition)
Costa (metacognition)
Flavell (metacognition)
Swartz & Perkins (metacognition)
Gardner (deep understanding)
Costa & Kallick (habits of mind)

Figure 1.5

Defining Brain-Compatible Classrooms

Brain-Compatible Classrooms
Principles*

Setting the Climate FOR Thinking

- Learning is enhanced by challenge and inhibited by threat.

- Emotions are critical to patterning.

- Learning involves both focused attention and peripherial perception.

Teaching the Skills OF Thinking

- The brain processes parts and wholes simultaneously.

- The brain has a spatial memory system (implicit) and a set of systems for rote learning (explicit).

STANDARDS FOR HIGH ACHIEVEMENT

Structuring the Interaction WITH Thinking

- The brain is a parallel processor.

- Learning engages the entire physiology.

- Each brain is unique.

- Understanding and remembering occur best when facts and skills are embedded in natural, spatial memory.

Thinking ABOUT Thinking

- The search for meaning is innate.

- The search for meaning occurs through patterning.

- Learning always involves conscious and unconscious processes.

*Based on Caine and Caine's twelve principles.

Figure 1.6

Brain-Compatible Classrooms
Implications for Learning

Setting the Climate FOR Thinking

Verbal and Nonverbal
 Signals
DOVE Guidelines
Emotional Intelligence
Moral Intelligence
Three-Story Intellect
Fat/Skinny Questions
People Search
Wait-Time
Response Strategies
Socratic Dialogue
Student Groupings
Blocks of Time
Year-Round Schools
Room Arrangement
Equipment and
 Supplies

Sensory Input
Language Stimulation
Learning Centers

Teaching the Skills OF Thinking

Microskills
• Collaborative Skills
• Thinking Skills
• Academic Content
 Skills and Concepts
• Technological Skills
• Performance Skills
Macroskills
• Problem-Solving Skills
• Decision-Making Skills
• Communication Skills
• Research Skills
• Word-Processing
 Skills
• Innovation Skills

• Production Skills
• Performance Skills
Skill Development
• Direct Instruction
• Development of Skill
 and Content Training
• Embedded
 Application
• Peak Performance
• FLOW

STANDARDS
FOR HIGH
ACHIEVEMENT

Structuring the Interaction WITH Thinking

Cooperative Structures
Graphic Organizers
Multiple Intelligences
• Verbal/Linguistic
• Logical/Mathematical
• Bodily/Kinesthetic
• Musical/Rhythmic
• Visual/Spatial
• Interpersonal/Social
• Intrapersonal/Introspective
• Naturalist/Physical World
Integrated Curriculum
• Performance Tasks
• Themes
• Problem-Based Learning
• Projects/Service Learning
• Case Studies

Thinking ABOUT Thinking

Personal Relevance
Construct Knowledge
Deep Understanding
Generalizations
Engagement
Cognitive Mediation
Metacognitive Reflection
Direct Application
Transfer Levels and Enhancing Transfer
Traditional Assessment
Dynamic Assessment
• Performance Assessment
• Learning Logs
• Mediated Journals

Figure 1.7

Defining Brain-Compatible Classrooms

Brain-Compatible Classrooms
Implications for Teaching

Setting the Climate FOR Thinking	Teaching the Skills OF Thinking
Satisfactory Teaching/Learning Scenario	Good Teaching/Learning Scenario

STANDARDS FOR HIGH ACHIEVEMENT

Structuring the Interaction WITH Thinking	Thinking ABOUT Thinking
Excellent Teaching/Learning Scenario	Superior Teaching/Learning Scenario

Figure 1.8

SkyLight Professional Development

Bibliography

Beane, J. ed. 1995. *Toward a coherent curriculum: 1995 yearbook of the ASCD.* Alexandria, VA: Association for Supervision and Curriculum Development.

Bloom, B. S. 1981. *All our children learning: A primer for parents, teachers, and educators.* New York: McGraw-Hill.

Brandt, R. 1988. On teaching thinking: A conversation with Arthur Costa. *Educational Leadership.* 45(7): 10–13.

Brooks, J. G., and M. G. Brooks. 1993. *In search of understanding: The case for the constructivist classroom.* Alexandria, VA: Association for Supervision and Curriculum Development.

Bruner, J. S. 1973. Readiness for learning. In *Beyond the information given: Studies in the psychology of knowing,* edited by J. Anglin. New York: Norton.

Caine, R. N., and G. Caine. 1991. *Making connections: Teaching and the human brain.* New York: Innovative Learning Publications/ Addison-Wesley Publications.

———. 1993. *Making connections: Teaching and the human brain,* 2nd ed. New York: Innovative Learning Publications/ Addison-Wesley Publications.

Coles, R. 1997. *The moral intelligence of children: How to raise a moral child.* New York: Random House.

Costa, A. 1991. *The school as a home for the mind.* Palatine, IL: IRI/SkyLight Training and Publishing.

Costa, A., and B. Kallick. 2000. *Discovering and exploring: Habits of mind.* Alexandria, VA: Association for Supervision and Curriculum Development.

Dewey, J. 1938. *Experience and education.* New York: Collier.

Diamond, M. 1988. *Enriching heredity: The impact of the environment on the anatomy of the brain.* New York: Free Press.

Epstein, H. 1978. *Education and the brain: The 77th yearbook of the National Society for the Study of Education.* Chicago: The Yearbook Committee and Associated Contributors, University of Chicago Press.

Feuerstein, R. 1980. *Instrumental Enrichment: An intervention program for cognitive modifiability.* Glenview, IL: Scott-Foresman Lifelong Learning Division.

Flavell, J. H. 1979. Metacognition and cognitive monitoring: A new area of cognitive-development inquiry. *American Psychologist.* 34: 906–911.

Fogarty, R., and J. Bellanca. 1993. *Patterns for thinking, Patterns for transfer.* Palatine, IL: IRI/SkyLight Training and Publishing.

Gardner, H. 1983. *Frames of mind: The theory of multiple intelligences.* New York: Basic Books.

———. 1993. *Multiple intelligences: The theory in practice*. New York: HarperCollins.

Gibbs, N. 1995. The EQ factor. *Time*, October. 146(14): 60–68.

Goleman, D. 1995. *Emotional intelligence: Why it can matter more than IQ*. New York: Bantam Books.

Goodlad, J. I. 1980. How laboratory schools go awry. *UCLA Educator*, winter, 21(2).

———. 1984. *A place called school: Prospects for the future*. New York: McGraw-Hill.

Gould, S. J. 1981. *The mismeasure of man*. New York: Norton.

Harmin, M. 1994. *Inspiring active learning: A handbook for teachers*. Alexandria, VA: Association for Supervision and Curriculum Development.

Hart, L. 1983. *Human brain, Human learning*. Kent, WA: Books for Educators.

Healy, J. M. 1987. *Your child's growing mind: A guide to learning and brain development from birth to adolescence* (A Main Street Book). New York: Doubleday.

———. 1990. *Endangered minds*. New York: Touchstone/ Simon and Schuster.

Isaacson, R. L. 1982. *Limbic system*, 2nd ed. New York: Plenum Press.

Jensen, E. 1996. *Completing the puzzle: A brain-based approach to learning*. Del Mar, CA: Turning Point Publishing.

Johnson, R., and D. Johnson. 1982. Cooperation in learning: Ignored but powerful. *Lyceum*, October.

Lozanov, G. 1978. *Suggestology and outlines of suggestology*. New York: Gordon and Breach.

Luria, A. 1976. *Working brain: An introduction to neuro-psychology*. New York: Gordon and Breach.

MacLean, P. D. 1969. New trends in man's evolution. In *A triune concept of the brain and behavior*. Paper presented at Queen's University, Ontario, Canada. Ann Arbor, MI: Books on Demand, University Microfilms International.

———. 1978. A mind of three minds: Educating the triune brain. In *Education and the brain*, edited by Jeanne Chall and Allan Mirsky. Chicago: University of Chicago Press.

Mayer, J. D., and P. Salovey. 1993. The intelligence of emotional intelligence. *Intelligence*. 17(4): 422–433.

O'Keefe, J., and L. Nadel. 1973. *The hippocampal syndrome: Persistence or something more?* Conference on Partial Reinforcement and Persistence Phenomena. Sussex, United Kingdom.

———. 1974. Maps in the brain. *New Scientist*, June 27.

———. 1975. *The psychology of space*. Invited address to the Canadian Psychological Association, Quebec City, Canada.

———. 1978. *The hippocampus as a cognitive map*. Oxford, England: Clarendon Press.

———. 1979. Precís of O'Keefe and Nadel's The hippocampus as a cognitive map, and author's response to commentaries. *The Behavioral and Brain Sciences*. 2: 487–534.

Ornstein, R., and D. Sobel. 1987. *The healing brain: Breakthrough discoveries about how the brain keeps us healthy*. New York: Simon and Schuster.

Palincsar, A. S., and A. Brown. 1984. Reciprocal teaching of comprehension-fostering and comprehension-monitoring activities. *Cognition and Instruction*. 1(2): 117–175.

Perkins, D. N. 1986. *Knowledge as design*. Hillsdale, NJ: Lawrence Erlbaum Associates.

Perkins, D. N., ed. 1995. *Outsmarting IQ: The emerging science of learnable intelligence*. New York: Free Press.

Perkins, D. N., and G. Salomon. 1988. Teaching for transfer. *Educational Leadership*. 46(1): 22–32.

———. 1989. Are cognitive skills context bound? *Educational Researcher*. 18(1): 16–25.

Piaget, J. 1970. Piaget's theory. In *Carmichael's manual of child psychology*, edited by P. Mussen. New York: Wiley.

Sousa, D. 1995. *How the brain learns: A classroom teacher's guide*. Reston, VA: National Association of Secondary Schools.

Sprenger, M. 1999. *Learning and memory: The brain in action*. Alexandria, VA: Association for Supervision and Curriculum Development.

Sternberg, R. J. 1986. *Intelligence applied: Understanding and increasing your intellectual skills*. New York: Harcourt Brace Jovanavich.

Swartz, R. J., and D. N. Perkins. 1989. *Teaching thinking: Issues and approaches*. Pacific Grove, CA: Midwest Publications.

Sylwester, R. 1995. *A celebration of neurons: An educator's guide to the human brain*. Alexandria, VA: Association for Supervision and Curriculum Development.

Vygotsky, L. S. 1978. *Mind in society: The development of higher psychological process*. Cambridge, MA: Harvard University Press.

Wolfe, P. 1996. *A staff developer's guide to the brain* (2 audiotapes). Front Royal, VA: National Cassette Services.

———. 2001. *Brain matters: Translating brain research into classroom practice*. Alexandria, VA: Association for Supervision and Curriculum Development.

Defining Brain-Compatible Classrooms

Mentors may use the following ideas with their protégés:

- Give the learning checklist (Blackline 1.1) to the protégé. Guide the protégé through the checklist to help determine progress in implementing brain-compatible learning strategies in the classroom. The checklist should help the protégé see areas of strength and areas that need improvement.

- Ask the protégé to use the reflection page (Blackline 1.2) to choose one strategy on which to focus for each of the four corners.

- Use any of the figures in this chapter (Figures 1.1–1.8) to review the components of a brain-compatible classroom.

- If a protégé needs more information on brain research, suggest Figure 1.5 as a reference list. For example, if a protégé wishes to learn more about active learning, he or she would look at Figure 1.5 to find researchers who focus on active learning. The protégé may use the bibliography and look up works for further reading.

- Figure 1.8 can be used as a tool for rating teaching. Guide the protégé to determine how to move from satisfactory to good to excellent to superior teaching.

Brain-Compatible Classrooms

Learning Checklist

Setting the Climate FOR Thinking

- ❏ Be aware of verbal and nonverbal behaviors.
- ❏ Establish classroom guidelines.
- ❏ Recognize emotional and moral intelligence.
- ❏ Ask high-level questions (fat/ skinny, three-story intellect).
- ❏ Probe for depth in answers (people searches, wait-time, response strategies, Socratic dialogue).
- ❏ Group students diversely (age, ability, etc.).
- ❏ Schedule blocks of time.
- ❏ Conduct a year-round school.
- ❏ Arrange room for learning.
- ❏ Create a rich environment (equipment, supplies, sensory input, language stimulation).
- ❏ Set up learning centers.

Teaching the Skills OF Thinking

- ❏ Promote collaboration (leadership, communication, conflict resolution, team building).
- ❏ Foster critical and creative thinking.
- ❏ Develop academic content skills and concepts (math, science, social studies, language arts).
- ❏ Incorporate technology (literacy, graphics).
- ❏ Require performance tasks (athletics, visual arts, performing arts, practical arts).
- ❏ Apply problem-solving and decision-making skills.
- ❏ Support communication.
- ❏ Build a knowledge base (research, word processing).
- ❏ Use innovation skills.
- ❏ Develop production skills.
- ❏ Incorporate embedded application.
- ❏ Incorporate performance skills.
- ❏ Use direct instruction.
- ❏ Develop skills and content learning.
- ❏ Identify peak performance and FLOW.

STANDARDS FOR HIGH ACHIEVEMENT

Structuring the Interaction WITH Thinking

- ❏ Use cooperative learning.
- ❏ Utilize graphic organizers.
- ❏ Target multiple intelligences.
- ❏ Design integrated curricula.
- ❏ Create performance tasks.
- ❏ Develop thematic units.
- ❏ Do problem-based learning.
- ❏ Design projects or service learning opportunities.
- ❏ Use case studies.

Thinking ABOUT Thinking

- ❏ Create personal relevance.
- ❏ Construct knowledge.
- ❏ Foster deep understanding.
- ❏ Make generalizations.
- ❏ Promote mindful engagement.
- ❏ Use mediation strategies.
- ❏ Embrace metacognition (plan, monitor, evaluate).
- ❏ Move to application.
- ❏ Shepherd the transfer of learning.
- ❏ Check for understanding (traditional assessment, dynamic assessment).

Teacher: _____   Date: _____

Blackline 1.1

Defining Brain-Compatible Classrooms

Brain-Compatible Classrooms

Reflection Page

Select one key area you would like to focus on under each section.

Setting the Climate FOR Thinking	Teaching the Skills OF Thinking

STANDARDS FOR HIGH ACHIEVEMENT

Structuring the Interaction WITH Thinking	Thinking ABOUT Thinking

Teacher: _____   Date: _____

An integrated lesson allows teachers to combine learning standards from several content areas and connect the activities and tasks. This helps students see cross-curricular relationships as well as the purpose for their learning. Skowron shares a model for designing a meaningful integrated lesson plan.

Integrated Instructional Design

by Jan Skowron

Integrated Instruction

Integrated instruction, sometimes referred to as thematic instruction, problem-based instruction, or experiential learning, most likely has its roots in the progressive education movement of the early 1900s (Rippa 1988, Drake 1993). John Dewey emphasized the advantages of engaging students in real-world experiences and criticized instructional methods that focused learning into separate, isolated compartments. His belief in the importance of experience as a method of teaching is shown in the following statement.

> Our whole policy of compulsory education rises or falls with our ability to make school life an interesting and absorbing experience to the child. In one sense, there is no such thing as compulsory education. We can have compulsory physical attendance at school; but education comes only through willing attention to and participation in school activities. It follows that the teacher must select these activities with reference to the child's interests, powers, and capacities. In no other way can she guarantee that the child will be present (Dewey 1913, ix).

Integrated Instructional Design

An Integrated Approach to Learning

Integrated instruction combines learning standards from different content areas within the same lesson or unit of study. The learning standards are connected through activities and tasks in a logical manner so students are able to understand relationships among the standards and the purpose of their learning. Assessment of student progress is likewise connected and embedded in the activities. An integrated approach to learning provides continuity and order for students. It helps them make sense of and see associations among the seeming randomness of educational objectives (Zemmelman, Daniels, and Hyde 1993). Genuine learning occurs as students see the connections among concepts and weave these connections into their own scheme of meaning (Beane 1993). An integrated curriculum helps students construct knowledge for themselves (Burke 1994). Integrated learning designs range from the combination of a few learning standards to total curriculum integration based on a major theme.

Why Integrated Instruction Is a Good Idea

Understanding relationships and connections is far more valuable than knowing isolated bits and pieces of information (Withrow, Long, and Marx 1999). Caine and Caine (1991) explain that the brain searches for patterns and connections within experiences to make sense of the world. Experiences that provide opportunities for students to make connections are likely to provide more lasting and deeper learning. The propensity of the human brain to search for patterns of meaning is the reasoning behind integrated instruction (Jensen 2000). Shanahan (1997) reports that student motivation in integrated learning settings is greater than in traditional settings, and integrated instruction produces positive attitudes toward learning. While few empirical studies have been done to test the effectiveness of integrated learning, proponents of this approach base their support on the positive experiences and observations of classrooms where integrated learning flourishes (Guthrie and McCann 1997). The theoretical basis for integrated instruction is also found in constructivist theory, which explains that learning occurs as a person builds meaning through direct experience (Ellis and Fouts 1997). (See Figure 2.1.)

Benefiting from Best Practice Models

The predominant factors that seem to deter teachers from using an integrated instructional approach are lack of time for planning and instruction, professional development, and practical models. Even when teachers are convinced of the effectiveness of integrated instruction and motivated to use it, the lack of practical models may discourage them (Gehrke 1993).

Teachers need time to plan, especially with one another, to integrate standards across content areas. Otherwise the task may be too monumental for any one teacher to assume (Jacobs 1991a). Just as students benefit from working in teams, so do teachers when there is a feeling of shared responsibility.

In spite of the advantages associated with integrated instruction, American education today, for the most part, remains structured around separate disciplines or content areas (Beane 1993, Ellis and Fouts 1997, Jacobs 1991a). At the high school level, the student's day is an assortment of seven or eight unrelated, disjointed time periods (Zemmelman, Daniels, and Hyde 1993). And, in the classroom where the curriculum is translated into instruction, instruction is most likely to be a series of isolated lessons. Some high schools have shown progress toward integrated learning by combining English, literature, history, and civics in an American studies course. Most often, this type of course is team taught by content-area certified teachers.

Integrated Instruction

Ellis and Fouts (1997) make several educationally sound arguments for integrated instruction:

Psychological/developmental—Learning occurs best when individuals see the connections among concepts.

Sociocultural—Current curriculum, especially at the secondary level, does not address the needs, interests, and capabilities of today's students. Updating through curriculum integration has the potential to resolve these inadequacies.

Motivational—Interest and motivation are enhanced through integrated learning activities when students see the purpose of their learning and are able to choose their learning activities.

Pedagogical—The traditional curriculum has become overloaded. Teachers are hard pressed to cover all the so-called essentials and do so in a meaningful way. Integrating learning concepts makes better use of classroom time.

Figure 2.1

Integrated Instructional Design

Students need time to actively engage in learning, process their learning, and reflect on their learning (Caine and Caine 1991, Fogarty 1996). The traditional forty-five minute time period schedule, predominant in today's high schools, does not lend itself to the type of teaching that promotes integrated, connected learning. Many teachers report that with a forty-five minute time period, there is little they can do other than the traditional lecture, question, respond strategy. Some middle schools and high schools have changed from the shorter periods to longer blocks of time to promote more connected learning through integrated instruction (Canady and Rettig 1996). Longer blocks of time enable teachers to actively involve students in learning.

If teachers are to change the way they teach, they need ongoing professional development (Withrow, Long, and Marx 1999). Effective professional development not only points out best practices, but also provides practical, realistic models—a structure for learning, transferring, and applying new approaches (Moye 1997). Professional development related to integrated instruction prepares teachers with strategies for successful implementation.

How to Begin

Integrating the curriculum can be a formidable task, but it becomes more manageable if approached in an organized, step-by-step manner. A clearly defined rationale for using integrated instruction and an organized plan to facilitate smooth implementation must exist. As Relan and Kimpston (1993) point out, there should be clear reasons for selecting an integrated approach over some other approach. Brophy and Alleman (1991) likewise explain that teachers must be selective and astute in planning curriculum integration and beware of integration merely for the sake of integration. There should be a logical connection among the learning standards incorporated into the integrated plan and a clear, direct connection between the standards and the teaching and learning activities.

One of the first planning steps in designing integrated instruction is to construct a calendar curriculum map that lists the topics of study in various content areas and their sequence through the school year. Heidi Hayes Jacobs (1991b, 1997) describes a process of calendar curriculum mapping where teachers plot out the topics that are being taught. Each teacher writes down the major topics of study for his or her content area for each month of the school year. An example of such a calendar curriculum map is shown in Figure 2.2. It is a general overview showing what is taught and when it is taught. This map is an "inventory" of content covered at a particular grade level. This approach to designing integrated instruction begins with the current curriculum rather than starting from scratch.

Curriculum Calendar Map for Grade 7 Team Preliminary Listing Prior to Alignment

	Language Arts	Social Studies	Science	Mathematics
September	Diary of Anne Frank	The Westward Movement	Interactions and Changes	Problem Solving
October				Decimals
November	Sarah Plain and Tall	The Civil War	Diversity of Living Things	Data Analysis
December				Fractions
January	To Kill a Mockingbird	Industrial Revolution, World War I	Force and Motion	Integers
February	Johnny Tremain		The Restless Earth	Ratio/Percents
March	Paul Bunyan and the Winter of the Blue Snow	The Great Depression	The Universe	Probability
April		World War II		Geometry
May	The Raven and the Coming of Daylight		Solutions	Intro to Algebra

Figure 2.2

Integrated Instructional Design

Each of the topics on the curriculum calendar map is associated with specific learning standards. These must be identified and analyzed to determine overlaps and gaps so that adjustments can be made accordingly. Realigning the standards in this way and connecting them to mutually supportive learning activities is central to planning for integrated instruction. The alignment of standards makes it easier to plan integrated lessons and units of study.

Some learning standards have a natural connection, some are mutually reinforcing, and some can be threaded through a "big idea" or theme.

Some learning standards have a natural connection. For example, combining graphing with reporting scientific data not only makes sense in terms of saving instructional time, it is also more meaningful for students. They use graphing for a real purpose.

Some learning standards are mutually reinforcing. For example, when students write about something they have read (short story) or done (science experiment), they communicate their comprehension and understanding and reinforce their writing skills.

Some learning standards are threaded through a "big idea." For example, the study of people in societies combines learning standards from history, geography, government and civics, economics, anthropology, and sociology (Lewis 1993). The focus or emphasis during such a unit of study may shift from history to economics to sociology depending on the learning standards being addressed.

The curriculum mapping procedure may also bring to light needed or desired changes in content. The planning process requires teachers to be open-minded and flexible in making changes to the curriculum. For example, the fact that a particular novel has always been taught at a particular time and grade level is not justification for having it remain so when another novel or reading activity may better reinforce and contribute to integrated learning.

Curriculum integration may be approached in a variety of ways. Robin Fogarty (1991) presents ten models of curriculum integration approaches. She begins by explaining the traditional, separate disciplines model and then describes the integrated models as summarized in Figure 2.3.

Any of the models described above may be used to integrate the curriculum. A discussion among staff members on the pros and cons of these models helps to build common understandings and to develop a rationale for using a particular type of integrated instruction.

A Planning Guide for Integrated Instruction

The Planning Guide for Integrated Instructional Design is a thinking process approach to guide decision-making for integrated instructional planning. It guides the teacher through the preliminary planning process using a series of key questions that are referenced to resources and pertinent information and comments. It is comprised of three sections: (1) Desired Results, Figure 2.4; (2) Lesson Design, Figure 2.7; and (3) Evidence of Learning, Figure 2.8. Each section has three columns: Planning Questions and Decisions, Planning Resources, and Notes and Comments.

Fogarty's Model of Curriculum Integration

Fragmented—The traditional model of separate and distinct disciplines, which fragments the subject areas.

Connected—Within each subject area, course content is connected topic to topic, concept to concept, one year's work to the next, and relates ideas(s) explicitly.

Nested—Within each subject area, the teacher targets multiple skills: a social skill, a thinking skill, and a content specific skill.

Sequenced—Topics or units of study are rearranged and sequenced to coincide with one another. Similar ideas are taught in concert while remaining separate subjects.

Shared—Shared planning and teaching take place in two disciplines in which overlapping concepts or ideas emerge as organizing elements.

Webbed—A major theme is selected and the learning concepts of all the disciplines are examined to determine a "fit" with the major theme. Once the learning concepts are outlined, instructional activities are designed around them. (This is probably the most popular approach to integrating the curriculum.)

Threaded—The metacurricular approach threads thinking skills, social skills, multiple intelligences, technology, and study skills through the various disciplines.

Integrated—This interdisciplinary approach matches subjects with overlaps in topics and concepts, using some team teaching in an authentic integrated model.

Immersed—The disciplines become part of the learner's lens of expertise; the learner filters all content through this lens and becomes immersed in his or her own experience.

Networked—The learner filters all learning through the expert's eye and makes internal connections that lead to external networks of experts in related fields.

Figure 2.3

The Planning Questions and Decisions column poses a series of key questions. The Planning Resources column lists the types of resources and data sources that will facilitate answering the questions in column one. The Notes and Comments column provides information that will further clarify and assist in answering questions in column one. A detailed explanation of each section follows.

Desired Results
Planning Question and Decision 1:
MAKE THE COMMITMENT

The first question: Why will integrated instruction best serve the students? A written statement affirming the value and use of integrated learning serves as a rationale, gives direction to the teaching staff, and communicates to parents and the community what students learn and how they will learn it.

Planning Question and Decision 2:
CONSTRUCT THE CURRICULUM CALENDAR MAP

Once an affirmative decision to use integrated instruction is made, all teachers involved participate in developing the curriculum calendar map. While it is possible for one teacher to design and implement integrated instruction for his or her classroom, the planning effort is more efficient when many teachers are involved. A schoolwide effort to integrate instruction includes all staff members in planning. A grade-level effort includes all teachers of that grade level.

Planning Questions and Decisions 3 and 4:
TRANSLATE CONTENT TO LEARNING STANDARDS

The next step in the planning process involves taking an in-depth look at the content and topics entered on the curriculum calendar map and translating them into learning standards. The Integrated Instructional Planner, Part 1 (Figure 2.5) is used to document the learning standards within the content areas that cluster around a major learning theme. This highlights and enables correction of redundancies and gaps in the curriculum. The priority of the learning standards is considered and decisions are made regarding which standards are to be emphasized. Standards designated as having a high priority due to a weakness determined through student assessment data receive greater emphasis and focus during instruction.

For integrated instruction to be effective, students must understand the patterns of meaning that are intended (Jensen 2000). Therefore, students must have a clear understanding of what they are expected to learn (learning standards) within the integrated activity. The Integrated Instructional Planner Part 1 may be shared with students to enable them to understand the purpose of the integrated activities. For young students, the standards may be rewritten and presented in using simple terminology. (Part 2 of the planner, Figure 2.6, is discussed later.)

Planning Questions and Decisions 5 and 6:
CONSIDER ASSESSMENT STRATEGIES

Student assessment in an integrated setting is best accomplished as a performance task related to the actual learning activities. Any instructional activity may serve as an assessment when the teacher designs a rubric for it. Embedding assessment in instruction is both effective and efficient. Assessment is directly related to what is being learned, and it is not a separate activity that requires additional time or preparation.

Planning Question and Decision 7:
MONITOR STUDENT PROGRESS

An important part of teaching is observing and monitoring students' progress as they engage in learning activities. Planning to do so ensures that this important part of the teaching and learning process is conducted.

Planning Question and Decision 8:
COMMUNICATING ACHIEVEMENT

Achievement measures how well the learning standards have been met. The manner in which learning progress and achievement are communicated may vary from written reports to informal conversations. Students need feedback on their progress with information on how to improve. Parents want to know how their students are progressing and how to help them.

Integrated Instructional Design

SECTION 1: DESIRED RESULTS
Use these questions to plan an integrated instructional design.

Planning Questions and Decisions	Information and Data Sources	Notes and Comments
1. How and why will teaching and learning be more effective if learning standards are integrated within lessons rather than taught separately?	Review professional literature on integrated instruction as it relates to the district curriculum, state standards, student needs based on test data (formal and informal), school improvement goals, district and school goals.	It is important to have a rationale for integrated instruction that is clearly communicated to parents and other stakeholders.
2. What connections exist among the learning standards?	Refer to the Curriculum Calendar Map example (Figure 2.2).	Determine what relationships already exist among the curriculum areas by constructing a curriculum map. Don't try to force objectives to fit into an integrated design. There should be a natural, easy coordination.
3. How will learning standards be organized and documented?	Refer to the Integrated Instruction Planner samples in Figures 2.5 and 2.6.	Construct a graphic showing the relationships of the learning standards across the content areas.
4. What standards are a higher priority than others?	Review student strengths and weaknesses as shown in assessment data.	Determine the level of importance of the standards. Higher priority standards should be given greater instructional time.
5. How will the learning standards be assessed? (Are combined or embedded assessments feasible?)	Review any required and optional assessments.	Planning for assessment is a recursive process. Assessment strategies and tools are tentatively outlined in the initial stages of instructional design, reconsidered and modified as the design emerges, and then finalized with the finished product.
6. What assessment materials are available and what materials need to be developed?	Review rubrics and assessments in district curriculum guides, teacher manuals, other sources.	
7. How will students' difficulties be recognized along the way?	Consider the use of formative assessments and observational techniques.	
8. How will assessment results be communicated to students and parents?	Consider report cards, grading scale, portfolios, and other means.	

Figure 2.4

SECTION 1: DESIRED RESULTS—INTEGRATED
Planning Questions and Decisions
Grade 5 Team

1. How and why will teaching and learning be more effective if learning standards are integrated within lessons rather than taught separately?

We have a modified departmentalized arrangement for grade five students. It seems we have been teaching the same concepts in several different classes. If we plan together we can eliminate this redundancy and have time for teaching other concepts. Also, our students will experience connections among the content areas and be involved in using information across the curriculum. We hope this will strengthen their learning and make it more meaningful.

2. What connections exist among the learning standards?

The standards we have identified are from reading, writing, listening/speaking, science, social studies, and fine arts. At this time we did not see a connection to any math standards or physical education standards but would like to build other units to incorporate these areas also. We, as teachers, are beginning to build connections in our minds. Perhaps this is the first step to helping our students do the same.

3. How will learning standards be organized and documented?

We are going to use the Integrated Instructional Planner, Part 1 as a starting point. We discussed how we would use this tool to provide our students with an overview of what they will learn. We might set up an assembly arrangement to kick this off.

4. What standards are a higher priority than others?

The way we planned this out, all the standards are important. Students will need some out of class time to work on their computer reports so we will need to plan for that. Otherwise, too much class time will be used.

5. How will the learning standards be assessed? (Are combined or embedded assessments feasible?)

We like the idea of using rubrics for the activities along the way rather than having a separate final assessment. The students' reports and presentations will be their final assessment. We reviewed the state standards and the district level requirements. We have even gone beyond with our fine arts standards. Marilyn (art teacher) convinced us that it would be a good connection to all the other content area standards.

6. What assessment materials are available and what materials need to be developed?

We have a writing rubric developed by the teachers that we will use for the writing components. We will develop a rubric with the students for the multimedia presentations they will do. They will use the rubric to evaluate their own presentation. We're cautious about having them evaluate each other. We'll see how it goes.

7. How will students' difficulties be recognized along the way?

We are going to have to have some pretty structured observational strategies to be sure everyone is progressing. Some of us want to administer a forced choice test mid-point and at the conclusion to be sure students are getting it. Maybe we'll do so this time to see how it works out.

8. How will assessment results be communicated to students and parents?

Portfolios! We will have students do a table of contents of their artifacts with a list of the learning standards incorporated in each artifact. We may invite parents to view the presentations – but with so many working during the day it may not be a good idea. Perhaps we can invite some other adults – the DARE officer, librarian, principal – to view the presentations.

Figure 2.4 (continued)

Integrated
Instructional Design

INTEGRATED INSTRUCTIONAL PLANNER – PART 1

Major Learning Theme or Big Idea

Interdependence of living things and the environment

Reading Standards/Benchmarks
1. Recognize compare/contrast text structure as embedded in informational text.
2. Recognize descriptive text structure.
3. Use context to determine word meanings: *habitats, regurgitate, prey.*
4. Use reference material (Internet) to obtain information.

Writing Standards/Benchmarks
1. Use report writing format to present information related to the topic of study.
2. Present information in a clear and coherent manner.
3. Use correct spelling and mechanics.
4. Use Hyper-Studio to generate report.

Listening and Speaking Standards/Benchmarks
1. Speak clearly and precisely using appropriate volume.
2. Use eye contact when speaking.
3.

Science Standards/Benchmarks
1. Wolves live in organized units.
2. Wolves have a communication system.
3. Wolves cooperate in hunting.
4. Wolves are an endangered species.
5. Wolves are part of the ecosystem of the tundra.

Physical Education Standards/Benchmarks
1.
2.   None Applicable
3.

Social Studies Standards/Benchmarks
1. Characteristics, location, and extent of the tundra
2.
3.

Fine Arts Standards/Benchmarks
1. Research artistic renderings of wolves— compare to photos of real wolves (optional).
2.
3.

Mathematics Standards/Benchmarks
1.
2.   None Applicable
3.

Figure 2.5

INTEGRATED INSTRUCTIONAL PLANNER – PART 2

LEARNING STANDARDS/ BENCHMARKS (skills, concepts, strategies, processes)	OPENING ACTIVITIES	TEACHING STRATEGIES/ STUDENT ACTIVITIES	STUDENT GROUPING ARRANGEMENT	MATERIALS AND RESOURCES	ASSESSMENT
Survey and predict what a reading text selection is about. Recognize text structure: (1) Compare/contrast is the minor text structure of gray wolf, arctic wolf, tundra wolf. (2) Description used as a major structure. Develop vocabulary specific to a unit of study: • habitats p. 3, 14 • regurgitate p. 6 • prey p. 7, 8–9, 11 • others to be determined during class discussion	Ask about prior experiences and background knowledge of wolves. Fill in Anticipation Guide worksheet. Preview selection (Book Walk). Predict the kind of information that will be learned from reading this text.		Whole class	Test: *Call of the Wolves* (Berger) Anticipation Guide Worksheet	Observe students to determine on-task behavior, level of text difficulty.
Research and organize major concepts: • Wolves live in organized units. • Wolves have a communication system. • Wolves cooperate in hunting. • Wolves are an endangered species. • Wolves are part of the tundra ecosystem.		Independent reading of text Discussion of text structure and context clues	Individual support group for less able readers Whole class	Text	Continue observation of students. Use observational checklist.
		Concept Mapping (after reading selection)	Small groups (jig-saw approach)	Chart paper, transparencies, markers	Student presentations of concept maps (Use Speaking Rubric to assess.)
Organize information in report format. Write to convey information (expository).		Report related to major concepts, i.e., compare and contrast wolf and human communication Review rubric for informational reports.		Internet resources Presentation software program	Written report (Use existing rubric for informational reports.)
CONCLUSIONS/CONNECTIONS/ REFLECTIONS • Speak clearly and distinctly to an audience. • Discuss prior and newly-acquired information.		Revisit Anticipation Guide. Discuss similarities and differences to *Julie of the Wolves, Call of the Wild.*	Whole group	Discussion questions	Share reports with other classes, parents/family.

Figure 2.6

Integrated Instructional Design

Planning Guide—INTEGRATED Instruction
SECTION 2: DESIGN

Consider these questions as a thinking guide as you plan a differentiated instructional design.

PLANNING QUESTIONS AND DECISIONS	INFORMATION AND DATA SOURCES	NOTES AND COMMENTS
1. What are the learning standards to be achieved?	Use the Integrated Instructional Planner, Part 1, completed in section one of this Planning Guide, to document the learning standards that will be taught.	Be sure to align the learning standards to the activities as shown on the Integrated Instructional Planner. Redundancies should be noted and eliminated.
2. What is a motivating opening for the unit?		Create interest and anticipation in the unit.
3. What are some possible teaching/learning strategies?	Curriculum guides, teaching manuals, professional literature, best practices information, etc., are sources of information for teaching and learning activities.	Use the Integrated Instructional Planner, Part 2, as you consider the planning questions in column one.
4. What materials are needed to support and enhance learning?	Check the materials and resources available through the school, library, community. Students may be asked to bring in related materials if needed and if they have access to them.	
5. What is the appropriate use of technology?	Check Internet sources and software programs.	
6. How will students be grouped?		If small group instruction is planned, consider how this will occur—needs based, interest based, other.
7. What opportunities will students have to reflect on their learning?		Remember to provide time for reflection and processing throughout the unit—not just at the end.

Figure 2.7

SkyLight Professional Development

Lesson Design

In planning integrated instruction, appropriate teaching strategies and learning activities are developed that are directly connected to the learning standards. A single activity may incorporate several learning standards. The complexity of the activities varies with the level of maturity and capabilities of the students and the expertise and confidence of the teacher.

The Integrated Instructional Planner, Part 2 (Figure 2.6) is an overview of how the learning standards are taught. It includes a statement of the learning standards in relation to teaching strategies and student activities.

SECTION 2: DESIGN—INTEGRATED Planning Questions and Decisions
Grade 5 Team

1. What are the learning standards to be achieved?
The major learning of this unit is: Interdependence of living things and the environment. The learning standards cover reading, writing, listening/speaking, science, and social studies. A fine arts objective is an included option. The Integrated Instructional Planner, Part 1 contains the specific list of all the standards.

2. What is a motivating opening for the unit?
All classes will attend the opening activity where the learning standards, purpose, and overview of activities will be described. (Parents could be invited to attend the opening.) Afterwards, students will convene in their teams to discuss what they already know about the topic and preview some of the resources they will use.

3. What are some possible teaching/learning strategies?
Cooperative activities will be balanced with independent activities. Some whole group instruction will be necessary. Guided reading strategies may be used with students who need more support.

4. What materials are needed to support and enhance learning?
Numerous trade books have been preselected and will be available for student use. Also see #6 below.

5. What is the appropriate use of technology?
Students will have opportunities to use the Internet for further research. Presentational software will be used to generate reports.

6. How will students be grouped?
There are four classrooms included in this unit. Two teachers will team teach their groups. All students will be brought together in the library for the presentations on the last three days.

7. What opportunities will students have to reflect on their learning?
Students will revisit the Anticipation Guide filled out at the beginning of their study of wolves. They will discuss similarities and differences of fiction and nonfiction selections on wolves.

(Continued on next page)

Figure 2.7 (continued)

Integrated Instructional Design

Planning Guide–INTEGRATED Instruction
SECTION 2: DESIGN
Use these questions to plan an integrated instructional design.

PLANNING QUESTIONS AND DECISIONS	INFORMATION AND DATA SOURCES	NOTES AND COMMENTS
8. What mini-lessons will be conducted?		Even when learning standards are integrated, it is necessary to develop specific lesson plans for day-to-day teaching. These lessons contain these components: • motivating opening • teaching/learning strategies • materials and resources • student groups • closure • follow-up practice • assessment
9. What forms of practice will be used?		Students may be grouped to address common needs.
10. How long will this unit take?	Calendar of school events, holidays, curriculum pacing guides, and testing schedules are sources of information for scheduling.	Develop a specific organized calendar and schedule for the activites.
11. Are there any foreseeable pitfalls in this lesson?		Think ahead to avoid potential difficulties.
12. What will I do if the lesson/unit doesn't work out?		A fall-back plan is helpful to avoid potential chaos.

Figure 2.7 (continued)

Evidence of Learning

The assessment of student learning is initially considered in section one of the Planning Guide for Integrated Instructional Design. When planning for the integrated unit nears completion, the assessment of student learning and expectations for performance are reconsidered and finalized. Performance assessments with clearly defined rubrics that spell out the criteria for performance and define expectations are appropriate to use with integrated lessons and units. An example of a

SECTION 2: DESIGN–INTEGRATED
Planning Questions and Decisions (continued)
Grade 5 Team

8. What mini-lessons will be conducted?
- *How to use presentational software (all students)*
- *Compare/contrast text structure in reading and writing (all students)*
- *Word study (group based on need)*

9. What forms of practice will be used?
Students who appear to have difficulty with reading vocabulary or report writing will be grouped together for additional support lessons relating to those skills.

10. How long will this unit take?
The study will begin on March 4 and continue for ten days. Students will work on this project for approximately two hours per day. The teachers will schedule mutually convenient times. The amount of time may vary depending on how the students progress.

11. Are there any foreseeable pitfalls in this lesson?
With all this activity going on, some students may be distracted or off-task. Also, some students may not participate fully in the cooperative groups. We'll have to monitor closely and facilitate and model appropriate learning behaviors.

12. What alternatives are there if the lesson doesn't work out?
A demonstration will be used if the student activity doesn't work out as planned. Students will observe and record their findings in their science logs.

Figure 2.7 (continued)

four-point scale rubric appears in Figure 2.9. It describes the level of performance for each of the criteria. The rubric is a tool for the teacher to use in assessing student learning and is also useful to communicate performance expectations to students and parents. Students use the rubric to plan how they will accomplish a task and to evaluate their own performance. An effective teaching/learning strategy is for students to participate in the construction of the rubric.

Integrated Instructional Design

Planning Guide—INTEGRATED Instruction
SECTION 3: EVIDENCE OF LEARNING
Use these questions to plan an integrated instructional design.

PLANNING QUESTIONS AND DECISIONS	INFORMATION AND DATA SOURCES	NOTES AND COMMENTS
1. How will students demonstrate their learning?	See curriculum resource information and best practices information related to types of assessment.	Refer to your planning notes in section one as you finalize decisions regarding assessment.
2. How will the assessment be scored?	Design appropriate rubrics. Consider student participation in design of rubrics.	Possible assessments to consider for integrated learning are usually performance based.
3. How will learning be reported?	Consider the development and use of student portfolios as a means of providing feedback to students and parents.	If a schoolwide grading scale is required, be sure to align rubric levels with the grading scale.
4. How will the assessment results be used?		Use assessment results to determine student strengths and weaknesses and plan the next lessons. When school report cards are in terms of specific content areas and classroom instruction is integrated, assessments need to be correlated to specific learning objectives. The Integrated Instructional Planner (Part 1) may be used to show this correlation by adding a column for the assessments.

Figure 2.8

SECTION 3: EVIDENCE OF LEARNING—INTEGRATED
Planning Questions and Decisions
Grade 5 Team

1. How will the students demonstrate their learning?	2. How will the assessment be scored?	3. How will learning be reported?	4. How will the assessment results be used?
a. Concept Map related to wolves (group task) b. Concept Map presentation to class (all members of group will have a part) c. Written reflection by each student on their participation in the group's work	a. Develop rubric for concept map activity. Distribute to students when assignment is given. b. Speaking/listening rubric to assess presentation of information c. No scoring – comments only	a. Group scores based on rubric b. Individual scores based on rubric c. Comments from the teacher	a. Feedback for students on their work as a group b. Feedback for students and teacher on how speaking/listening skills are used c. Feedback for teacher on how students participated in the group work
Selected response test (20 items)	Answer key (20 items, 5 points each); sign up to use scantron for scoring	Go over test items with students. Grades will be determined according to the schoolwide grading scale.	Determine which students need reinforcement of factual information. Students make corrections as necessary. Include results in quarterly report card grade.
Written report—specific topic related to wolves selected by each student	Writing rubric (district)	Copy of rubric showing performance level will be returned to students. Teacher comments will be included as appropriate.	The rubric will provide feedback to the student. A total of 10 points for this assignment will be included in the quarterly report card grade.
Report—group task Students will use information from their individual reports to create a computer-generated presentation.	Rubric on presentation of reports	Copy of rubric for each group will be scored. Teacher comments will be included.	Feedback for students and teacher on how students worked as a group.
Portfolios—All assessments above will be included with an explanation of the learning standards included in each one.	Rubric developed by teacher and students	Students will share portfolios with parents.	Feedback for students, teachers, and parents on group and individual participation in this unit.

Figure 2.8 (continued)

Scoring Rubric for a Story Map

	Attempted (1)	Developing (2)	Developed (3)	Accomplished (4)
Setting	Shows no evidence of understanding time or place.	Identifies a time and place.	Identifies time and place and provides some description.	Identifies detailed components of time and place with extensive description.
Characters	Does not identify characters or incorrectly lists characters.	Lists some characters. May provide limited description.	Lists main characters and includes some roles, traits, and/or relationships.	Identifies all main characters; clearly defines their roles, traits, and/or relationships.
Problem	Identifies incorrect problem.	Shows limited or incomplete understanding of the problem.	States the main problem clearly.	States the problem completely and elaborates reasons, background, etc.
Events	Lists incorrect events.	States some major events.	States major events in proper sequence.	States all major events clearly and in proper sequence with some elaboration.
Solution	Identifies incorrect solution.	Identifies partial solution.	States the solution clearly.	States the solution clearly and explains why it resolves the problem.
Personal Reaction	Does not provide any personal reaction or connection to prior knowledge.	Provides very limited personal reaction.	Provides personal reaction and explains some connections to prior knowledge and other learning.	Personal reaction and connections are logically explained.

Using the Integrated Instructional Design Planning Guide

The Integrated Instructional Design Planning Guide is a thinking process approach to planning instruction. Preservice teachers and novice teachers will find it helpful to follow all the steps in using the planning guide. Teachers who have little or no previous experience in planning integrated instruction will find the planning guide a supportive scaffold in their initial efforts. As a result, subsequent planning will be easier. Experienced teachers with an understanding of instructional design may find that they need only review the questions and activities and focus on those areas that will enhance their planning efforts. An example of how a fifth-grade teaching team completed the Planning Guide was shown throughout this selection. The team used the guide to structure their discussion and begin their planning.

1. Read the planning guide in its entirety

Become familiar with the planning guide before you begin using it. This will save you time in the long run. Get the "big picture" in mind before filling in the details.

2. Think it through

Begin with Section 1: Desired Results. Think about the questions in column one and write down your thoughts and reactions to the planning questions. Consult the data and information sources suggested in column two and note the reminders and supplemental information in column three. Add notes and comments of your own that will be helpful in subsequent planning. Planning questions may be deleted or added to fit your situation. Continue through Section 2: Lesson Design and Section 3: Evidence of Learning.

3. Synthesize information

Step two above has led you to study and analyze the current curriculum and begin planning integrated instruction. The information you have obtained is now synthesized and translated onto the Integrated Instructional Planner (Figures 2.5 and 2.6).

Summary of General Planning Steps for Integrated Learning

The Integrated Instructional Design Planning Guide contains the detailed description of how to plan for integrated instruction. The steps below are a general outline of the process.

1. Think through the process of integrated instruction using the Integrated Instructional Design Planning Guide.
2. Determine rationale for using an integrated learning approach.
3. Discuss and select an integration model (Figure 2.3).
4. Develop a Curriculum Calendar Map.
5. Align topics of study on the Curriculum Calendar Map.
6. Document learning standards and connections on the Integrated Instructional Planner, Part 1.
7. Develop the instructional overview (for Integrated Instructional Planner). Determine and develop specific lesson plans as needed.

BIBLIOGRAPHY

Beane, J. A. 1993. Problems and possibilities for an integrative curriculum. In *Integrating the curricula*, ed. R. Fogarty, 69–83. Arlington Heights, IL: IRI/SkyLight Publishing, Inc.

Brophy, J., and J. Alleman. 1991. A caveat: Curriculum integration isn't always a good idea. *Eduational Leadership.* 49(2): 66–70.

Burke, K. 1994. *How to assess authentic learning.* Arlington Heights, IL: SkyLight Training and Publishing, Inc.

———. 1999. *How to assess authentic learning,* 3rd ed. Arlington Heights, IL: SkyLight Training and Publishing.

Caine, R., and G. Caine. 1991. *Making connections: Teaching and the human brain.* Alexandria, VA: Association for Supervision and Curriculum Development.

Canady, R., and M. Rettig. 1996. Models of block scheduling. In *Block scheduling: Time to learn.* Arlington Heights, IL: SkyLight Training and Publishing.

Dewey, J. 1913. *Interest and effort in education.* Boston: Houghton Mifflin.

Drake, S. M. 1993. *Planning integrated curriculum.* Alexandria, VA: Association for Supervision and Curriculum Development.

Ellis, A. K., and J. T. Fouts. 1997. *Research on educational innovations.* Larchmont, NY: Eye on Education.

Fogarty, R. 1991. *How to integrate the curricula.* Arlington Heights, IL: IRI/SkyLight Publishing.

———. 1996. *Block scheduling: A collection of articles.* Arlington Heights, IL: SkyLight Training and Publishing.

———. 1997. *Brain-compatible classrooms.* Arlington Heights, IL: SkyLight Training and Publishing, Inc.

Gehrke, N. J. 1993. Explorations of teachers' development of integrative curriculums. In *Integrating the curricula*, ed. R. Fogarty. Arlington Heights, IL: IRI/SkyLight Publishing, Inc.

Guthrie, J., and A. McCann. 1997. Characteristics of classrooms that promote motivations and strategies for learning. In *Reading engagement: Motivating readers through integrated instruction,* ed. J. Guthrie and A. Wigfield, 128–148. Newark, DE: International Reading Association.

Jacobs, H. 1991a. On interdisciplinary curriculum: A conversation with Heidi Hayes Jacobs. *Educational Leadership.* 49(2): 24–26.

———. 1991b. Planning for curriculum integration. *Educational Leadership.* 49(2): 27–28.

———. 1997. *Mapping the big picture.* Alexandria, VA: Association for Supervision and Curriculum Development.

Jensen, E. 2000. *Brain based learning.* Del Mar, CA: Turning Point Publishing.

Lewis, A. 1993. Getting unstuck: Curriculum as a tool of reform. In *Integrating the curricula*, ed. R. Fogarty, 49–60. Arlington Heights, IL: IRI/SkyLight Publishing, Inc.

Moye, V. 1997. *Conditions that support transfer for change,* Arlington Heights, IL: IRI/SkyLight Training and Publishing.

Relan, A., and R. Kimpston. 1993. Curriculum integration: A critical analysis of practical and conceptual issues. In *Integrating the curricula*, ed. R. Fogarty, 31–47. Arlington Heights, IL: IRI/SkyLight Publishing, Inc.

Rippa, S. A. 1988. *Education in a free society.* New York: Longman.

Shanahan, T. 1997. Reading-writing relationships, thematic units, inquiry learning. . . In pursuit of effective integrated literacy instruction. *Reading Teacher.* 51(1): 12–19.

Withrow, F., H. Long, and G. Marx. 1999. *Preparing schools and school systems for the 21st century.* Arlington, VA: American Association of School Administrators.

Zemelman, S., H. Daniels, and A. Hyde. 1993. *Best practice: New standards for teaching and learning in America's schools.* Portsmouth, NH: Heinemann.

Mentors may use the following six blackline masters as they coach protégés in how to plan integrated lessons:

- Curriculum Calendar Map
- Section 1 Desired Results—Integrated: Planning Questions and Decisions
- Section 2 Design—Integrated: Planning Questions and Decisions
- Section 3 Evidence of Learning—Integrated: Planning Questions and Decisions
- Integrated Instructional Planner, Part 1
- Integrated Instructional Planner, Part 2

CURRICULUM CALENDAR MAP

	Language Arts	Social Studies	Science	Mathematics	Music	Art	Phys. Ed.
September							
October							
November							
December							
January							
February							
March							
April							
May							

Blackline 2.1

SECTION 1: DESIRED RESULTS – INTEGRATED
Planning Questions and Decisions

1. How and why will teaching and learning be more effective if learning standards are integrated within lessons rather than taught separately?

2. What connections exist among the learning standards?

3. How will learning standards be organized and documented?

4. What standards are a higher priority than others?

5. How will the learning standards be assessed? (Are combined or embedded assessments feasible?)

6. What assessment materials are available and what materials need to be developed?

7. How will students' difficulties be recognized along the way?

8. How will assessment results be communicated to students and parents?

SECTION 2: DESIGN – INTEGRATED
Planning Questions and Decisions

1. What are the learning standards to be achieved?

2. What is a motivating opening for the unit?

3. What are some possible teaching/learning strategies?

4. What materials are needed to support and enhance learning?

5. What is the appropriate use of technology?

6. How will students be grouped?

7. What opportunities will students have to reflect on their learning?

8. What mini-lessons will be conducted?

9. What forms of practice will be used?

10. How long will this unit take?

11. Are there any foreseeable pitfalls in this lesson?

12. What will I do if the lesson/unit doesn't work out?

Blackline 2.3

SECTION 3: EVIDENCE OF LEARNING – INTEGRATED
Planning Questions and Decisions

1. How will students demonstrate their learning?

2. How will the assessment be scored?

3. How will learning be reported?

4. How will the assessment results be used?

INTEGRATED INSTRUCTIONAL PLANNER – PART 1

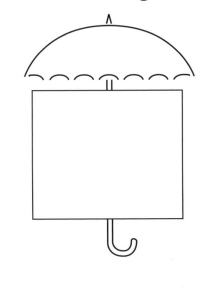

Major Learning Theme or Big Idea

Reading Standards/Benchmarks
1.
2.
3.
4.

Writing Standards/Benchmarks
1.
2.
3.
4.

Listening/Speaking Standards/Benchmarks
1.
2.
3.

Science Standards/Benchmarks
1.
2.
3.

Physical Education Standards/ Benchmarks
1.
2.
3.

Social Studies Standards/Benchmarks
1.
2.
3.

Fine Arts Standards/Benchmarks
1.
2.
3.

Mathematics Standards/Benchmarks
1.
2.
3.

Integrated
Instructional Design

INTEGRATED INSTRUCTIONAL PLANNER – PART 2						
Learning Standards/Benchmarks (skills, concepts, strategies, processes)	**Opening Activities**	**Teaching Strategies/Student Activities**	**Student Grouping Arrangement**	**Materials and Resources**	**Assessment**	
Conclusions/Connections/Reflections						

Blackline 2.6

Fogarty and Stoehr provide additional concrete examples of how themes serve as highly visible organizers for curriculum design. Themes make it easy for teachers to integrate curricular content and motivate student learning as well as help students understand the "big ideas" and key concepts.

Themes

by **Robin Fogarty and Judy Stoehr**

Why Bother?

Probably the most common form of curriculum integration is the thematic learning unit. From preschool classrooms to college-level practicums, themes act as umbrellas. They range from primary topics such as *bears* and *gardens* to themes for older groups such as *the solar system* and *the human mind*. Themes provide highly visible organizers for curriculum design, making it easy for teachers and teacher teams to coordinate curricular content. Themes ignite learning for students and act as a hook.

Themes as Organizing Centers

The following are organizing centers teachers can use to find appropriate themes:

Topics: dinosaurs, bears, rain forests
Concepts: patterns, discoveries, relationships
Events: field trips, musicals, spaghetti dinners
Projects: inventions, murals, quilts
Novels: *To Kill a Mockingbird, The Old Man and the Sea*
Films: *Twelve Angry Men, Star Wars, Gettysburg*
Songs: "Scarborough Fair," "We Are the World"

Adapted from *Integrating Curricula with Multiple Intelligences: Teams Themes and Threads* by Robin Fogarty and Judy Stoehr, pp. 84–134. © 1995 by IRI/SkyLight Training and Publishing, Inc. Used with permission.

Topics

Topics tend to be subject related, concrete, and narrower than conceptual themes. Topical themes encompass science topics such as the *solar system, mammals,* or *simple machines,* as well as social studies topics that include the *Civil War, Canada,* or *deserts.* Sometimes topics evolve from an art focus, such as *doodles* or *native crafts,* while other topics are rooted in technology, like *computers* or *codes.* Still other topics emerge from literature. Among typical literature-based topics are *heroes, mysteries,* or *travel,* and more generic topics such as *biographies* or *discoveries.*

Concepts

Concepts are broader ideas than topics. They are more abstract and global in nature. The distinguishing element of conceptual themes is their ability to reach out to many disciplines and defy subject matter boundaries.

Patterns is a conceptual theme that branches out to all content. This theme abounds in math (geometric designs, tessellations and algebraic notations, numeric progressions, etc.) and in science (periodic table of elements, branching patterns, waves, genetic compositions, etc.). The same is true of patterns in history (history repeats itself), economics (cycles of the stock market), and geography (ocean currents, tectonic plates). Naturally, art is rich with patterns (color, texture, design) as is music (rhythm, beat, melody). (There are patterns in health, patterns in business, and patterns in technology.) There are even patterns in physical education and sports (the figure eight in skating). The concept of patterns is rich and fertile and includes all aspects of the school curricula. Possible themes include *cycles, change, harmony, diversity, relationships, fear, love, hate, prejudice, tolerance, courage,* and *responsibility.* Each has the ability to stretch across several disciplines and areas of subject matter content.

Events

Events act like a magnetic field, organizing all activities toward a forceful center. An event might be simple, such as a *spaghetti dinner* for the class, a *reception for the old-folks home,* or a *guest speaker.* However, it may also be large scale, such as a *fashion show,* a *three-day outdoor educational trip,* a *school play,* a *musical,* or an *eighth grade trip to Washington, D.C.* Regardless of the size or magnitude of the event, it rallies the same energetic effect on all it touches.

Sometimes an event is deliberately planned to be a high-profile culmination of a curriculum project. For example, one school organized a literature-based unit for fiction reading called "Up, Up, and Away!" As students read, they collected tokens for each book. The goal for the school was one thousand books (one thousand tokens). The pay off? If they reached the magic number, the principal would sit all day in a hot air balloon above the school. Needless to say, it created all kinds of reading activity.

Projects

Some projects can be almost overwhelming, such as *building a house* or a *solar-powered car.* Some projects are a little more manageable, such as *creating a package* that can protect an uncooked egg dropped from a height of eight feet or *producing a school yearbook.* Other projects can be simple in comparison, such as *science fair projects, piñatas, jack-o-lanterns,* or *window-sill gardens.* Whatever the project, big or small, long or short, it has the power to elicit every student's focused energy.

Novels and Films

There is nothing as compelling to a diverse audience as a good novel or first-rate film. The story line, setting, characters, plot, subplots, major and minor themes, and, of course, climax all provide fertile ground for exploring ideas. Imagine the exciting curriculum ideas that could be inspired by *Moby Dick, Old Yeller, The Phantom Tollbooth, Twelve Angry Men,* or *Journey to the Center of the Earth.* The possibilities for meaningful thematic units are limitless.

SkyLight Professional Development

Section I: Designing Learning Experiences | 67

Songs

Songs, along with drama, sculpture, dance, and other art forms, are the memory of a culture: Its victories and tragedies, its heroes and villains, its hopes and despair are all common themes of songs handed down from generation to generation within every culture. Songs' stories, settings, characters, and plots are no less exciting than those of novels or films. They are a perfect centerpiece for the integrated curriculum, both for what they are and what they can do as a bridge to other learning.

Songs such as "Shenandoah," "I've Been Working on the Railroad," and "Home on the Range" each tell a story about a time, a place, a group of people in the history of the United States. "Follow the Drinking Gourd" captures students' interest and imagination as they learn that it is an African-American song about slavery and the Underground Railroad. Consider the lessons that could develop from songs such as "Abraham, Martin, and John," "Fifty Nifty United States," "It's a Small World," "Free at Last," "Lift Ev'ry Voice and Sing," "I'm in the Army Now," "One Tin Soldier," "Waltzing Matilda," "So Long, Frank Lloyd Wright," and many, many more. These lessons capture the interest and imagination of students, motivating them to learn about and understand the world, both past and present. Lessons such as these offer yet another dimension to integrating the curriculum through multiple intelligences.

Themes as Catalysts

Students are another primary reason for using themes in the K–12 or college classroom. Themes ignite learning for students and provide highly visible, all-encompassing umbrellas for curriculum and instruction. As students immerse themselves in a thematic unit, they realize how all of the activities connect under the umbrella of the theme. Themes as catalysts have kid appeal and are relevant, purposeful, meaningful, holistic, and contextual.

Kid Appeal

Keeping in mind the fact that themes ignite student interest, it becomes paramount that theme selections have "kid appeal." In fact, why not involve the students themselves in the selection of themes? Let them brainstorm lists of ideas to provide genuine impact in the selection process. Imagine the excitement the *atomic bomb* as a theme would generate. This topic has much more kid appeal than the concept of *nuclear energy*. Although topical themes may be selected because they are compatible to students' interests, the bigger ideas can remain the curricular focus for planning.

Relevant, Purposeful, and Meaningful

Themes not only provide the motivation or hook for students, they also make learning more relevant. Once students see the connection between things they're learning in class and things they're using in life, learning at school becomes purposeful and meaningful. Thus, by connecting lessons to situations outside of the classroom, students realize the relevance of academic tasks. They understand that calculating an area is not a mere exercise, but rather an equation that can help them determine such things as how much paint to buy to repaint their bedrooms.

Holistic and Contextual

Combining integrated learning with applied learning is similar to marrying academia to vocational education, tech prep to academic subjects, or the practical to the theoretical. It is exciting and relevant for kids. It also provides a holistic model of instruction and curriculum that fosters learning in context. Students can learn one-to-one correspondence by passing out straws. They can learn about the Pythagorean theorem as it applies to cutting rafters for a house. And, they can learn about writing by publishing a school paper. Through application, academic content is easily integrated with situations outside of the classroom. Learning is automatically and meaningfully transferred from learning the text to learning the *context*. Not only is contextual learning more helpful for students, it's also an efficient model for teachers. By embedding learning in relevant, holistic contexts, skill building is enhanced through applied problem solving. In summary, contextual learning, supported by thematic teaching, provides an efficient and often time-saving model for curriculum design.

Who Says?

Voices from the field that promote thematic teaching span the United States. There is Jacobs in New York, Lounsbury in Florida, Beane and Fogarty in Illinois, Vars in Ohio, Grady in Colorado, and Kovalik in Washington. While each presents an experienced voice with practical and easy-to-implement ideas, each also has his or her own tenor.

Jacobs

Jacobs' design options for interdisciplinary curriculum feature six ideas: discipline-based, parallel, multidisciplinary, interdisciplinary, integrated day, and complete programs. Several of the options support the use of themes as organizing centers. Jacobs' *Interdisciplinary Curriculum: Design and Implementation* (1990) provides a collection of essays delineating the process of developing thematic units. Perkin's article "Selecting Fertile Themes for Integrated Learning" is included in this especially rich anthology. Perkins' examination of two themes (transportation and argument and evidence) reveals the keys to fertile themes.

Vars

Vars' *Interdisciplinary Teaching: Why and How* (1993) is a classic middle school book. Originally published as a monograph in 1987, Vars second edition provides an expanded resource. Specifically, thematic units are targeted through the core curriculum and feed off student issues and concerns. Curriculum themes, according to Vars, incorporate content, skills, and concepts as well as personal and social concerns. The result is often a problem-centered thematic unit such as *maturing, production and consumption,* or *policy making.*

Lounsbury

Another voice from the middle school movement is John Lounsbury. An editor of the 1992 edition of *Connecting Curriculum through Interdisciplinary Instruction,* he intertwines the development of interdisciplinary instruction with the idea of teaming. (He says the letters in the word team stand for "together everyone achieves more.") In *Doda* (1992), Lounsbury uses an interdisciplinary web to create thematic units such as *Chinese culture, architecture,* and *aviation.*

Fogarty

Fogarty's ten views of integrated curricula also provide options or models similar to Jacobs'. Fogarty's (1991) models include ten ideas: fragmented, connected, nested, sequenced, shared, webbed, threaded, integrated, immersed, and networked. (To read more about Fogarty's work, see Selection 1, Defining Brain-Compatible Classrooms; for more on Fogarty's ten models, see selection 2, page 41.)

Beane

Beane (1993), yet another familiar voice from the middle schools, is a longtime advocate of curriculum integration. His belief that themes, questions, and activities should be generated by the students themselves puts an authentic learner-centered focus on thematic instruction. Stressing the idea of students generating essential questions to frame a theme is a major component of Beane's work.

Themes

Hundreds of Themes

Dinosaurs; The Future; Man vs. Nature; Whales; Myths; Robots; Time After Time; The Dawn of Civilization; Inventions; Friendship; Bears; Environment; Up, Up, and Away; Old Favorites; America the Beautiful; Our Canadian Neighbors; Across the Sea; Simple Machines; Shoes; Win or Lose?; Animals; Long Ago; Change; Patterns; Survival; Why Man Creates; Biases; Media; Biography; The Renaissance; How Dry Is the Desert?; The Ice Age; The Solar System; Water; Friend or Foe?; Cultural Diversity; Sound; Light; Insects; Cemetery Study; The Mind; Birds; Under the Sea; Around the World; Pyramids; War; War and Peace; Native Americans; The Circus; Hats; Shapes; Statistics; The Shrinking Globe; Conflicts; Transportation; Argument and Evidence; Beginnings; Perseverance; Family Treasures; Pilots and Passengers; Connections; When Time Began; 2020; Profiles in Courage; Fear; Trade; Exploration; Discovery; Love; Citizenship; Food, Clothing, and Shelter; The Community; Zoos; Nature's Fury; Dreams and Nightmares; Skyscrapers; Volcanoes; Earthquakes and Other Natural Disasters; The Weather; Heroes; Male vs. Female; Creatures; Craters; Submarines; Fish; Seashells; Colors; Rainbows; Reptiles; Technology; Television: Good or Evil?; Tragedy; Romance; Space; Spiders; Pioneers; Halloween; Holidays; The Wild West; Careers; Wisdom; Courage; Authority; Nutrition; Wellness and Fitness; Global Economy; Latin America; Natural Wonders; Death and Dying; Pets; Decisions; Mysteries; Magic; Mammals

Grady

Grady's approach to interdisciplinary curriculum uses themes as umbrella ideas to connect the disciplines. Her work at the Mid-continent Regional Educational Laboratory (McREL) in Colorado utilizes the ideas of standards and benchmarks as guides to integrated thematic learning that targets key goals. Grady uses the ideas of developing "chunks" of integrated curriculum with the driving force of "critical content."

Kovalik

ITI: The Model: Integrated Thematic Instruction is a major work by Kovalik (1993). Based on brain research, teaching strategies, and curriculum development, Kovalik's model uses a yearlong theme as the "heart and soul" of the classroom. The yearlong theme is a big idea with a "kid-grabbing twist" (Kovalik & Olsen, 1993). Using theme titles such as "What Makes It Tick?" or "You Can't Fool Mother Nature," Kovalik illustrates ways to evaluate a theme, identify key points, and find multiple resources. Skills and concepts are targets for thematic instruction.

GUIDEBOOK

I Hear It!

Themes
(to the tune of M-O-T-H-E-R)

T is for the themes we think of daily.
H is for the honing of our lists.
E means we extrapolate criteria.
M means we manipulate the theme.
E expands activities and learning.
S is for selecting key goals.
Put them all together, they spell
   THEMES.
They open up the world for me.

Themes are fun, inviting, and doable, and they make learning exciting for students and for teachers. Themes also organize content and create manageable chunks of connected ideas. But, there are many questions about how we can make these themes work for us. How do we infuse integrity into our thematic units? How do we manipulate themes for real accountability? How do we align themes with our valued goals? How do we think about themes before plunging in? The answer to these questions is as simple as T-H-E-M-E-S (see Figures 3.1–3.3).

More Themes

Sports; You; Skeletons; Music, Ballet, and Drama; Games Around the World; Antarctica; Fair-Weather Friends; Hobbies and Collections; Collectibles; Superheroes; Presidents; Choices; Honesty; Farms; Industrialization; The Paper Chase; Science Fiction; Family Living; The Computer Age; The Arts; Islands; The Written Word; News; The City; Opera; Famous Battles; Newspapers; Headline News; Superstitions; Legends; Texas; Mexico; Egypt; Favorite Places; Oregon Trail; Cluster; The Moon; Hemingway; The American Dream; The Young and the Old; Bridges; Currency; Language; A Picture Is Worth a Thousand Words; Caring; Animals at Work; Critics' Choices; Film; Human Connections; Archeology; Humor; Drugs: Beneficial or Harmful; Addiction; Plants; Senses; Magnets; Both Sides of the Issue; The Research Search; Famous People; Fame or Fortune?; Competition; Cooperation; Leadership; Tongue Twisters; Fables; Tall-Tales; Riddles; Controversy; Gardens; Witches, Ghosts, and Goblins; A Sign of the Times; Flowers; Celebrations of Life; Anecdotes; Afterthoughts; The Universe; Truth; Moral Dilemmas; Ethics; Pigs; Rain Forests; Evolution; Night and Day; Why Do People Develop Habits?; There's No Place Like Home; The Ugly American; Tourists; The Sky Above; Pollution; Handicaps; Fantasy; The Middle East; Faces; Clowns; Masks; Faulkner; The American Novelist; Leverage; Debate; Cartoons; The Changing Tide; Megatrends; Warm Fuzzies; Creative Features; Frogs, Toads, and Princesses; Fairy Tales; The World of Work; Ways of Knowing; Man Through Art; Happiness; Picture This; Every Ending Is a Beginning; Short Cuts; Fashion; Prey; Talk, Tales, and Tidbits; Seasons; Wheels; Whatchamacallits!

Themes

Themes

Think of themes		Generate; brainstorm 20–30 ideas; gather and collect in an ongoing manner.
Hone the list		Sort the themes into 3 categories: concepts, topics, problems; sift and select 3 (one from each category).
Extrapolate the criteria		Reflect and project reasons why a theme is valued; develop criteria to use it again.
Manipulate the theme		Reflect on possible questions: pose a question as the thematic focus; refine into a higher-order question with a "how" or "why."
Expand into activities		Generate viable activities; list relevant learning episodes; include activities for all the multiple intelligences and the various curriculum areas.
Select goals and assessments		Delineate aims and objectives; align activities to the valued goals and standards; determine assessment strategies.

Figure 3.1

Think about themes by generating a lengthy list. As a faculty or team, brainstorm an initial list of twenty, thirty, or fifty ideas. Post the list on large paper in the teacher's lounge. Commit to doubling the list by the end of the week. Then start "stealing" ideas from everywhere. Gather ideas from books, journals, neighboring districts, other teachers, old units, and textbook concepts. Collect as many different ideas as possible. Think of the various disciplines and themes in your studies. Create a list with the students, and assign another list for homework to get the parents involved. Do whatever it takes to compile a longer list of "candidate" themes than the one listed earlier. Challenge yourselves: try to add to the list without duplicating any words already listed.

Hone the list. Just because you've brainstormed, collected, gathered, and listed one hundred themes does not mean that all of them are great (at least for your purposes). Sort out the ideas by dividing them into a list of three distinct sections. Label the sections as topics, concepts, and problems. Discuss or define what a concept is, which things are topics, and where the problems are. Or, sort out the ideas on the list and see what defining elements occur in the sorting process. Then, categorize the ideas as topics, concepts, or problems. With your colleagues and/or teammates, select three "champion" themes—one from each of the categories (e.g., a topical theme—dinosaurs; a conceptual theme—systems; and a problematic theme—How Does Man Survive?) Display the champion themes for all to see. Use whatever method necessary to reach an agreement on the three. Then, take a moment to reflect on how your team finally reached its decision.

Extrapolate criteria. Think about tug-of-war discussions that have resulted in champion themes. Recall the reasons, rationale, and persuasive arguments that convinced everyone a particular theme had merit or was better than another. Justify your choices. Know why one theme stands out above the rest. Dialogue with team members and discover their reasons for choosing certain themes. List the emergent criteria on large paper and post them next to the champion themes. Be clear about the criteria for selecting themes, because they are revisited each time a new theme is needed. Then, select one of the three themes to work with further.

Manipulate the theme. Massage the theme. Reflect on possible questions that naturally occur. What do you want to know? What are the essential questions—the questions that pique interest and invite investigation? Capture the questions of the children. Pose questions of value and notice how the thematic focus is transformed and raised to higher levels. Search for questions that provoke the mind and incite emotion. Think about how, why, and where. Transpose the theme into a question that evokes curiosity and intrigue—a question that drives the theme and brings all on board. Don't hurry through this part. As Francis Bacon once said, "A prudent question is one-half of wisdom." Process the theme by postulating all kinds of questions; refine them until a final question takes shape.

Expand into activities. Hook into a theme (and a question) and produce activities that are triggered by this theme. "Web" the theme out to the various curricular areas: math, science, social studies, language arts, art, music, health, PE, and technology (Fogarty, 1991). Think of more activities for integrated learning than can be done. Include activities that involve multiple intelligences. Create a fun and exciting atmosphere as you recall, borrow, and invent appropriate and appealing activities for students. And, of course, include student choices and interests in an expanded and elaborated web.

Select key goals and assessments. Armed with the valued learner goals that comprise aims and objectives, take time to focus on the traditional curricular areas in the web—math, science, social studies, etc.—and examine each of the activities for alignment with expected goals. Use this step to "selectively abandon" and "judiciously include" activities. Once you have an organizing theme or question, you can literally generate hundreds of activities. The task now is to refine the thematic unit with only those activities that truly target significant goals. Each activity, in whatever subject area, needs to be rich enough to provide fertile ground for thoughtful learning and mindful production. Once the activities are refined and aligned, an assessment is easily made with authentic measures such as portfolios and performances.

Figure 3.1 (continued)

Middle School or High School Theme

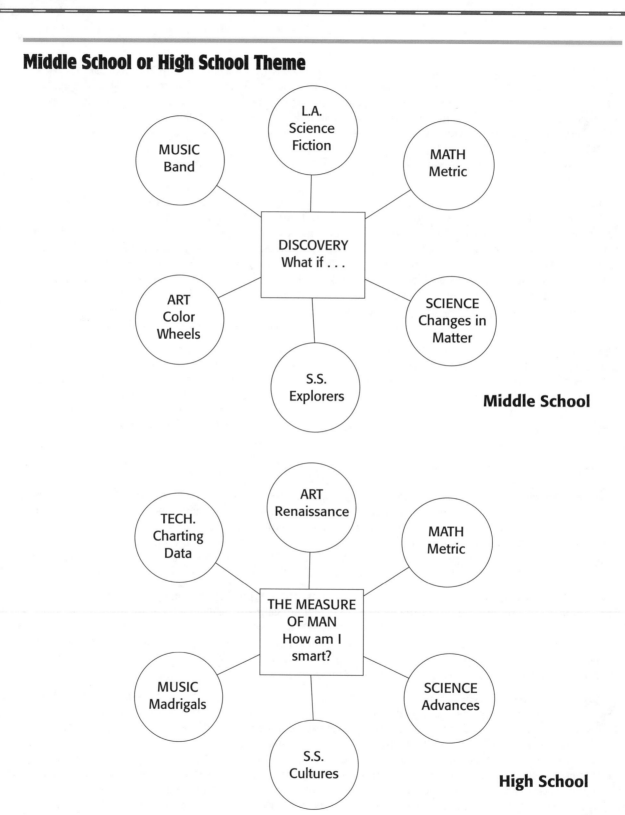

Figure 3.2

Illustrated Themes

Think of themes

Friends
The World
Animals
Harmony
The Arts

Argument and
  Evidence
Inventions
Cultures
Neighbors

People,
  Places, Things
Old Favorites
Time After
  Time

Hone the list

TOPICS	CONCEPTS	PROBLEMS
Dinosaurs	Patterns	Hostages
Bears	Cycles	Health Care
Environment	Conflict	School
Plants	Change	Funding

Extrapolate the criteria

CRITERIA FOR A FERTILE THEME

1. Relevant to students
2. Many resources available
3. Broad enough for all curriculum areas
4. Intrigues teachers and students

Manipulate the theme

Environment—Feast or Famine?
Citizenship—How Am I a Good Citizen?
Creativity—Why Does Man Create?
The American Dream—Fantasy or Reality?
Desert—How Dry Is the Desert?

Expand into activities

MUSIC Band
L.A. Science Fiction
MATH Metric
DISCOVERY What if . . .
ART Color Wheels
S.S. Explorers
SCIENCE Changes in Matter

Select goals and assessments

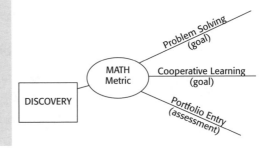

DISCOVERY

MATH Metric

Problem Solving (goal)

Cooperative Learning (goal)

Portfolio Entry (assessment)

Figure 3.3

Themes

Selected Theme

Themes may be deductively developed with a selected theme. The *selected theme* is chosen from a bank of theme ideas. We will look at a few vignettes that exemplify how selected themes come about.

Deductive Process/Webbed to Subject Matter: *How Courage Is Like the Rain: A Philosophy Study for the Senior Cluster*

> Courage? What does it mean? What comes to mind? Hero. Sudden. Unexpected. Save a child. Train track rescue. *Profiles in Courage.* Inner self. Recognition. War hero. Medals. Purple Heart. Strength. Cowardice. *Catch-22.* Moral courage lion. *The Wizard of Oz.* Stand up! Stand out! Famous. High dive. Risk. Bungee jump. Untested. Undetected. Under pressure. Surprise, like a summer shower. Rain.
>
> The brainstorm flows through its natural cycle: a burst of ideas, a lull, reignited associations, silliness, novelty, and a final winding down. The teacher pounces on the final word, *rain,* and asks, "How is courage like rain?" Heads together, pens poised, the small groups discuss possible comparisons and one team writes on a large piece of poster paper. As the student writes, he thinks out loud: "Courage is like rain because both . . . hmm . . . both can happen suddenly; they can come upon you unexpectedly and . . . Wait, I've got it . . . they often result in a change for you. If you get caught in the rain and get wet, you change your clothes. If you act in a courageous way it may change how you feel about yourself."

So goes the latest scenario in the senior cluster. Staffed with a teacher team that consists of a guest artist, a visiting attorney, a guidance counselor, and a literature teacher, this philosophy study targets students from the senior cluster levels: incoming freshmen through graduating seniors. Designed around the discipline of philosophy, interdisciplinary approaches to subject matter expose students to content through dilemma and to the paradox and ambiguity of universally compelling philosophical issues: truth, justice, equality, authority, wisdom, courage, life, death, and love. Each is selected as a theme to study.

Themes can be explored in myriad domains. For example, in an experiment with authority, students can read about historically renowned figures of authority such as Hitler, Stalin, and McCarthy. They can compare these historical figures with authority figures in their own lives. In turn, literature can become a springboard for historical simulations, real-life role plays, personal journals, and depictions of authority through visual and performing arts. Following is an example of how a theme is explored by a language arts teacher and students.

> TEACHER: Courage is like rain . . . isn't that a fresh idea? Let's explore some of the ideas a bit further. For example, what do you mean when you say courage is unexpected? Give us a real illustration.

> STUDENT #1: Well, when you step on the high dive and you look down, you're really afraid of the fall. Yet, you prepare, just as you've done in practice many times before; you proceed through your rituals of standing at the invisibly marked spot, stepping deliberately through the approach, focusing yourself mentally, and performing the precision dive with skill and grace. That's courage, if you ask me.

> TEACHER: I agree. That's certainly a grand display of physical courage. What else?

> STUDENT #2: Standing up for what you believe in, in front of your friends, when you know you're in the minority. I think that shows courage.

COURAGE

Assignment:

Please prepare an answer to the essential question "How Common Is Courage?" You may use one or any combination of the following expressive forms:
- Art
- Music
- Drama
- Writing
- Speaking
- Other

You may work by yourself or in collaboration with one or two others.

Presentations begin next week. You will have 25 minutes to present and 5 minutes for feedback. Please sign up for a time.

TEACHER: Tell us more about that.

STUDENT #3: Maybe you like classical music because you've had to learn it and play it in orchestra, but your friends want to listen to hard rock or rap. Even though it's a simple example, we can really pressure each other to the point that it does take courage to stick to your own ideas.

TEACHER: That's so true, isn't it? How about one more example of courage?

STUDENT #4: Cowards can be courageous. My grandpa says that a lot of guys in the war ended up as decorated heroes, but they weren't all that heroic in the beginning. Once their plane was shot down or they found themselves in prison camp, their courage got them through.

STUDENT #5: Yeah! It's like when someone rescues a kid from a fire or rushes into the street and throws a child from the path of a car—the courage just happens suddenly, unexpectedly. And someone who seems more like a coward in other situations proves himself a hero with courage.

Various subjects are integrated in this example. The fertile themes of courage, trust, and love are transformed into an investigative question and then easily "webbed" out to various disciplines for appropriate instructional activities (see Figure 3.4). In turn, they are aligned with key goals (Fogarty, 1991).

To evaluate the study of courage, students are required to respond to certain questions for their portfolio or performance assessment. Presentations are as varied as their presenters. Creativity flourishes and debate is lively as students grapple with something unknown to them. After all, who really *knows* how common courage is?

Webbed Model: Selected Themes

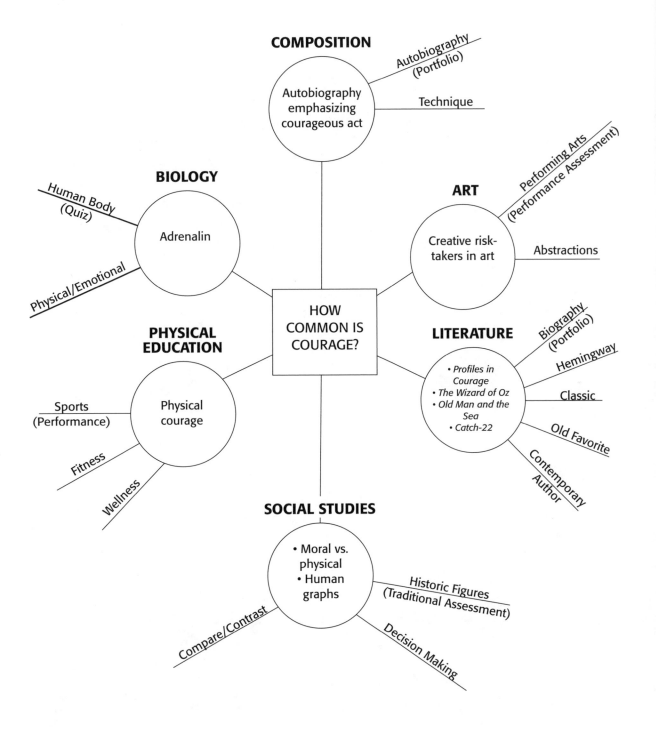

Figure 3.4

Themes

Can We Talk?

Themes as organizing centers for developing curriculum and for igniting learning are, without a doubt, useful approaches to integrating the curricula. Within the planning process, perhaps the most critical step is exploring the theme for breadth and depth. To explore a theme, hold a "question session" in the staff room with the teacher team. Brainstorming with students also enriches the question bank and the teams' search for key questions to hook students with. Survey the following list in Figure 3.5 to see the kinds of "hook" questions other teams have generated.

After reviewing the "hooks," brainstorm about any topic with your teammates and generate questions. See Figure 3.6 to understand how the brainstorming process usually works.

"Hook" Questions or Statements for Themes

Theme	Question/Statement
Information Highway	Am I lost?
Water	Water, water everywhere . . .
Cultural Diversity	Who do you think you are?
Enterprise	Why work together?
Families	Family matters
Ecology	Man vs. nature
Milwaukee	A great place on a great lake?
Computers	Friend or foe?
Technology	Good, bad, ugly?
Responsibility	Who me?
Adolescence	What will my friends think?
Parenthood	Pants or pantyhose?
Crime	Gang up on crime!
Conflict	Fighting fair?
Time	How does time fly?
Choices	Will I or won't I?
Communication	Are you getting the message?
Travelers	Discoverers or intruders?
Travel	Which way are we going?
Goals	Where am I? Where am I going?
Circus	Is life a circus?
Survival	Instinct or extinct?
Well-Being	Who's in charge?
Relationships	Love 'em or leave 'em?
Leadership	Consensus vs. confusion?
Violence	Is might right?

Figure 3.5

Themes

The Brainstorm Cycle

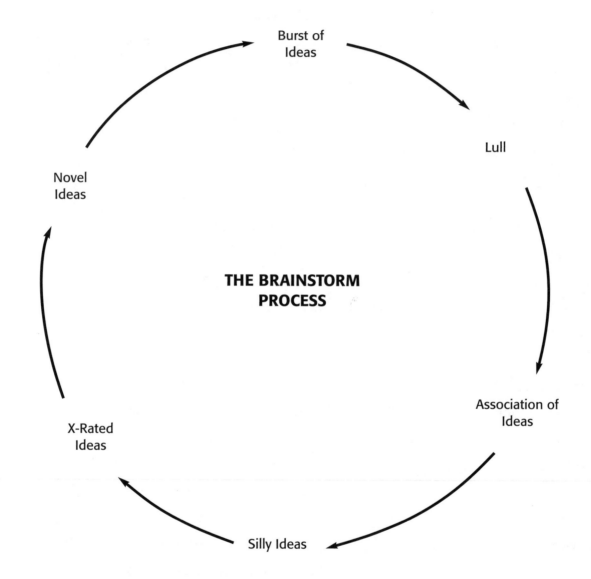

Burst of Ideas

Lull

Novel Ideas

THE BRAINSTORM PROCESS

X-Rated Ideas

Association of Ideas

Silly Ideas

Figure 3.6

BIBLIOGRAPHY

Ashton-Warner, S. 1963. *Teacher.* New York: Simon & Schuster.

Beane, J. A. 1993, September. Problems and possibilities for an integrative curriculum. *Middle School Journal,* pp. 18–23.

Burke, K. A. 1993. *The mindful school: How to assess authentic learning.* Palatine, IL: IRI/Skylight Publishing.

———. 1999. *How to assess authentic learning,* 3rd ed. Arlington Heights, IL: SkyLight Training and Publishing.

Fogarty, R. 1991. *The mindful school: How to integrate the curricula.* Palatine, IL: IRI/Skylight Publishing.

———. 2002. *How to integrate the curricula,* 2nd ed. Arlington Heights, IL: SkyLight Professional Development.

Jacobs, H. H., ed. 1990. *Interdisciplinary curriculum: Design and implementation.* Alexandria, VA: Association for Supervision and Curriculum Development.

Kovalik, S. 1993. *ITI: The model: Integrated thematic instruction.* Oak Creek, AZ: Books for Educators.

Lounsbury, J. H., ed. 1992. *Connecting curriculum through interdisciplinary instruction.* Columbus, OH: National Middle School Association.

Vars, G. F. 1993. *Interdisciplinary teaching: Why and how.* Columbus, OH: National Middle School Association.

Mentors can demonstrate to protégés how to design an integrated thematic unit.

- Blackline 3.1 can be used when a theme has already been selected.
- Blackline 3.2 can be used to refine and hone a selected theme.

Themes

Theme Web—Selected Theme

Use the Web graphic organizer to create an integrated thematic unit.

LANGUAGE ARTS

MUSIC

MATH

THEME

ART

SCIENCE

SOCIAL STUDIES

"Hook" Questions or Statements for Themes

List the selected theme and the essential questions related to the theme. Use the essential question(s) to plan the thematic unit activities.

| Theme |

Question/Statement

Question/Statement

Question/Statement

Question/Statement

Question/Statement

The Blueprints approach to cooperative learning advocates creating mixed ability or heterogeneous groups in which students use higher-order thinking skills to learn for understanding and transfer in all subject areas. Bellanca and Fogarty provide a repertoire of interactive strategies mentors can share with their protégés.

The Blueprints Approach to Cooperative Groups

by **James Bellanca and Robin Fogarty**

The best things and the best people rise out of their separateness; I'm against a homogenized society because I want the cream to rise.
—Robert Frost

"How do I get started?" is the most frequently asked question by classroom teachers new to cooperative learning. They are in the forming phase. They know well that the first lessons in the first week of school set the tone for the year. The best starts for cooperative learning are made prior to any formal introduction of cooperative learning. By beginning with planning and preparing for the what, why, and how of cooperative learning, teachers can introduce a cooperative climate in the classroom.

Teachers who have used homogeneous groups (e.g., lab groups in chemistry), may wonder "What is different about the Blueprints approach to cooperative groups?" Teachers who have played the role

Adapted from *Blueprints for Achievement in the Cooperative Classroom*, 3rd edition by James Bellanca and Robin Fogarty. © 2002 by Pearson Education Inc. Used with permission.

The Blueprints Approach to Cooperative Groups

WHAT IS A COOPERATIVE GROUP?
- 2-5 students
- Teacher-selected
- Mixed by ability, motivation, gender, race
- Shared academic goal
- Targeted social skills
- Self-assessing

Q. WHEN DO I START USING COOPERATIVE GROUPS?
A. Start using cooperative groups right away. Cooperative learning takes time to develop. The sooner you start, no matter how small a start, the better. It is best to start with informal structures (e.g., think-pair-share, prediction pairs) before proceeding to more formal structures (e.g., jigsaw, graphic organizers).

THREE LEVELS OF INSTRUCTION

3 Transfer

2 Deep Understanding

1 Cooperative Climate

---

of information giver ask, "Why use cooperative groups?" These are good questions.

The answer to the first question, "What is different about the Blueprints approach to cooperative groups?" is twofold. First, Blueprints introduces a very unique approach to cooperation; it asks the teacher to form a cooperative classroom that creates a context for higher achievement by all students. Second, Blueprints introduces tools for creating mixed ability or heterogeneous groups in which students can learn for understanding and transfer in all subject areas.

The answer to the second question—"Why use cooperative groups?"—is more complicated. First, the research shows that the Blueprints approach increases students' academic performance and improves their social skills. By providing learning tools, Blueprints especially helps low performers become higher achievers and develop the social skills to interact with each other and their teachers in more positive ways. Second, the Blueprints approach benefits teachers. As they teach students how to use the cognitive tools, they see the fruits of their labor in higher test scores and increased student academic performance. As they teach students the social skills of cooperative learning, they see student behavior improve and student time on task increase.

What is this thing called cooperative learning? How does it differ from traditional grouping procedures in the classroom? How does it change the teacher's role? Cooperative learning is an instructional model for teaching students how to learn together. It uses heterogeneous groups as a tool for creating a more cooperative classroom in which students' achievement, self-esteem, responsibility, high-level thinking, and favorable attitudes toward school increase dramatically.

Cooperative groups include two to five students of different ability, skill, motivation, gender, or racial origin who work to achieve a single learning goal. In the cooperative classroom, teachers use a variety of structures and strategies to build on-task attention, trust, and shared success.

Specs

Cooperative learning structures may be informal or formal. The basic difference between the two is that formal structures require the use of specific tools—roles, guidelines, success criteria, and group assessment strategies—that define how participants interact to achieve the common goal; informal structures only require the students to interact with each other to achieve a single goal.

Informal Structures

The easiest way to start creating a cooperative classroom is to try a few informal cooperative learning strategies. Informal structures enable students to sample, experience, and enjoy cooperative learning. At the same time, informal structures help teachers see how the new approach works with their students and to gauge their own comfort level in managing the increased activity in the classroom. Teachers may include informal approaches in their standard lessons with little modification. These informal strategies quickly and easily initiate cognitive rehearsal and unite teams in the classroom.

Q. WHAT IS MEANT BY A SINGLE ACADEMIC GOAL?

A. A group of students applies collaborative social skills to achieve a single academic goal. All group members share the goal and work together as a single unit to achieve it. Individual goals give way to and focus on the group goal at all levels of academic work.

At the first level, the factual level, the group works as a unit to ensure each member "gets all the facts." For instance, if the common goal is to recall the definitions of ten key vocabulary words, the members help each other learn the words.

At the second level, the processing level, the group works to include all members in the process of meeting the goal. For example, if the goal is to challenge the group to compare the attributes of two authors, then each member contributes to the comparison.

At the third level, the transfer level, the group works to meet a complex goal (e.g., to solve a complex problem). Again, it is the group, not each individual working alone, that is responsible for the group's success. Think of a cooperative group as a group of lifeguards at a beach. One day, when the waves are high, the lifeguards spot a swimmer in distress beyond the breakers. Each guard knows he or she cannot swim through the breakers alone. Together, two—a male and female—jump into their boat. They work as a team with one goal—to get over the breakers and save the swimmer. One goal, different abilities.

The Blueprints Approach to Cooperative Groups

Q. WHAT IS COGNITIVE REHEARSAL?
A. Cognitive rehearsal means that students verbally share, explain, or assess their ideas or concepts with each other. Cooperative learning and cognitive organizers are instructional models used to facilitate cognitive rehearsal.

Cognitive rehearsal, a key concept for understanding cooperative learning, rests on the principle that the one who talks is the one who learns. In traditional classrooms where the teacher talks to students ninety percent of the time, it is the teacher who benefits from cognitive rehearsal. The teacher talks and learns while the students passively record information in their heads, notebooks, or computers, which rewards students with better memories. On the other hand, when students answer questions or discuss the material with the teacher, they benefit intellectually. Students also benefit when they interact with each other in small groups.

Informal cooperative learning starts students on the way to serious cognitive rehearsal. The key is to have student pairs spend at least two minutes at the beginning of a cooperative lesson preparing for new content, explaining a thought, or assessing what they have learned.

The informal strategies for promoting cognitive rehearsal do not require roles, guidelines, and other methods used in formal group tasks. Each of the eight informal strategies (see Figure 4.1) takes little more than two to five minutes of face-to-face interaction. The teacher just decides when to use a tool, prepares instructions, and goes to it!

Informal Cooperative Structures

Think-Pair-Share

Explain Why

Business Cards

KWL

Prediction Pairs

We Bags

I Learned Mail-Gram

Pair Review

Figure 4.1

Think-Pair-Share

The think-pair-share rehearsal strategy can be used to

- help students summarize key points after a lecture,
- begin a new topic or unit by having students discuss prior knowledge,
- stimulate student thinking about an important piece of information,
- check students' understanding of a topic,
- bring closure to a lesson,
- deepen students' short-term memories, or
- promote student transfer of a concept.

With each of these uses of the think-pair-share strategy, give similar instructions:

Before the lecture. To start, say something like this: "Today, I am going to describe (topic). After I define each term, I'm going to ask you to (a, b, c, d, or e) with a partner." Fill in the second blank with one of the following: (a) summarize the key points, (b) describe what you already know about the topic, (c) pick one idea of importance to you and explain it, (d) tell how the information is important to you, or (e) explain something new you learned about the topic. Sample student ideas after 10–20 seconds.

After the lecture (or at appropriate intervals during a longer lecture). After an appropriate amount of time, ask students to turn to the person on their (right or left side), and take turns doing one of the activities (a, b, c, d, or e; see above). Allow time (2–3 minutes) for each person to share.

Explain Why

Explain why encourages students to rehearse their reasons for selecting answers. Before a lesson, ask students three to five multiple choice questions. After students answer each question, invite several students to explain why they selected their answers. Write students' answers on the board and explain to students that they will discover the correct answers as they study the lesson.

Business Cards

Business cards is a motivational strategy for rehearsal that involves the entire class. First, give each student a 3" x 5" index card and explain the purpose of a business card (e.g., to greet other people, to tell about yourself, or to explain an idea).

Then, model how to complete the business card being used. Display the card on an overhead or whiteboard and give the following instructions:

1. Write your first name in the middle of the card using capital letters (e.g., TOM).
2. Write the name of your school beneath your name (e.g., ML King School).
3. In the upper right corner of the card, write a success you have had this week at school, home, or play (e.g., made a friend, got a 95 on a quiz).
4. In the upper left corner, write your learning goal for this week (e.g., improve vocabulary quiz score, finish a paper).
5. In the lower right corner, write a benefit for doing your homework (e.g., higher grades).
6. In the lower left corner, write the title of your favorite book (e.g., *Curious George, The Grapes of Wrath*).
7. Demonstrate your best cooperative skill (e. g., give a pat on the back, smile, or give an "Atta boy").

Finally, after all students have completed their cards, instruct everyone to find a partner. After the pairs settle, each student should choose one of the corner topics (success, goal, benefit, or favorite) and explain to their partner why they selected the topic. After one or two minutes, ask students to switch partners and select a different corner to share. Student continue switching until all four corner topics have been discussed.

KWL

KWL stands for what we Know, what we Want to know, and what we Learned. Introduced by Ogle in 1986, this cognitive rehearsal strategy helps with pre-lesson diagnosis. Here is how it works:

1. Ask students to find a partner. Announce the unit or lesson title (e.g., safety, photosynthesis, *Moby Dick,* or whole numbers).

2. Give each pair a worksheet with three column headings at the top: What We Know, What We Want to Know; and What We Learned. Invite pairs to list all they know about the topic in the first column and all they want to know about the topic in the second column. Match the pairs into foursomes so they can share their lists.

3. After finishing the unit, allow time for student pairs to write what they learned in the third column. Encourage students to discuss and their answers.

Prediction Pairs

Prediction pairs may be used when students can share an activity (e.g., reading a book). Begin by having students select a partner. Give each prediction pair a book or short story to read together. Let partners choose who will act as recorder and who will act as reader. Ask recorders in each pair create a chart with two columns: What Will Happen Next and Reasons Based on Content.

Explain that after the reader reads each page aloud, the pair should predict what will happen next in the story. The recorder should write the predictions on the chart in the What Will Happen Next column. Predictions might be "incidents" both partners agree to. Then, the recorder should list the pair's reasons for the predictions in the Reasons Based on Content column. The pair should include supporting evidence from the pages they have read.

After students' complete an appropriate number of pages, invite pairs to share their prediction charts with another pair.

We Bags

To use the informal strategy we bags, ask students to select a partner and give each pair a paper bag. Invite the pairs to decorate the bags with their names, favorite books or foods, or names of places they have visited. Then, ask the groups to fill their bags with objects that have special meaning to them. When pairs are finished decorating and filling their bags, tell them to join another pair. Each person should introduce his or her partner to the foursome by discussing each item in the bag.

I Learned Mail-Gram

The I learned mail-gram strategy supports rehearsal after a lesson. Invite each student to complete and sign a mail-gram (a card) that has the stem, "I learned . . .". Next, match students into pairs to share their mail-grams. Rotate sharing pairs several times.

Pair Review

Pair review works well as a closure task for short lessons. Ask students to form pairs. Then, divide the lesson's information into two equal parts and ask one student to review the first half and the other student to review the second. Be explicit as to what each member should look for in the text (e.g., three key ideas; definitions of five vocabulary words).

After students have independently reviewed their half of the material, ask them to share their findings with their partners. Be sure to specify how many ideas each partner should share.

After pairs finish sharing with each other, ask them to rank the most important words, ideas, or concepts they found, and list the reasons for their rankings. This activity encourages deeper processing and strengthens students' short- and long-term recall of items or concepts. When students use graphic organizers, such as a ladder or steps, to record their ideas, their recall is further enhanced. Use pair reviews for checking homework, reviewing pre-tests, recalling prior knowledge, or renewing old acquaintances.

GUIDEBOOK

Hints for Implementing Informal Structures

To prevent students from taking advantage of the looser structure of these strategies, be sure to walk students through their first cooperative experience. When the teacher devotes time to explaining the reasons for each step, students begin to understand the underlying value as well as the steps of the process. For example, if KWL is chosen as a beginning strategy, start by announcing what students are going to do (work with the partner), why they are going to do it (to help each other), and what the common goal is (recall what they know about a topic). Next, tell students how to do the task (move your chairs quietly, put your heads together, and quietly talk with each other). Set a tight time limit for the work. When they finish their charts, ask pairs to share their ideas with another pair or the whole class. When the task is done, be sure to compliment the students on how well they did the task and the quality of their answers.

Formal Structures

After students are comfortable working in pairs, it is time to upgrade the level of cooperative work and use formal task groups. Task groups increase the amount of student-to-student cognitive rehearsal in a lesson.

Task Groups

Initial task groups should include three students, preferably of different ability or motivation. Task groups are more formal than the informal pair activities described in the previous section. That is, task groups are structured explicitly to include:

- roles,
- cooperative guidelines,
- criteria for success in meeting a group goal, and
- a group assessment strategy.

Q. WHAT ARE TASK GROUPS?
A. Task groups are formal group structures with
- roles,
- cooperative guidelines,
- criteria for success,
- a group goal,
- a group processing strategy, and
- the ability to gather information, process concepts, or make applications.

The Blueprints Approach to Cooperative Groups

Task groups support various models of instruction and can be used with any content lesson in the curriculum. In the direct instruction model, a teacher designs formal cooperative task groups with an anticipatory set, input, guided practice, or closure. In an inquiry lesson, a teacher creates cooperative lessons for gathering information, processing concepts, or making applications. Tasks as simple as learning vocabulary and practicing computation or as complex as contrasting two authors' styles or testing a physics hypothesis benefit from formal cooperative structures.

Introducing the Jigsaw

To start students in the more formal cooperative task groups, introduce them to the procedures in a simple, fun way. After they demonstrate a working knowledge of the procedures, move into content. One exceptionally useful structure to start with is the jigsaw. Two forms of jigsaws are introduced—the simple portmanteau jigsaw and the more complex concept jigsaw.

THE JIGSAW PORTMANTEAU An easy way to introduce the jigsaw strategy is to use a jigsaw to learn vocabulary. To make it fun, students can create new words made up of two words put together. These are called *portmanteau words,* because they blend different concepts in a word that has a meaning of its own. (For some examples of portmanteau words, see Figure 4.2.)

Try the lesson shown in Figure 4.2. This simple lesson demonstrates a round-robin jigsaw procedure with roles, guidelines, and group processing. Keep the list of new portmanteau words short so students can easily see and feel a "jigsaw" and learn the jigsaw procedures. In the processing that concludes the task, highlight the benefits of roles, guidelines, and jigsaw pieces for learning the words. After students demonstrate that they know how to jigsaw, use the same model to learn formal vocabulary words.

A Sample Starter: The Jigsaw Portmanteau

1. Select nine portmanteau words. Try these words created by students who learned the jigsaw portmanteau in their classes:

   Customerania (or customephrenia): the tendency of every salesperson in a store to ask "May I help you?" when you are just looking

   Leaftover: the tiny piece of greenery stuck between someone's front teeth after eating spinach salad or soufflé

   Socdroop: the tendency of socks which have lost their elastic to work their way down below the ankle

   Chateauincinerade: the very, very well done steak that was accidentally left in the microwave for three hours

   Linebind: when you go to the bank and are delighted that the line is short only to discover the person in front of you is depositing $500 in pennies

   McLag: having to wait longer for your order at a fast-food hamburger joint than at a restaurant

   Aussification: what happens to most Americans who spend a long time in Australia

   Acceleryeller: the person who thinks that when the stoplight changes to yellow it means to step on the gas

   Diffizzication: what happens to any opened carbonated drink after sitting around for three days

2. Divide the class into trios. Assign each group member three words. Give the following instructions:

   STEP 1: Learn the definitions of the three words. Draw a picture of each word. (You will use the sketch to teach the other members).

   STEP 2: Conduct the first round of teaching and checking—each member teaches one word to the other members. Check that everyone understands the definition for each word. (Have each member review the definition.) Coach as needed.

   STEP 3: Conduct a second round of teaching and checking.

   STEP 4: Conduct a third round of teaching and checking.

   STEP 5: Do a double check; make sure all groups members know all the words.

   STEP 6: Take a quiz.

   STEP 7: As a group, list the learning strategies you used to learn the vocabulary (e.g., check after each round, make and explain a sketch, give encouragement, etc.).

3. All students must know all the words within the fifteen minutes allowed for the exercise. To help, have one member quiz the other group members after each round of three and for the total nine. Then, after all the rounds, quiz the students.

Figure 4.2

THE CONCEPT JIGSAW A more formal type of jigsaw is the content jigsaw. This jigsaw can be used to gather a large amount of information in a short amount of time. By dividing the gathering task among the group members, the teacher sets the stage for an in-depth discussion of the core content. Let's look at the steps in the jigsaw procedure (see Figure 4.3).

Steps for the Jigsaw

1. Assign the information-gathering task.
2. Allot time for each student to work alone and gather his or her fair share of the information.
3. Structure the groups.
4. Monitor the groups at work.
5. Assign time for the group assessment.
6. Assess individual knowledge with a quiz or written essay.

Figure 4.3

QUESTIONS FROM THE THREE-STORY INTELLECT

First-Story Verbs:

Count
Describe
Name
Recall
Tell

Second-Story Verbs:

Compare
Distinguish
Explain why
Analyze
Solve

Third-Story Verbs:

Estimate
Evaluate
Predict
Imagine
Judge

STEP 1: Assign the information-gathering task. For example the teacher may jigsaw reading a textbook chapter in various ways:

- Divide the textbook chapter into three equal parts and ask each student to read one part.
- Assign three readings from different sources and ask each student to read one source and report to the group.
- Pose three questions about the textbook chapter, one question for each of the stories in the three-story intellect model. Then, student A reads to answer the first-story question (for facts), student B reads to answer the second-story question (for understanding), and student C reads to answer the third-story question (for transfer).

STEP 2: Allot time for students to work alone and gather their fair share of the information. For less motivated students, allot time in class for coaching and checking. For more motivated students, make this a homework assignment.

STEP 3. Structure the groups. Take time to establish the structure. Highlight the single goal and review the guidelines for cooperation. Assign roles (recorder, timekeeper, and task checker) and review role responsibilities if necessary. Emphasize the targeted social skill (e.g., active listening). Set up the assessment criteria and rubric. The assessment should focus on how well the group worked together and the quality of the product. Keep individuals accountable but include a group presentation of the finished task.

STEP 4: Monitor the groups at work. Coach and check for understanding as needed and help students keep their attention on the single goal.

STEP 5: Assign time for the group assessment. Be sure to include an assessment of the group process using a tool such as Mrs. Potter's questions (Figure 4.4) or the PMI (Figure 4.5) as well as an assessment of each individual's contributions to the product.

Mrs. Potter's Questions

- What were you supposed to do?
- What did you do well?
- What would you do differently next time?
- Do you need any help?

Figure 4.4

PMI

- What I liked (Pluses)
- What I didn't like (Minuses)
- Questions or thoughts (Intriguing questions)

Figure 4.5

The Blueprints Approach to Cooperative Groups

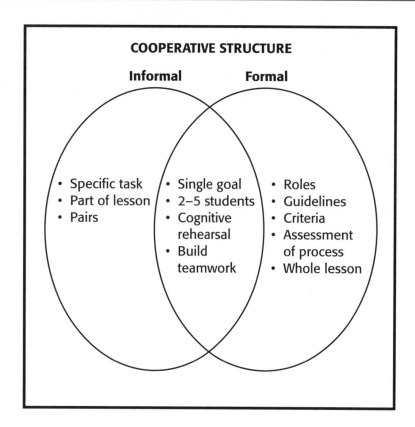

COOPERATIVE STRUCTURE

Informal   **Formal**

- Specific task
- Part of lesson
- Pairs

- Single goal
- 2–5 students
- Cognitive rehearsal
- Build teamwork

- Roles
- Guidelines
- Criteria
- Assessment of process
- Whole lesson

STEP 6. Assess individual knowledge with a quiz or written essay. Even if tracking and ability grouping are the norm in a middle or high school classroom, teachers may structure content jigsaws or other formal cooperative tasks to meet the academic standard.

Consider an example taken from third-year English. The school tracks students into advanced placement (AP), average, and remedial groupings, and, students within each track exhibit a wide range of reading and writing abilities. The standard requires all students to analyze a significant American novel. To apply this standard equally and fairly to all students, teachers assign the same book, Hawthorne's *Scarlet Letter,* to students in all tracks. For departmental tests, each student must know the names and the importance of six major characters, twelve symbols, and nine events in the story. In addition, each student is expected to explain, using textual evidence, why a specific character made a certain moral decision. Finally, each student must write an essay about one or more characters. (The essay is graded by the teacher.) No collaboration is allowed during the assessment.

Although the assessment is individualistic, teachers use formal cooperative learning to maintain this standard in the AP and remedial classes.

In the AP class, students form cooperative task groups. Each group selects one contemporary film to compare with the novel. Students are given a worksheet with questions about character, theme, cultural references, symbolism, and setting.

Each group jigsaws the questions; group members choose a part of the jigsaw to use as their focus when reading the novel. After students have read the novel, each group member takes one-half of a class period to lead the small group in a discussion of the novel from his or her focus. After all members have shared, the group synthesizes its understandings and prepares group members to write individual essays comparing the novel with the selected film. In addition, the group prepares and makes a presentation to the entire class. When all groups have presented, the teacher guides a closing discussion of the novel, emphasizing department-mandated facts and the moral decisions of the major characters. Finally, students individually take the test and write an essay.

In the remedial class, the teacher and the students spend ten days doing a chapter-by-chapter analysis of the text. Each class period begins with a review of the prior night's reading assignment, including characters, symbols, and important events. Then, the teacher guides think-pair-share discussion of the importance of the elements identified that day. At the end of chapter study, the teacher assigns students to formal task groups, and each student in every task group is asked to become an expert on two characters, four symbols, and three events (based on the standard). Each group must also create a mind map that combines all these features—characters, symbols, and events. For each element, the responsible student finds the text to support the group's position on the element. Groups spend three days drawing their mind maps and preparing for an all-class presentation. Presentations are graded by a rubric that highlights the accuracy of the quoted sources. After the presentations, the groups prepare members for a final examination on these elements. The examination tests factual knowledge and requires each student to write an essay explaining why a character made the decisions he did. Each test receives an individual grade.

The Blueprints Approach to Cooperative Groups

After the Introduction

After students have completed a formal cooperative task, it is very important that they look back and debrief about *what* and *how* they learned. For the simple vocabulary jigsaw (the portmanteau), this may entail taking a few minutes to assess individual knowledge. For other more complex cooperative tasks such as the content jigsaw, debriefing is an essential cognitive rehearsal. Debriefing reinforces the idea that cooperation improves individual achievement and solidifies students' recall and understanding of the core information. The simple jigsaw lesson, the portmanteau, demonstrates very powerfully to students that working together gives them better academic results than working alone. When students participate in heterogeneous groups (groups in which members differ in ability or motivation), they discover that each individual, whether they are higher or lower performers, score better by working as a team. Students also discover that assessment of content mastery is best done individually, but assessment of the group process is best done by the group.

During the time students are working in groups, what does the teacher do? Not only do students' roles change, but also the teacher's role shifts dramatically in a cooperative classroom (see Figure 4.6).

The changed teacher role hints at the differences between traditional groups and cooperative groups in a thinking classroom (see Figure 4.7).

As Slavin (1977a), Johnson and Johnson (1974), and other researchers of cooperative learning have shown, cooperative groups increase students mastery of the basic skills. Reading and mathematics scores go up, grades improve, and students report that they prefer working together. But there is more, as Joyce reported in his meta-analysis of the effects of cooperative learning: "Cooperative learning procedures facilitate learning across all curriculum areas and ages, improving self-esteem, social skill and solidarity and academic learning goals ranging from the acquisition of information and skill through the modes of inquiry of academic disciplines" (Joyce, Weil, and Calhoun 2000, p. 15).

The Teacher's Role

From the traditional classroom:

- dispensing information from the front of the classroom
- performing for and entertaining passive students
- rewarding and punishing
- preparing for standardized tests
- grading workbooks and tests at the teacher's desk
- emphasizing teacher-student and student-material interactions

To the cooperative, achieving classroom:

- planning dynamic lessons for transfer of learning
- teaching students how to learn
- developing student responsibility through coaching and monitoring
- promoting active learning
- facilitating student self-evaluation
- encouraging and cheerleading mastery of skills and concepts
- extending participation
- intervening and correcting in the groups
- motivating high-level thinking
- building group skills
- balancing teacher-to-student, student-to-material, and student-to-student interactions

Figure 4.6

How Cooperative Groups Differ from Traditional Learning Groups

Traditional Learning Groups

One goal and/or task is learned at a time.

Groups break up when product or task is finished.

Social skills are assumed; they are not explicitly taught.

One leader gets main role.

Group is evaluated without looking at individual efforts.

Teacher grades product.

Homogeneous groups are created.

Students are only responsible for themselves.

Each student relies on him- or herself.

No cooperative structure is included.

Cooperative Learning Groups

Higher-order thinking is woven into every lesson.

Teacher focuses on group interaction.

Social skills are explicitly taught.

Roles are shared and mixed.

Individual contribution to group goal is evaluated.

Group looks back and processes its interactions and group work.

Groups are heterogeneous; students with different characteristics are mixed and matched.

Members share responsibility for group.

Students rely on each other.

Cooperative structure is evident.

Figure 4.7

What Joyce points out is the most significant insight yet into the potential power of cooperative learning. As much as "pure" cooperative learning accomplishes when used as a stand-alone strategy, it provides a greater opportunity when combined with strategies that challenge students to think more skillfully, solve problems, or generate new concepts. In essence, the combinations that Joyce noted provide windows of opportunity that have exponential effects on student learning.

BUILD

Marcus and McDonald's (1990) acronym, BUILD, highlights the variables that produce the powerful results identified in the research on cooperative learning (see Figure 4.8). A lesson designed with all these BUILD variables is a robust and force-ful cooperative learning event that has a high likelihood of get-ting excellent results. But, the likelihood that a lesson will have the powerful effects mentioned in the research decreases as the number of BUILD variables in the lesson decreases.

The BUILD Acronym

B = Build in higher-order thinking to challenge students.

U = Unite the teams so students form bonds of trust.

I = Invite individual accountability.

L = Look back and debrief what and how students learned.

D = Develop students' social skills.

(Adapted from Marcus and McDonald 1990.)

Figure 4.8

For each BUILD variable, the teacher can select from dozens of strategies to design each cooperative thinking lesson. Note in the portmanteau jigsaw or in the sample lessons at the end of this chapter how the lesson uses each of the variables. Teachers may use many strategies with the BUILD structure:

student and teacher questions, graphic organizers, jigsaws and group investigations, problem solving, problem-based learning modules, and team projects. BUILD guides teachers in creating a strong, formal cooperative structure and serves as a framework for criteria to assess the quality of the cooperative task.

The BUILD Structure as Rubric

Teachers create a BUILD structure by using the five steps in cooperative lesson planning.

Build in higher-order thinking. To create cooperative groups in which student learning, achievement, and self-esteem are increased significantly, the teacher must build higher-level thinking into the tasks. Creating high-level thinking challenges automatically boosts cooperation because the group members recognize that they need help from the group to meet the challenge. Conversely, if the task is too easy, such as a simple fill-in-the-blank worksheet, students realize that they can do the task more quickly, more easily, and better by working alone without collaborators. High challenge fosters high collaboration. In turn, higher-level metacognitive discussion promotes the desired transfer.

Unite the team to form bonds of trust. When teachers tailor high-level cognitive tasks for the group, members form a united team—a team with a "sink or swim together" posture. When students know that they all make it together but none makes it alone, their motivation to cooperate is sparked naturally. Interdependence by team members to accomplish individual as well as group goals is an absolute key to the high-performance classroom.

Invite individual accountability. Another critical element to cooperative groups is helping each student know that he or she is accountable personally for achieving the group goal and learning the material. Often, students new to cooperative models are unskilled at learning and being accountable for the total picture at the same time. High-performing classrooms, on the

> **Q. WHAT KIND OF CLASSROOM INTERACTIONS DO WE USE?**
> **A.** To BUILD thinking in the cooperative classroom, three types of interactions to consider:
>
> STUDENT-TEACHER = How teachers question and respond to students
>
> STUDENT-STUDENT = How students talk and work with each other
>
> STUDENT-INFORMATION = How students deal with the material

SkyLight Professional Development

Section I: Designing Learning Experiences | 107

other hand, gradually adopt deliberate, visible, and, sophisti-cated steps to invite individual accountability. These graduated moves range from quick, individual quizzes to more elaborate, independent, and appropriate applications of what a student has learned.

Look back and debrief what and how students learned. Taking time to look over what the group has done—planning, monitoring, and evaluating academic and cooperative tasks—is another critical element in the high-performing classroom. This metacognitive model promotes further application and transfer from the lesson and also fosters cognitive rehearsal among the group members. Without group processing time or group processing formats, little, if any, transfer takes place. Yet, when students evaluate their group behaviors and task results, they exhibit noticeable tendencies toward meaningful transfer.

Develop students' social skills. A final element for high-functioning cooperative learning teams is the teacher's explicit attention to developing students' social skills. These skills are needed for communicating, building trust, promoting leader-ship, and resolving conflicts. Students develop into valuable, contributing, and empathetic members of groups when they have acquired specific social skills: active listening behaviors (e.g., paraphrasing, affirming, and clarifying), leadership skills (e.g., encouraging others), and conflict resolution skills (e.g., disagreeing with ideas but not people, listening to others' points of view, and seeking consensus).

Applying the BUILD Rubric to a Lesson

As noted, a second important value of the BUILD model is its use as a rubric for evaluating a lesson's alignment with the cooperative framework. Figure 4.9 shows a rubric that teachers can use to plan and assess the potential effectiveness of their cooperative lessons.

Without teachers deliberately integrating the five BUILD attributes, groups function simply as study groups, which have a much lower impact on achievement. However, when teachers emphasize BUILD, formal cooperative groups develop the cohesion that facilitates higher-achievement levels.

Rubric for BUILD

To what degree does this lesson:

	1	2	3	4
Build in higher-order thinking	All facts and recall	Implied thinking	Application of specific skill	High challenge thinking and reflecting
Unite the team	Task can be done alone	Uses roles and guidelines	Has common-goal structures	Supports common goal
Invite individual responsibility	No reason to work together	Uses one strategy	Uses two strategies	Uses three or more strategies
Look back and review	Not called for	Content review	Content and cooperation review	All three functions—content, cooperation, cognition—reviewed
Develop social skills	Not done	Forced by structure	Encouraged by structure taught and reviewed	Expectation integrated

Figure 4.9

Summary

When introducing cooperative learning, begin with informal strategies. Teach students a strategy such as think-pair-share, and use it each day. Add other informal strategies gradually. Introduce simple, formal strategies to give variety to cooperative instruction when students have developed a climate of cooperation. Return to the informal strategies and concentrate on building cooperation if students regress in their abilities to work together.

BIBLIOGRAPHY

Johnson, D. W., and R. Johnson. (1974). Instructional goal structure: Cooperative, competitive, or individualistic. *Review of Educational Research,* 44, 213-240.

Joyce, B. R., M. Weil, and E. Calhoun. 2001. *Models of teaching,* 6th ed. Boston, MA: Allyn & Bacon.

Marcus, S. A., and P. McDonald. 1990. *Tools for the cooperative classroom.* Palatine, IL: Skylight.

Ogle, D. S. 1986. K-W-L group instructional strategy. In *Teaching Reading as Thinking.* A. S. Palinscar, D. S. Ogle, B. F. Jones, and E. G. Carr, eds. Alexandria, VA: Association for Supervision and Curriculum Development.

Three sample lessons are provided on the pages that follow:

• T-E-A-M (Together Each Achieves More) (elementary)

• Cooperative? Competitive? or Individualistic? (middle)

• Torn Circles (secondary)

All three sample lessons give ideas for using cooperative groups. Protégés can work with their mentors to adapt these lessons to meet their own classroom needs.

BLUEPRINT: ELEMENTARY LESSON

T-E-A-M (Together Each Achieves More)

SETTING UP THE SCAFFOLDING

Students are used to working on individual tasks in school. Cooperative learning disrupts the game they have learned to play. This lesson helps students learn that working together increases individual achievement and is important to high performance—Together Each Achieves More (TEAM). In cooperative learning, students must prove that they have learned with meaning rather than merely memorizing content. Three questions are associated with this high-content, high-challenge, and high-support lesson: What does each child understand? How has each student improved his or her thinking skills? What has each learned about working with others as a team member?

WORKING THE CREW

Use the think-pair-share and explain why strategies for this lesson. First, show the word TEAM on an overhead. Invite students to think about times when they participated in a team and to answer this question: What did it take for team members to win the challenge together? Tell students to form pairs. Ask pairs to join their lists and agree on three answers to the question. Invite pairs to share answers with the whole class. List unduplicated answers on the board. Ask students to explain why the pair selected a specific answer. When the list is complete (about 3–5 minutes), invite students to select some examples from the list that match with T-E-A-M. Make a list.

REFLECTING ON THE DESIGN

Conclude by asking students how this activity helped their concept of teamwork. Call on individuals who have not yet spoken, if possible. Remember to wait for answers and give as many as students as possible the opportunity to respond.

BLUEPRINT: MIDDLE SCHOOL LESSON

Cooperative? Competitive? Or Individualistic?

SETTING UP THE SCAFFOLDING

On the materials table, place a pile of old magazines, one pair of scissors for every three students, a pad of newsprint with crayons or markers, and several rolls of masking tape. Tell the students that they are going to study three ways people work together. On the board, write the words *cooperative, competitive,* and *individualistic.* Draw a T-chart under each.

COOPERATIVE		COMPETITIVE		INDIVIDUALISTIC	
Looks Like	Sounds Like	Looks Like	Sounds Like	Looks Like	Sounds Like

Define each word. Write the definition under the word and add examples.

- Cooperative: when two or more people work together toward a single goal (e.g., football players, airplane crew)

- Competitive: when one or more persons work against each other toward a single goal (e.g., two football teams try to win the game, race car drivers try to win a race)

- Individualistic: when one person works alone to reach a goal (e.g., a mountain climber, a house painter) according to a set criterion (80 percent, etc.)

Ask members of the class to add other examples.

WORKING THE CREW

Divide the class into teams by asking them to count off by threes. Tell them that each three-person team is going to work toward a single goal. Before the students do the task, however, prepare the teams with materials and instructions.

Give each trio one hanger, 24" of string, one 8" X 11" tagboard, one pot of paste, one pair of scissors, and one magazine. Assign the roles of cutter (cuts out selected pictures), paster (pastes on squares) and arranger (ties pictures to hanger). The cooperative goal is to make a mobile using pictures (from the magazine) glued to tagboard squares (see Figure 2.12). The middle piece of each mobile has one of the following team words: cooperation, competition, or individualism. Assign each group one of the themes and tell the groups that their pictures must represent their assigned themes.

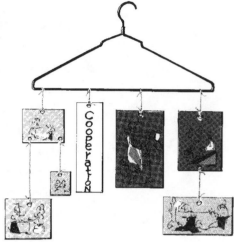

Allow 10 minutes for teams to construct their mobiles. Give teams another 3 minutes to ensure that each member can explain the picture selections made for their theme. When a member can explain the selections, then he or she signs the mobile. After all members have signed their finished mobiles, hang the mobiles throughout the room.

Figure 2.12

REFLECTING ON THE DESIGN

To explore how the students feel about the concepts of cooperation, competition, and individualism, ask them to give examples of positive and negative feelings about each of these three ways to interact.

For social skill processing, ask students to describe a cooperating behavior they used today.

For cognitive processing, simply have students describe their products (the mobiles).

For metacognitive reflection, tell groups to talk about how they thought through the task. What did they do first? Second? Third? Reinforce the value of cooperation by telling them that they will do many tasks during the year in which they will work cooperatively to think critically and creatively.

BLUEPRINT: SECONDARY SCHOOL LESSON

Torn Circles

SETTING UP THE SCAFFOLDING

On the board or on a transparency, write the words and describe the three types of interactions:

- Cooperative: when two or more people work together toward a single goal (e.g., football players, airplane crew)
- Competitive: when one or more persons work against each other toward a single goal (e.g., two football teams try to win the game, race car drivers try to win a race)
- Individualistic: when one person works alone to reach a goal (e.g., a mountain climber, a house painter)

Elicit definitions of the words from students with sports examples of the three types of interactions:

- Cooperation: seesaw, leap frog
- Competition: Olympic, tug of war
- Individualistic: swimming, tightrope walking

Divide the class into teams of three and assign the roles:

- Material's manager: Gets the stuff.
- Reporter: Gives report.
- Observer: Talks about feelings.

WORKING THE CREW

Explain to the students that the Torn Circles activity is a quick, but graphically concrete, example of the three types of social interactions. Ask them to focus on how they feel as they sample the three distinct interactions.

Competitive Task

Instruct students to each, by themselves, take a sheet of scratch paper (gathered by the material's manager) and tear a circle. The goal is to tear the roundest circle in the group. Reiterate, "The winning circle will be judged by others for roundness."

After the individuals complete the task, instruct them to select the "best" circle in their groups of threes.

After the "winner" from each group is selected, have each side of the room select the three roundest circles.

Ask the six finalists, one at a time, to place their circles on the overhead projector and, using a pseudo "applause meter," judge the best circle in the room. (First-place, second-place and third-place winners may be chosen.)

After the competition is over, ask students to describe how they are feeling in their groups of three. Ask reporters to sample the feelings experienced by their groups. Gather a list of words that describe students' feelings on the competitive tasks (e.g., anxious, stupid, angry, nervous).

Individualistic Task

Instruct students that again, they are to individually tear shapes. However, this time the torn shapes must meet these criteria:

- two straight sides
- two curves
- one hole

Any and all torn shapes that meet the criteria earn a 100 percent grade for the participants.

Again, talk with students about how they felt during this interaction. Gather words that describe their feelings when trying to meet individual criteria (e.g., successful, non-threatened, satisfied, a winner).

Cooperative task

Instruct students that in this last interaction they are to each contribute a piece for a final collage comprised of three pieces. The final collage design should symbolize cooperation. Ask each student trio to design a collage that symbolizes cooperation using the group's three torn pieces.

Again, ask student what feelings they experienced as they cooperatively completed this task. Gather words that describe their feelings (e.g., supported, teamwork, pride, trust).

REFLECTING ON THE DESIGN

Throughout the three interactions, students focused on their feelings. Take time to compare and contrast the three lists of words describing the different feelings students had during the activities.

To process socially, ask students to describe a social situation in which someone acted inappropriately.

The Blueprints Approach to Cooperative Groups

To process cognitively, check that students understand the three types of interactions. Ask students to role-play in groups of six these three words: *competitive, individualistic, cooperative.*

Finally, lead students to metacognitively transfer the concepts beyond this one situation by directing each student to make an entry in his or her log. (The log is a student notebook of ideas, thoughts, notes, and so forth that may be referred to and added to throughout the year).) Have students complete one of the following lead-ins in their logs:

Cooperation is like _____ because both _____.
Competition differs from cooperation because _____.
The hardest part about cooperating is _____.

SkyLight Professional Development

Level 2

MENTORING GUIDEBOOK

SECTION II

Assessing
Student Work

One of beginning teachers' chief complaints is the tremendous workload they have, including a seemingly endless flow of paperwork. Induction team members can share tricks of the trade for reducing the time needed to create learning materials, plan lessons, grade student work, and complete administrative paperwork.

—Gordon and Maxey 2000

ssessment may be a challenge for mentors as they guide their protégés in how to assess for understanding. As educators, mentors may be struggling with their own assessment issues. Even though grading objective quizzes, homework, and paper-and-pencil tests are important, today's teachers also need to know how to assess more subjective work such as students' performances and projects. Authentic assessments include designing performance tasks to integrate curriculum objectives and standards, and creating rubrics to evaluate student work. (Creating performance tasks and rubrics are addressed in *Mentoring Guidebook Level 1: Starting the Journey.*) One time-consuming component in today's classroom is the tremendous emphasis placed on preparing students for the high-stakes standardized tests that, in some cases, determine whether or not a student passes a grade level or graduates from school. When people talked about "evaluation" 20 years ago, they usually meant mid-terms, finals, and traditional letter grades. Today's teacher, however, is responsible for developing a repertoire of authentic assessment tools to measure each student's attainment of standards, to be able to differentiate assessments to meet the needs of diverse students, and to report progress to all the major stakeholders.

Wiggins (1993) defines assessment as a "comprehensive, multifaceted analysis of performance; [that] must be judgment-based and personal . . . assessment done properly should begin conversations about performance, not end them" (13). Sometimes, mentor teachers are learning about these new techniques along with their protégés. The newly graduated novice teacher fresh from a college of education may have much more experience using these performance-based tools than the mentor does. Often, the recent graduate has already developed rubrics and completed a professional portfolio as part of the graduation requirement. Mentors, therefore, may need to pull in other teachers more familiar with performance assessments to provide feedback along the mentoring journey. Since the mentor/protégé relationship is collaborative, beginning teachers can also share their expertise in a mutual exchange of ideas. In a positive mentoring experience, both parties grow professionally when they learn from each other.

In Selection 5, **Teacher-Made Tests**, I review some of the basic steps for designing a quality teacher-made test. Most teachers took a course in college dealing with tests and measurements. In addition to learning the definition of the *mean, median,* and *mode,* they also developed multiple-choice tests to turn in to their professors as part of the course requirements. This assignment usually was much more difficult than anticipated. When the new graduates start teaching, therefore, they might prefer to use the book or workbook tests provided by the publisher rather than take the time and effort to construct their own tests, even though many book tests do not assess levels of thinking that require more than recall and comprehension. The time requirements for creating valid teacher-made tests might overwhelm the new teacher, especially if he or she teaches several different classes or teaches students with a wide range of ability levels. Selection 5 helps beginning teachers—and mentors—review the characteristics of effective teacher-made tests and provides tips for how to construct test questions, develop better tests, and make modifications for students with special needs. Even though new teachers cannot always develop their own tests, they will at least know how to recognize a valid test and how to adapt commercial tests to meet the needs of their students.

The last selection in this section explores one assessment tool in depth: the portfolio. Selection 6, **Portfolios**, defines the portfolio and its uses. A portfolio can be the framework to collect, select, and reflect on student work. The student, teacher, and parent can review a student's work and see growth and development over time. Teachers can also use the portfolio as evidence the student is on track for meeting the standards and curriculum goals. Portfolios become more focused on accountability when students and teachers select key arti-facts to show how the students are meeting each standard. Often, each artifact is labeled with a specific standard and a checklist or rubric is attached to indicate the quality of the piece or the student's progress in meeting the standards.

The heart and soul of any portfolio is reflection. Students share what they learned and most importantly, share how they feel about their learning. According to Rolheiser, Bower, and Stevahn (2000), "Adding an element of reflection fosters the critical thinking and decision making necessary for continuous learning and improvement" (31). Many new teachers have completed their own professional portfolios during their pre-service training, so they may be familiar with the importance of reflection. Mentors, moreover, can share their own experiences implementing portfolios or, if the mentor is unfamiliar with the portfolio process, protégés can be referred to another teacher who uses portfolios. The mentor can also recommend video programs and distance learning courses that model the portfo-lio process. Assessing 150 portfolios can also be daunting. Sample rubrics are provided to assist teachers in the evaluation process. Burke, Fogarty, and Belgrad (2002) suggest using a "weighted" portfolio rubric so items focused on standards or curriculum goals receive more emphasis.

The key to learning this "new generation" of assessments is to learn *together*. Even veteran teachers face the challenge of assessing so many students, so often, in so many contexts. Hopefully, this section on assessment will trigger meaningful conversations among mentors, protégés, and peer teachers faced with similar challenges. It is interesting that Wiggins (1993) says the word *assess* is a form of the Latin verb *assidere* which means "to sit with." He says "In an assessment, one 'sits with' the learner. It is something we do *with* and *for* the stu-dent, not something we do *to* the student" (14). The etymology of *assess* could also describe the mentor/protégé relationship. The mentor fosters the concept of working *with* and *for* the novice as they learn about new ways to use teacher-made tests and portfolios in the evaluation process. Together the mentor and novice explore new methods to assess students' work and share ideas, insights, and concerns about the importance of implementing quality assessments to monitor and to measure student learning.

REFERENCES

Burke, K., R. Fogarty, and S. Belgrad. 2002. *The portfolio connection: Student work linked to standards*, 2nd ed. Arlington Heights, IL: SkyLight Professional Development.

Gordon, S. P., and S. Maxey. 2000. *How to help beginning teachers succeed*, 2nd ed. Alexandria, VA: Association for Supervision and Curriculum Development.

Rohleiser, C., B. Bower, and L. Stevahn. 2000. *The portfolio organizer: Succeeding with portfolios in your classroom*. Alexandria, VA: Association for Supervision and Curriculum Development.

Wiggins, G. P. 1993. *Assessing student performance: Exploring the purpose and limits of testing*. San Francisco: Jossey-Bass, Inc.

Even though the public's attention seems focused on standardized tests, effective teacher-made tests correlated to learning standards provide a valid and reliable method to determine what students have learned and what they still need to know. The mentor can help the protégé develop meaningful tests to assess students' understanding of the curriuculum.

Teacher-Made Tests

by **Kay Burke**

While large-scale standardized tests may appear to have great influence at specific times . . . . Without question, teachers are the drivers of the assessment systems that determine the effectiveness of schools.
—Stiggins, 1994

What Are Teacher-Made Tests?

Teacher-made tests are written or oral assessments that are not commercially produced or standardized—in other words, a test a teacher designs specifically for his or her students. *Testing* refers to any kind of school activity that results in some type of mark or comment being entered in a checklist, grade book, or anecdotal record. The term *test,* however, refers to a more structured oral or written evaluation of student achievement. *Examinations* are tests that are school scheduled, tend to cover more of the curriculum, and count more than other forms of evaluation (Board of Education for the City of Etobicoke, 1987). *Teacher-made tests* can consist of a variety of formats, including matching items, fill-in-the-blank items, true-false questions, or essays.

Adapted from *How to Assess Authentic Learning,* 3rd edition, by Kay Burke, pp. 95–111. © 1999 by SkyLight Training and Publishing, Inc. Used with permission.

Tests can be important parts of the teaching and learning process if they are integrated into daily classroom teaching and are constructed to be part of the learning process—not just the culminating event. They allow students to see their own progress and allow teachers to make adjustments to their instruction on a daily basis. "But one of the most serious problems of evaluation is the fact that a primary means of assessment—the test itself—is often severely flawed or misused" (Hills, 1991, p. 541).

Constructing a good teacher-made test is very time consuming and difficult; moreover, it is hard to understand why something so essential to the learning process has been virtually ignored in teacher preservice or inservice training. Veteran teachers have relied on commercially made tests in workbooks or on their own often inadequate teacher-made tests for most of their evaluations. Teachers have often neglected addressing this aspect of instruction because they were not trained to write effective tests and few administrators could offer guidance.

One of the problems with teacher-made tests is their emphasis on lower-level thinking. A study conducted by the Cleveland Public Schools (Fleming and Chambers, 1983, as cited in Stiggins, 1985) examined over 300 teacher-made, paper-and-pencil tests. The results of the study found that teachers appeared to need training in how to do the following:

1. plan and write longer tests;
2. write unambiguous paper-and-pencil test items; and
3. measure skills beyond recall of facts (Stiggins, 1985, p. 72).

The research also found that teachers often overlooked quality-control factors like establishing written criteria for performances or planning scoring procedures in advance. Wiggins notes that "course-specific tests also have glaring weaknesses, not only because they are often too low level and content heavy. They are rarely designed to be authentic tests of intellectual ability; as with standardized tests, teacher-designed finals are usually intended to be quickly read and scored" (Wiggins, 1989, p. 123).

In addition, many teacher-made tests emphasize verbal-linguistic intelligence, and poor readers are at a disadvantage no matter how much content they know. Teacher-made tests do not carry the same importance as standardized tests in public relations between the school and the community. Even though many of them have the same objective-style format that allows for easy comparisons, they are not seen as reliable and valid. Teacher-made tests are often subject to question because they differ greatly from class to class; their quality is open to debate. Stiggins (1994) notes that although standardized, large-scale assessments command all the media attention, it's the day-to-day classroom assessments that have the greatest impact on student learning. He says, "Nearly all the assessment events that take place in a student's life happen at the behest of the teacher. They align most closely with day-to-day instruction and are most influential in terms of their contribution to student, teacher, and parent decision making" (p. 438).

Since colleges of education are just beginning to require teachers to take courses in assessment, many teachers have entered the classroom with very little training in how to create meaningful tests. They either remember the types of tests they took as students or they model the tests on ones provided by their fellow teachers or in workbooks. Unfortunately, most of the tests teachers took as students were multiple-choice, recall tests that covered content. Teachers have had very little practice constructing problem-solving situations on tests to measure the application of skills and higher-order thinking.

Why Do We Need Better Teacher-Made Tests?

Even though parents and the media value published test scores, most teachers do not rely on standardized tests to tell them what their students know and don't know. Standardized tests occur so infrequently that one aggregate score is not very helpful in determining future instructional goals. Teacher-made tests, however, allow teachers to make decisions that keep instruction moving. Teachers can make changes immediately to meet the needs of their students. "They [teachers] rely most heavily on assessments provided as part of instructional materials and assessments they design and construct themselves—and very little on standardized tests or test scores" (Stiggins, 1985, p. 69).

The key to teacher-made tests is to make them a part of assessment—not separate from it. Tests should be instructional and ongoing. Rather than being "after-the-fact" to find out what students did not learn, they should be more "before-the-fact" to target essential learnings and standards. Popham (1999) warns that teacher-made tests should not be instructional afterthoughts. They should be prepared prior to instruction in order for the teacher to target appropriate instructional activities for students. "Assessment instruments prepared prior to instruction operationalize a teacher's instructional intentions. . . . The better you understand where you're going, the more efficiently you can get there" (p.12).

Teachers also need to make adjustments in their tests for the various learning styles, multiple intelligences, and learning problems of the students in their classes. It would be impossible to address every student's needs on every test, but efforts should be made to construct tests that motivate students to learn, provide choices, and make allowances for individual differences.

Multiple Intelligences

Gardner's (1983) theory of multiple intelligences calls for multiple assessments for the multiple intelligences. An effective teacher-made test should address more than one or two intelligences. Teachers who include strategies and tools such as graphic organizers, student choice, and opportunities for oral answers meet the needs of their diverse students.

Learning Modalities

Teachers need to construct tests that can be adjusted for students' learning modalities and to make modifications for at-risk students. Frender (1990) defines learning modalities as ways of using sensory information to learn. Three of the five senses are primarily used in learning, storing, and recalling information. Because students learn from and communicate best with someone who shares their dominant modality, it is important for teachers to know the characteristics of their students so that they can at least alter their instructional styles and tests to match the learning styles of all the students.

Frender has identified many characteristics of the three styles of learning. The Types of Learners Chart (Figure 5.1) lists the characteristics that could most likely influence student test-taking skills.

Types of Learners

VISUAL LEARNERS	AUDITORY LEARNERS	KINESTHETIC LEARNERS
mind sometimes strays during verbal activities	talks to self	in motion most of the time
organized in approach to tasks	easily distracted	reading is not a priority
likes to read	has difficulty with written directions	poor speller
usually a good speller	likes to be read to	likes to solve problems by physically walking through them
memorizes by seeing graphics and pictures	memorizes by steps in a sequence	enjoys handling objects
finds verbal instructions difficult	enjoys listening activities	enjoys doing activities

(Adapted from Frender, 1990, p. 25)

Figure 5.1

Teacher-Made Tests

Modifications for Students with Special Needs

With the movement toward inclusive classrooms, teachers need to be able to meet the needs of students with learning disabilities, behavior exceptionalities, physical exceptionalities, and intellectual exceptionalities. In addition, as today's society is a "salad bowl" of many ethnic groups, teacher-made tests must allow opportunities to succeed for students whose first language is not English. Many schools have now detracked, thereby merging all levels of students (gifted, average, remedial) into one inclusive class. It would be impossible to use one objective test to measure the growth and development of all students. Authentic tests can celebrate diversity by allowing students a wide variety of ways to demonstrate what they know and what they can do.

Teacher-made tests can be constructed to meet the needs of all students by providing many opportunities to measure what students can do instead of just measuring their ability to read, write, and take tests. The modifications listed in Figure 5.2 can be made to help ensure success on tests for all students, especially those with special needs who are most at risk of failing tests.

How Can We Design Better Teacher-Made Tests?

Most teachers will not have time to rewrite all their tests to conform to the guidelines (see Figure 5.3). However, it is important to make sure new tests are designed to meet student needs—and truly reflect learning. If, as Wiggins (1989) suggests, "we should teach to the authentic test," students should also be brought into the test-making process. They can help construct meaningful tests based on essential learnings. Brown (1989) recommends that teachers draw students into the development of tests. He maintains that nothing helps a person master a subject better than having to ask and debate fundamental questions about what is most important about that

Guidelines for Teacher-Made Tests

1. Read instructions orally.

2. Rephrase oral instructions if needed.

3. Ask students to repeat directions to make sure they understand.

4. Monitor carefully to make sure all students understand directions for the test.

5. Provide alternative evaluations—oral testing, use of tapes, test given in another room, dictation.

6. Provide a clock so students can monitor themselves.

7. Give examples of each type of question (oral and written).

8. Leave enough space for answers.

9. Use visual demonstrations.

10. Use white paper because colored paper is sometimes distracting.

11. Do not crowd or clutter the test.

12. Give choices.

13. Go from concrete to abstract.

14. Don't deduct for spelling or grammar on tests.

15. Use some take-home tests.

16. Provide manipulative experiences whenever possible.

17. Allow students to use notes and textbooks during some tests (open book tests).

18. Allow students to write down key math or science formulas (so that students are not penalized for poor memory).

19. Include visuals like graphic organizers on tests.

20. Give specific point values for each group of questions.

21. List criteria for essay questions.

22. Provide immediate feedback on all tests.

23. Allow students to correct mistakes and/or to retake tests to improve scores and understand what they didn't understand on the first test.

(Adapted from material distributed by the Board of Education for the City of Etobicoke, 1987, pp. 204-214)

Figure 5.2

subject—and how someone could tell if he or she has mastered it. "Students of all ages who create some of their own examinations are forced to reflect on what they have studied and make judgments about it" (Brown, 1989, p. 115).

SkyLight Professional Development   Section II: Assessing Student Work | 129

Guidelines for Teacher-Made Tests

The following guidelines may help in the construction of better teacher-made tests:

1. Create the test before beginning the unit.
2. Make sure the test is correlated to course objectives or learning standards and benchmarks.
3. Give clear directions for each section of the test.
4. Arrange the questions from simple to complex.
5. Give point values for each section (e.g., true/false [2 points each])
6. Vary the question types (true/false, fill-in-the-blank, multiple choice, essay, matching). Limit to ten questions per type.
7. Group question types together.
8. Type or print clearly. (Leave space between questions to facilitate easy reading and writing.)
9. Make sure appropriate reading level is used.
10. Include a variety of visual, oral, and kinesthetic tasks.
11. Make allowances for students with special needs.
12. Give students some choice in the questions they select (e.g., a choice of graphic organizers or essay questions).
13. Vary levels of questions by using the three-story intellect verbs to cover gathering, processing, and application questions.
14. Provide a grading scale so students know what score constitutes a certain grade (e.g., 93–100 = A; 85–92 = B; 75–84 = C; 70–74 = D; Below 70 = Not Yet!).
15. Give sufficient time for all students to finish. (The teacher should be able to work through the test in one-third to one-half the time given students.)

Figure 5.3

Constructing Effective Tests

Constructing better teacher-made tests begins with objective evaluation (see Figure 5.4). Obviously, it is important to select test items that will measure whether students have achieved the significant learning objectives, benchmarks, or standards that have been targeted. Essays, graphic organizers, oral performances, and artistic presentations measure meaningful learning and can all be included on teacher-made tests. Because of time constraints, however, many teachers choose to use objective-style questions (see Figure 5.5). Objective-style questions have highly specific, predetermined answers that require a short response.

Even though objective-style questions can play a role in the assessment process, they, like standardized tests, must be put in the proper perspective.

Objective Types of Evaluation

A well-developed objective test . .

ADVANTAGES	DISADVANTAGES
• can evaluate skills quickly and efficiently • can prevent students from "writing around" the answer • can prevent students' grades from being influenced by writing skills, spelling, grammar, and neatness • can be easily analyzed (item analysis) • prevents biased grading by teacher • can be used for diagnostic or pre-test purposes • can be given to large groups	• requires mostly recall of facts • does not allow students to demonstrate writing skills • often requires a disproportionate amount of reading (penalizes poor readers) • can be ambiguous and confusing (especially to younger students) • usually has a specific, pre-determined answer • can be very time-consuming to construct • promotes guessing • is often used year after year despite differing needs of students

Adapted from the Board of Education for the City of Etobicoke, 1987, pp. 157–158.

Figure 5.4

"Evaluation should be a learning experience for both the student and the teacher. However, objective-style testing is frequently ineffective as a learning experience for either the student or the teacher because objective-style questions too often require only the recall of facts and do not allow the student to display thinking processes or the teacher to observe them" (Board of Education for the City of Etobicoke, 1987, p. 156).

A good evaluation program does not have to include objective-style tests; however, if it does, the questions should be well-constructed and the objective-style tests should be balanced by other authentic assessments.

Misconceptions About Objective Tests

Often critics of authentic assessment point out that evaluating products, performances, and portfolios is too "subjective," and the teachers could assign a grade because they liked or didn't like a student or could base the grade upon outside variables like neatness, attendance, or behavior. These same critics point

Tips For Constructing Test Questions

True-False Items
- Avoid absolute words like "all," "never," and "always."
- Make sure items are clearly true or false rather than ambiguous.
- Limit true-false questions to ten.
- Consider asking students to make false questions true to encourage higher-order thinking.

Matching Items
- Limit list to between five and ten items.
- Use homogeneous lists. (Don't mix names with dates.)
- Give clear instructions. (Write letter, number, etc.)
- Give more choices than there are questions.

Multiple-Choice Items
- State main idea in the core or stem of the question.
- Use reasonable incorrect choices. (Avoid ridiculous choices.)
- Make options the same length (nothing very long or very short).
- Include multiple correct answers (a and b, all of the above).

Completion Items
- Structure for a brief, specific answer for each item.
- Avoid passages lifted directly from text (emphasis on memorization).
- Use blanks of equal length.
- Avoid multiple blanks that sometimes make a sentence too confusing.

Essay Items
- Avoid all-encompassing questions ("Discuss" is ambiguous . . . tell all you know about a subject).
- Define criteria for evaluation.
- Give point value.
- Use some higher-order thinking verbs like *predict* or *compare and contrast* rather than all recall verbs like *list* and *name*.

Adapted from Board of Education for the City of Etobicoke, 1987, pp. 112–187.

Figure 5.5

to objective tests being fairer or more valid and reliable. Since most well-written selected-response test items frame challenges that allow for just one best answer or a limited set of acceptable answers, it leads to the "objective" evaluation of responses as being right or wrong. However, Stiggins (1994) warns that when the teacher selects the test items for inclusion in the final test, he or she is making a subjective judgment as to the meaning and importance of the material to be tested. ". . . [A]ll assessments, regardless of their format, involve judgment on the part of the assessor. Therefore, all assessments reflect the biases of that assessor" (p. 103). Teachers should examine both the advantages and disadvantages of objective-style tests and then determine the role they will play in the evaluation process.

Questioning Techniques and Three-Story Intellect Verbs

Bellanca and Fogarty (1991) have created a graphic based on Bloom's Taxonomy called the Three-Story Intellect (see Figure 5.6) to show what verbs teachers can use when they ask questions. First-story verbs like *count, describe,* and *match* ask students to gather or recall information. Second-story verbs like *reason, compare,* and *analyze* ask students to process information. And third-story verbs like *evaluate, imagine,* and *speculate* ask students to apply information. An effective teacher-made test includes verbs from all three stories of the intellect. Many teachers use this graphic as a guide when they ask questions in class and when they create teacher-made tests that encourage higher-order thinking.

The Three-Story Intellect Review (see Blackline 5.3 at the end of this selection) provides a method to analzye tests to determine how many questions address each of the three levels of learning—gathering, processing, and applying. A well-balanced test should include questions from all levels to assess students' recall of factual information, their ability to process that information and, most important, their ability to apply that information by doing something with it. Stiggins (1994) observes that it is teachers and the assessments they create that have the most impact on student learning and drive the assessment systems in schools.

Teacher-Made Tests

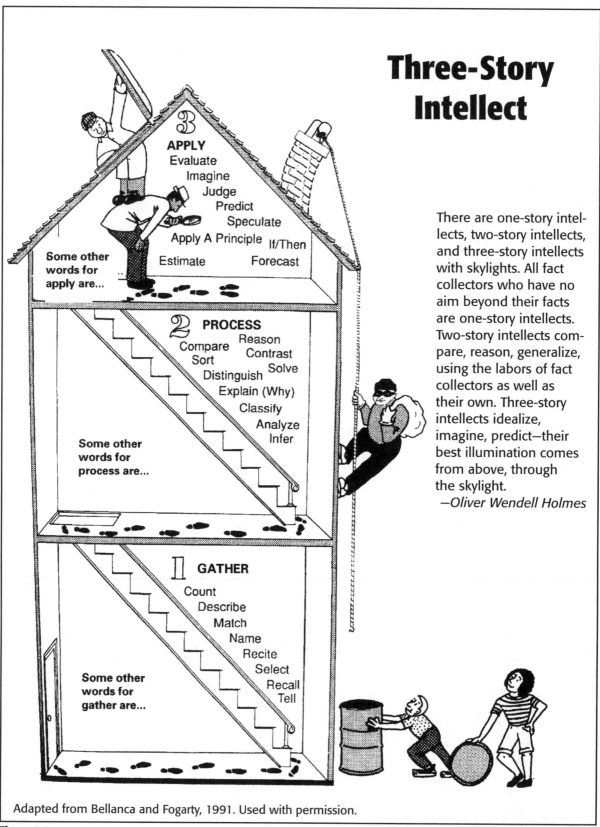

Three-Story Intellect

③ **APPLY**
Evaluate
Imagine
Judge
Predict
Speculate
Apply A Principle   If/Then
Estimate   Forecast

Some other words for apply are...

② **PROCESS**
Reason
Compare   Contrast
Sort   Solve
Distinguish
Explain (Why)
Classify
Analyze
Infer

Some other words for process are...

① **GATHER**
Count
Describe
Match
Name
Recite
Select
Recall
Tell

Some other words for gather are...

There are one-story intellects, two-story intellects, and three-story intellects with skylights. All fact collectors who have no aim beyond their facts are one-story intellects. Two-story intellects compare, reason, generalize, using the labors of fact collectors as well as their own. Three-story intellects idealize, imagine, predict—their best illumination comes from above, through the skylight.
—*Oliver Wendell Holmes*

Adapted from Bellanca and Fogarty, 1991. Used with permission.

Figure 5.6

BIBLIOGRAPHY

Bellanca, J. A. and R. Fogarty. 1991. *Blueprints for thinking in the cooperative classroom,* 2nd ed. Palatine, IL: IRI/Skylight Publishing, Inc.

———. 2002. *Blueprints for achievement in the cooperative class-room,* 3rd ed. Arlington Heights, IL: SkyLight Training and Publishing.

Board of Education for the City of Etobicoke. 1987. Making the grade: Evaluating student progress. Scarborough, Ontario, Canada: Prentice-Hall Canada.

Brown, R. 1989, April. Testing and thoughtfulness. *Educational Leadership* pp. 113–115.

Frender, G. 1990. *Learning to learn: Strengthening study skills and brain power.* Nashville, TN: Incentive Publications.

Gardner, H. 1983. *Frames of mind: The theory of multiple intelligences.* New York: Basic Books.

Hills, J. R. 1991, March. Apathy concerning grading and testing. *Phi Delta Kappan,* pp. 540–545.

Popham, W. J. 1999. *Classroom assessment: What teachers need to know,* 2nd ed. Boston: Allyn and Bacon.

Stiggins, R. J. 1985, October. Improving assessment where it means the most: In the classroom. *Educational Leadership* pp. 69–74.

———. 1994. *Student-centered classroom assessment.* New York: MacMillan College Publishing Co.

Wiggins, G. 1989, April. Teaching to the (authentic) test. *Educational Leadership* pp. 121–127.

- Mentors can show their protégés the examples of test questions on Blackline 5.1. Mentors can ask protégés to create sample questions for each of the four categories—graphic organizer and matching, true/false, and essay questions.
- Protégés can use the checklist in Blackline 5.2 when creating tests.
- Mentors can give Blackline 5.3 to their protégés to analyze and compare commercially-made and teacher-made tests against the three-story intellect model.
- Mentors and protégés can use Blackline 5.4 to reflect on what they have learned about teacher-made tests. Reflection is an important part of creating teacher-made-tests—reflecting on the process can help improve efforts.

Teacher-Made Tests

Examples

MATCHING QUESTIONS
Social Studies Test on Southeastern United States

Directions: (Three points each.) Fill in the letter from Column B that the phrase in Column A is describing.

Column A		Column B
C	1. Changing crops from one year to another.	A. Cotton
G	2. Separated cotton seeds from cotton.	B. Tobacco
K	3. Someone who visits a place for pleasure.	C. Crop Rotation
A	4. Once referred to as "white gold."	D. Service Jobs
E	5. Biggest farms in Southeast.	E. Plantations
B	6. First cash crop.	F. Erosion
I	7. Crops grown to earn money.	G. Cotton Gin
D	8. Jobs in which people are served in some way.	H. Slave Labor
		I. Cash Crops
		J. Ranches
		K. Tourist

(Courtesy of Nancy Minske, Wheeling, Illinois)

GRAPHIC ORGANIZER
History

TRUE/FALSE QUESTIONS
English

Directions: Please circle true next to the number if the statement is true; circle false if the statement is in any way false (2 points each). You will receive an additional 2 points if you rewrite the false statements to make them true.

(T) or F   1. Mark Twain wrote *Huckleberry Finn.*
Rewrite: _____
_____

T or (F)   2. Tom Sawyer is the protagonist in *Huckleberry Finn.*
Rewrite: Tom Sawyer appears in *Huckleberry Finn,* but Huck is the protagonist.

(T) or F   3. Mark Twain's real name is Samuel Clemens.
Rewrite: _____
_____

T or (F)   4. The runaway slave, Jim, hid on Hanibal Island after he left Aunt Polly.
Rewrite: Jim hid on Jackson Island.

T or (F)   5. Mark Twain was a wealthy man all of his life.
Rewrite: Twain made a lot of money, but he went backrupt by investing in bad businesses.

ESSAY QUESTIONS
Science

Point Value: 20

Directions: Select one of the following topics for your essay question. Your essay will be evaluated on the following criteria:

• accuracy of information
• organization of information
• use of support statements
• clarity and effectiveness

Select *one* topic.

1. Predict what will happen if the ozone layer continues to deplete at its current rate.
2. Evaluate the effectiveness of our government's research and regulations regarding acid rain.
3. Speculate what will happen if a cure for AIDS is not found within five years.
4. Compare and contrast the bubonic plague to AIDS. You may draw a Venn diagram to help you organize your thoughts before you write.

The Big Ten Teacher-Made Test Checklist

Test: _____ Date:_____

Grade Level/Class:_____

_____ 1. I wrote my test before I taught the subject matter.

_____ 2. I have listed my standards and benchmarks on the test.

_____ 3. I have listed my grading scale on the test.

_____ 4. I have varied the question types to include _____ types.

_____ 5. I have provided point values for each section.

_____ 6. I have included tasks to address the multiple intelligences and learning modalities of my students.

_____ 7. I have given students some choice of questions.

_____ 8. I have used all three levels of the Three-Story Intellect verbs in my questions.

_____ 9. I have made allowances for students with special needs.

___10. I have made sure that all students have time to finish the test.

Signature: _____ Date: _____

Three-Story Intellect Verbs Review

1. Analyze one of your own teacher-made tests. Classify the questions by marking them first, second, or third level according to the Three-Story Intellect. Tally the results.

   a. Number of first-story gathering questions. _____

   b. Number of second-story processing questions. _____

   c. Number of third-story applying questions. _____

2. Analyze a chapter test from a textbook or any commercially prepared content test in terms of the guidelines used above. Tally the results.

   a. Number of first-story gathering questions. _____

   b. Number of second-story processing questions. _____

   c. Number of third-story applying questions. _____

3. Compare and contrast the analysis of your original teacher-made test to your analysis of the commercially prepared test. Comment on your findings.

4. Construct an original teacher-made test to use with your students. Follow the guidelines discussed in this chapter and use The Big Ten Teacher-Made Test Checklist (Blackline 5.2).

Teacher-Made Tests Reflection Page

3 List three things you have learned about teacher-made tests.
1._____
2._____
3._____

2 List two things you would like to try on your next teacher-made test.
1._____
2._____
_____

1 List one comment you have about teacher-made tests.
1._____
_____
_____

Portfolios provide a framework for teachers to collect student work correlated to standards and curriculum goals. Mentors can help new teachers develop techniques to help students organize their portfolios to document their learning.

Portfolios

by Kay Burke

A portfolio is more than just a container full of stuff. It's a systematic and organized collection of evidence used by the teacher and student to monitor growth of the student's knowledge, skills, and attitudes in a specific subject area.—Vavrus, 1990

What Is a Portfolio?

"A portfolio is a collection of student work gathered for a particular purpose that exhibits to the student and others the student's efforts, progress or achievement in one or more areas." This working definition of portfolios was developed at the Northwest Regional Educational Laboratory in Portland, Oregon (cited in Johnson and Rose, 1997, p. 6). Tierney, Carter, and Desai (1991) define portfolios as ongoing assessments that are composed of purposeful collections that examine achievement, effort, improvement, and processes, such as selecting, comparing, sharing, self-evaluation, and goal setting (cited in Johnson and Rose, 1997, p. 6). A portfolio is more than just a collection of stuff randomly organized and stuck in a folder. There is a purpose and a focus to a portfolio. The organization and the contents of portfolios differ according to the purpose and the type of the portfolio (see Figure 6.1).

Portfolios

Additional items that could be included in a portfolio are reflections or comments from peers about the artifacts; comments from parents or significant others; descriptions of major concepts learned; and bibliography of sources used.

Purpose of the Portfolio

The first step in creating a portfolio is to determine the purpose of the portfolio. The contents need to be aligned to the purpose or rationale for implementing portfolios. A portfolio can be used to:

1. Document meeting district, state, or national standards.
2. Connect several subject areas to provide an "integrated" assessment of the student.
3. Chronicle a student's growth and development over extended periods of a semester, year, or clusters of grades (K–2, 3–5, 7–9, 10–12).
4. Document the key concepts taught by teachers.
5. Share at a job interview, promotion, or college entrance review.

The purpose of the portfolio will determine the type of portfolio and the process to be used in developing the portfolio. It is not unusual for a portfolio to combine several purposes to meet the needs of the students or school.

Types of Portfolios

Once the primary purpose for creating a portfolio has been determined, educators must select the type of portfolio that would best fulfill the purpose (see Figure 6.2). These types may also be combined to correlate with the purpose for creating the portfolio.

Hansen (1992) advocates using self-created literacy portfolios by asking students to include what they are like outside the classroom. Students can include pictures of relatives, awards or ribbons they have won in athletic events, lists of books or

A Portfolio May Contain

1. *A Creative Cover*—to depict the subject area or the author

2. *A Letter to the Reader*—to explain the cover and to welcome the readers

3. *A Table of Contents*—to display organization

4. *Six or Seven Student Artifacts*—to showcase work selected by teachers and students

5. *Reflections*—to reveal student insight

6. *Self-Evaluation*—to analyze strengths and weaknesses

7. *Goal-Setting Page*—to set new short-term and long-term goals

8. *Conference Questions* (optional)—to provide the audience with key questions

Figure 6.1

Types of Portfolios

1. *Writing*—dated writing samples to show process and product

2. *Process Folios*—first and second drafts of assignments along with final product to show growth

3. *Literacy*—combination of reading, writing, speaking, and listening pieces

4. *Best-Work*—student and teacher selections of the student's best work

5. *Unit*—one unit of study (Egypt, angles, frogs, elections)

6. *Integrated*—a thematic study that brings in different disciplines (e.g., "Health and Wellness"—language arts, science, math, health, and physical education)

7. *Year-long*—key artifacts from entire year to show growth and development

8. *Career*—important artifacts (resumés, recommendations, commendations) collected for showcase employability

9. *Standards*—evidence to document meeting standards

Figure 6.2

magazines about rock stars, sports, hobbies, or anything that interests them. The key to the portfolio is the discussion the items generate. Every adult and student involved in a literacy portfolio project creates a literacy portfolio. "Whether or not we know ourselves better than anyone else does, our portfolios give us the opportunity to get to know ourselves better" (Hansen, 1992, p. 66). Krogness (1991) suggests that students list their goals at the beginning of each year. The goal-setting allows them to learn what they value and focus their attention on meeting their goals.

Why Should We Use Portfolios?

The portfolio helps the classroom environment become a seamless web of instruction and assessment. "If carefully assembled, portfolios become an intersection of instruction and assessment; they are not just instruction or just assessment, but, rather, both. Together, instruction and assessment give more than either give separately" (Paulson, Paulson, and Meyer 1991, p. 61).

Wolf (1989), Vavrus (1990), Paulson et al. (1991), Lazear (1991), and many others recommend using portfolios because they can be used as the following:

- Tools for discussion with peers, teachers, and parents
- Demonstrations of students' skills and understanding
- Opportunities for students to reflect on their work metacognitively
- Chances to examine current goals and set new ones
- Documentation of students' development and growth in abilities, attitudes, and expressions
- Demonstrations of different learning styles, multiple intelligences, cultural diversity
- Options for students to make critical choices about what they select for their portfolio
- Evidence to examine that traces the development of students' learning
- Connections between prior knowledge and new learning

Purves, Quattrini, and Sullivan (1995) maintain that port-folios provide documentation for other people to judge a person's quality as a performer, artist, or writer. They state, "A portfolio is an amplified resumé. It seeks to show the person off to the world, to say, 'Here is what I have done; look at it as an indicator of what I can do'" (p. 3). Indeed, discussing key artifacts during a job interview adds a richer dimension to the quality of the experience.

Searfoss (cited in Glazer and Brown, 1993) also talks about the importance of blending instruction and assessment. The final product is important, but the process is equally important and probably conveys more about how the student learns. "Assessing process means we cannot act alone; we need our students involved in observing and monitoring their own products. By helping students focus on process, we guide them to discover for themselves how they can continually improve a product as they create it. Students learn how to 'fit things' as they arise, rather than waiting until the teacher identifies them as 'incorrect' or 'unclear'" (p. 16). The process of metacognition —thinking about one's thinking—helps students become more self-reflective and more empowered as stakeholders in their own learning.

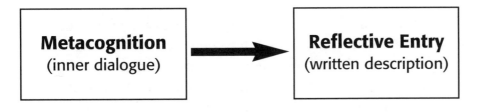

SkyLight Professional Development

Section II: Assessing Student Work | 145

Portfolios

How Can We Implement Portfolios?

Educators have developed a variety of creative and intricate portfolio systems, but for teachers just embarking on the portfolio journey, it might be best to start simply. The portfolio process in its simplest form includes three basic steps (Figure 6.3).

The Portfolio Process

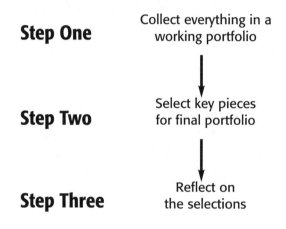

Step One — Collect everything in a working portfolio

Step Two — Select key pieces for final portfolio

Step Three — Reflect on the selections

Figure 6.3

The Collection Process

Educators, in most cases, recognize the benefits of using portfolios to show the growth and development of their students. Unfortunately, they also recognize the tremendous organizational problems and increased time commitment associated with implementing a portfolio system.

To simplify the implementation of the system, note the first step in the collection process is to develop a working portfolio. The working portfolio is where students store all the items they have collected before they make their selections for the final, or showcase, portfolio. Various methods for storing items include:

- large cardboard boxes
- cereal boxes
- file folders
- accordion files
- computer disks
- videos or CD-ROMs
- file cabinets

Working Portfolios

This process is similar to traditional assessment because students usually collect their work. Work should still be sent home and brought back. Teachers may choose to make a copy of very important assignments before they are sent home, just in case of loss or damage. Even if students lose some of their work, there should still be enough work left from which to choose for the final portfolio. This first step is not much different than a teacher asking students to keep a folder or a notebook of their work.

Variety of Artifacts

One of the characteristics of working portfolios that sets them apart from more traditional writing folders, however, is that they should contain a variety of works that reflect different modalities. Students should have more than just worksheets or homework assignments in their working portfolio; they should collect artifacts including cassette tapes, videotapes, pictures, projects, performances, rough drafts, journals, logs, artwork, musical work, computer disks, and assignments that feature work from all the multiple intelligences. If the portfolio is to create a true portrait of the student as a learner, it needs to be richly textured and comprehensive, and it needs to assess more than just one of the multiple intelligences—in this case, usually the verbal/linguistic intelligence. A writing folder is a writing folder. A portfolio is much more.

Selection Process

After most of the quarter or semester is spent collecting items, the selection process (see Figure 6.4) usually involves three major questions:

1. **Who** should select the items that go into the final portfolio?
2. **What** items should be selected?
3. **When** should these items be selected?

Who Should Select Items?

In most cases, both teachers and students select the items to be included in the final portfolio. The teacher needs to show evidence that the students met school goals or standards and that they understand the basic concepts of the course. If students were allowed to choose all the items, they would probably select their best work or favorites, but those items wouldn't necessarily provide a balanced analysis that documents learning. After the teacher has selected some general items, then students should have freedom to choose items which they want to include to showcase their strengths and talents.

Selection Process

Portfolio	Purpose
1. Teacher choice	to meet course
2. Teacher choice	objectives and
3. Teacher choice	standards
4. Student choice	to allow for
5. Student choice	individual choice and
6. Student choice	showcase best work
7. Peer or parent choice	to involve others
8. Reflection	
9. Self-assessment	to encourage self-evaluation
10. Goal-setting	

Figure 6.4

In addition, parents and peers are sometimes asked to select items for the portfolio and write a comment or reflection about the piece or pieces. The selection process could vary, however, depending on the purpose and type of the portfolio. If the purpose of the portfolio were to meet district standards, then the teacher would have to request pieces that provide evidence of meeting those standards. Sometimes the selection could involve both the teacher and the student. For instance, the teacher may need to include a narrative writing piece to meet standards, but the student can choose which one of his or her narrative pieces to include. The teacher sets the parameters, but the student has some choice within those parameters.

What Should Be Selected?

The motto that educators need to adopt for the selection process if they are going to maintain their sanity and make this process manageable is: "Less is more." It is not necessary to include all of the artifacts in the final portfolio. Even though some students think all of their work is wonderful and they "just can't eliminate anything," the very process of reviewing their work and deciding what is appropriate is metacognitive. Most portfolios contain seven to twelve items. Teachers should not have to bring a wagon to school to haul home portfolios. Keep it simple. Fewer items provide more opportunities for in-depth discussion and more targeted feedback and analysis.

Many teachers like to include selection criteria such as: "Select a piece that is your most unsatisfying piece and discuss why" or "Select the piece you would like to do over and tell why" or "Select the piece that you just don't understand and explain why." These criteria provide insightful information about the learner and the process he or she is going through. By viewing the "not so best" work, the audience gets a truer picture of the student's strengths and weaknesses and why he or she set goals for improvement. If students only select their "Best Work" for all portfolios, the students may increase their self-esteem, but the students, teachers, and parents may have a distorted or "rose-colored" opinion of the students' abilities. The evidence in the final portfolio needs to reflect both strengths and weaknesses and correlate to traditional assessments such as teacher-made tests and standardized tests. The portfolio grade will probably be higher than traditional test grades because students have more time to revise and perfect their work. The "Best Work" portfolio sometimes appears "fluffy" and portrays a portfolio as a "scrapbook of stuff" rather than a collection of evidence that the student met learning standards, district goals, or course objectives. The portfolio also needs to include rigorous assessments to document a student's ability and help teachers modify their instruction or adapt the curriculum to meet the students' needs.

When Should Items Be Selected?

A timeline for data gathering is essential. For some components of the portfolio, the timeline will indicate critical points in the academic year: beginning, middle, and end of year. For other components, a schedule of regular data gathering may be daily, weekly, and monthly.—Shaklee et al., 1997

The timing for selecting items for the final portfolio depends once again on the purpose and type of portfolio (see Figure 6.5 for scenarios). Many teachers find it more manageable to have the students complete unit portfolios throughout the year. Once the unit is complete, the teacher saves the portfolio contents and returns the notebook or permanent final portfolio container to the students for their next unit portfolio. At the end of the year, the teacher distributes the four or five unit portfolios and asks students to select items for their final year-long portfolio. The students then choose from about ten to twelve items based upon selection criteria such as the following:

1. Select one item from the beginning of the year and a similar item from the end of the year and comment on your growth.
2. Select your favorite artifact and explain why.
3. Select your least favorite artifact and explain why.
4. Select an artifact that will surprise people. Explain.

Timeline Scenarios

Unit Portfolio
1. Collect items for three or four weeks.
2. Select and reflect on items two weeks prior to the end of unit.
3. Conduct conferences in the last week.
4. Grade the last week.

Semester Portfolio
1. Collect items the entire semester.
2. Select seven to ten final items for the portfolio four weeks before the end of the semester.
3. Allow one week for students to select, reflect, and organize the portfolios.
4. Allow one week for conferences.
5. Allow one week for grading.

Year-Long Portfolio
1. Collect one to two items each week.
2. Review all items at end of each quarter and select three or four items. Date all items.
3. Repeat each quarter—students write reflections on each item.
4. Four weeks before end of school, select final ten to twelve items for the portfolio.
5. Allow two to three weeks for reflection, organization, and conferencing.
6. Allow one to two weeks for grading.

Figure 6.5

Reflection Process

"Most of the best research on cognitive development suggests that it is extremely important to create situations in which students must think about their own thinking, reflect on the ways in which they learn and why they fail to learn. It's clear that the more students are aware of their own learning processes, the more likely they are to establish goals for their education and the more deeply engaged they are in those processes" (Mills-Courts and Amiran 1991, p. 103). Reflection is the heart and soul of the portfolio, but reflection doesn't just happen. Teachers need to experiment with a variety of strategies to encourage students to use metacognitive strategies to think about their learning.

Portfolios

Labeling

The first and easiest step in the reflection process involves asking students to attach a label to each artifact in the portfolio. The labels could include things like:

- "Best Work"
- "Most Difficult"
- "Most Creative"
- "A Nightmare"
- "First Draft—More to Come"

Another strategy to introduce students to the reflection process is to have them select different-size sticky notes upon which to write their reflections, reactions, or descriptions. They then attach the sticky notes to each item. They may rewrite this initial reflection when they select the piece for their final portfolio; other times, they'll just edit it slightly. Sometimes they'll include their initial reflection from when they completed an item and then add another reflection—"Upon Further Reflection"—to provide insight after more time has elapsed.

Stem Questions

Some students become adept at writing descriptions and reflections of their work without any prompts. Many students, however, stare at their portfolio pieces and have no idea what to write. Teachers can "prime the pump" by either assigning a stem question or allowing students to select a stem to complete. See Figure 6.6 for examples.

Reflective Stems

1. This piece shows I've met standard #_____ because . . .
2. This piece shows I really understand the content because . . .
3. This piece showcases my _____ intelligence because . . .
4. If I could show this piece to anyone—living or dead—I would show it to _____ because . . .
5. People who knew me last year would never believe this piece because . . .
6. This piece was my greatest challenge because . . .
7. My (parents, friend, teacher) liked this piece because . . .
8. One thing I have learned about myself is . . .

Figure 6.6

Mirror Page

Another method to help students gain insight into their work is to ask them to organize their portfolio so that the item or piece of evidence is on one page; on the opposite page the student writes a description of the piece, followed by a reflection or reaction to it. The proximity of the reflection to the piece of evidence helps the portfolio creator as well as the reader focus on examining the piece more carefully by referring to the elements being described.

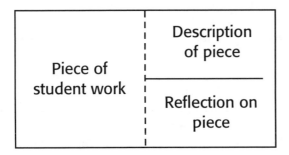

The description requires the student to explain the concept in the piece and share his or her understanding of its importance. Also, the description provides the teacher with a more in-depth analysis of student learning. The description could be elaborated upon during the conference, but it helps to clarify whether or not the student understands the basic concept of the assignment. The reflection, on the other hand, helps the student understand how he or she feels about the piece by asking himself or herself questions such as:

1. What does this piece show about me?
2. What did I do well in this piece?
3. What do I still need to practice?
4. What help do I need?

Student Reflection

One seventh-grade student was asked to include in his portfolio his most difficult math assignment and write why it was his most difficult piece. He included an assignment on word problems and wrote the following piece, entitled "My Most Difficult Work."

> "If I had to choose one, I would choose the word problems that we did. I found them the most difficult out of the things that we did. I found them the most difficult because I had to think about them for a while before I could get an answer especially since I work at a slow pace. We didn't have enough time for me to be able to take my time and think them over. I was able to find the answer most of the time but other kids work at a faster rate than I do so they were able to get more of the answers. I was glad we got to work in groups because it showed me that I was not the only kid who was having trouble with them. I think that it also helped me because some people could understand parts of the problem better than others and we could also learn how they found out the answers which will help us out in the future. I am going to try to correct it by getting a book on word problems and tips on how to solve them. I am also going to be an engineer so I will need to get good at them and take classes that deal with them when I get older."

The teacher had thought mathematics came very easily to the student. She said she gained new insight into the student as a learner and a person by reading his reflection. Her comment: "I ask you, does this child understand the content, the process, and himself?" (personal correspondence, 1996).

A portfolio without reflections is a notebook of stuff! The power of the portfolio is derived from the descriptions, reactions, processing patterns, and metacognitive reflections that help students achieve their goals. Conducting teacher-student conferences and peer conferences to discuss the portfolios helps synthesize the learning and celebrate the successes. The three basic steps remain the key: Collect-Select-Reflect! For educators and students just beginning the portfolio process, start small! Once the first portfolios are produced, the process can be altered, extended, and elaborated upon to meet the needs of the teacher, the school, and, most important, the student.

BIBLIOGRAPHY

de Bono, E. 1992. *Serious creativity.* New York: HarperCollins.

Glazer, S. M., and C. S. Brown. 1993. *Portfolios and beyond: Collaborative assessment in reading and writing.* Norwood, MA: Christopher-Gordon Publishers.

Hansen, J. 1992, May. Literacy portfolios: Helping students know themselves. *Educational Leadership,* 66–68.

Johnson, N. J., and L. M. Rose. 1997. *Portfolios: Clarifying, classifying, and enhancing.* Lancaster: Basil Technomic Publishing Company.

Krogness, M. M. 1991. A question of values. *English Journal,* 80(6), 28–33.

Lazear, D. 1991. *Seven ways of teaching: The artistry of teaching with multiple intelligences.* Palatine, IL: IRI/Skylight Publishing, Inc.

Mills-Courts, K., and M. R. Amiran. 1991. Metacognition and the use of portfolios. In P. Belanoff and M. Dickson, eds. *Portfolios: Process and product* (pp. 101–111). Portsmouth, NH: Boynton and Cook Publishers.

Paulson, F. L., P. R. Paulson, and C. A. Meyer. 1991, February. What makes a portfolio a portfolio? *Educational Leadership,* 60–63.

Purves, A. C., J. A. Quattrini, and C. I. Sullivan. 1995. *Creating the writing portfolio: A guide to students.* Lincolnwood, IL: NTC Publishing Group.

Shaklee, B. D., N. E. Barbour, R. Ambrose, and S. J. Hansford. 1997. *Designing and using portfolios.* Boston: Allyn and Bacon.

Tierney, R. J., M. A. Carter, and L. E. Desai. 1991. *Portfolio assessment in the reading-writing classroom.* Norwood, MA: Christopher-Gordon Publishers.

Wolf, D. 1989, April. Portfolio assessment: Sampling student work. *Educational Leadership,* 35–39.

Vavrus, L. 1990, August. Put portfolios to the test. *Instructor,* 48–53.

- Mentors and protégés can refer to the portfolio contents examples in Blackline 6.1 to help them decide what they might ask students to collect for their portfolios.
- Mentors can help protégés create their own rubrics for portfolios using Blackline 6.2 or protégés can adapt the rubric in Blackline 6.3 to meet their needs.
- Mentors can ask protégés to complete the reflection in Blackline 6.4. Protégés can then discuss their feelings on portfolios with their mentors.
- Mentors can help protégés plan for portfolios using Blackline 6.5.

Portfolios

Examples

PRIMARY
LANGUAGE ARTS PORTFOLIO
Integrated Unit on Spiders

Table of Contents

1. Letter to parents about what students have learned
2. Book review of Charlotte's Web
3. Web of characteristics of spiders
4. Water-color picture of spiders
5. Tape of student reading story about spiders
6. Original short story (first and final drafts) about a spider
7. Science report on arachnids
8. Spider rap song
9. Pictures of group project on spiders
10. Self-assessment using a criteria checklist

MIDDLE SCHOOL
GEOMETRY PORTFOLIO

Table of Contents

1. My Math Phobia Journal
2. Two geometry tests—corrections included
3. Glossary of geometry terms
4. Drawings of geometric shapes
5. Three problem-solving logs
6. String geometric design
7. Video of group project on angles
8. Essay on video, *Why Math?*
9. Research on math-related careers
10. Self-evaluation of portfolio using rubrics
11. Goal-setting for next quarter

HIGH SCHOOL
BIOLOGY PORTFOLIO

Table of Contents

1. Reports on careers related to the field of biology
2. One lab report
3. One problem-solving log
4. Pamphlet on diabetes (group project)
5. Video of group presentation on the circulatory system
6. Essay on germ warfare
7. Research paper on AIDS
8. Tape-recorded interview with college biology professor about AIDS
9. Self-evaluation of portfolio using rubric
10. Goal-setting web

COLLEGE
AMERICAN HISTORY PORTFOLIO

Table of Contents

1. Annotated bibliographies of five books about the Civil War
2. Reading list of fifty books and articles related to the Civil War
3. One abstract of a research article
4. Tape of interview with local historian
5. Journal entries of trip to Gettysburg
6. Map of the Battle of Gettysburg
7. Video of oral presentation on Pickett's charge
8. Research paper on military tactics used at the Battle of Gettysburg
9. Venn diagram comparing Battle of Gettysburg and Battle of Chancellorsville
10. Critique of TV miniseries The Civil War
11. Peer evaluation of portfolio using rubric

GUIDEBOOK

Criteria for Grading a Portfolio

1. Circle three criteria that could be used to assess a final portfolio:

accuracy	evidence of understanding	organization
completeness	form (mechanics)	reflectiveness
creativity	growth	visual appeal

2. Develop three subpoints that could explain each criterion more fully.

   Example: Evidence of Understanding
   • Knowledge of content
   • Ability to problem solve
   • Application of ideas

3. Create a checklist to evaluate a portfolio.

Portfolio Checklist

Criteria and Subpoints	Does Not Meet Expectations 1	In Progress to Meet Expectations 2	Meets Expectations 3	Exceeds Expectations 4
•				
•				
•				
•				
•				
•				
•				
•				
•				

MENTORING

Weighted Rubric for Portfolio

Student:_____ Subject:_____ Date:_____

Goal/Standard: Use reading, writing, listening, and speaking skills to research and apply information for specific purposes.

Criteria	Indicators	1	2	3	4	Score
Form	• Spelling • Grammar • Sentence structure	2–3 errors	1–2 errors	0 errors	0 errors and a high level of writing	__ x 3 __ (12)
Visual Appeal	• Cover • Artwork • Graphics	Missing 2 elements	Missing 1 element	All 3 elements included	All 3 elements are creatively and visually appealing	__ x 4 __ (16)
Organization	• Complete-ness • Timeliness • Table of Contents	Missing 2 elements	Missing 1 element	All 3 elements included	All 3 elements demonstrate high level of organization	__ x 5 __ (20)
Knowledge of Key Concepts	• Key concepts • Evidence of under-standing • Application	Evidence of key concepts included in portfolio	Evidence of basic level of understand-ing of key concepts	Evidence of high level of understand-ing of key concepts	Evidence of ability to apply knowl-edge to new situations	__ x 6 __ (24)
Reflections	• One per piece • Depth of reflection • Ability to self-assess	Missing 2 or more reflections	Missing 1 reflection	Insightful reflections for each piece	Reflections show insightful-ness and ability to self-assess	__ x 7 __ (28)

Comments:

Scale
A = _____
B = _____
C = _____
D = _____

Final Score: _____
(100)

Final Grade:_____

Portfolios Reflection Page

Review this PMI graphic organizer (de Bono, 1992) and write your own ideas about the pluses, minuses, and interesting aspects of portfolios.

Use of Portfolios

Plus
Minus
Interesting

Portfolios

Portfolio Planner

Purpose of portfolio:_____

_____

Type:_____

Timeline:_____

Working Portfolio	Final Portfolio

Generate items to collect.

_____   _____

_____   _____

_____   _____

Create three stem questions for reflections.

1. _____

2. _____

3. _____

Level 2

MENTORING GUIDEBOOK

SECTION III

Establishing Learning Communities

Building shared responsibility for student learning is an ongoing, iterative journey, filled with unanticipated turns and unexpected side roads.

—Conzemius and O'Neill 2001

long the road to professional growth, mentors are required to play different roles. Protégés embarking on the teaching journey "may perceive their roles as directly responsive to the school system's mandated curriculum, regardless of their students' prior knowledge or preferences in their own learning" (Joseph-Bolotin and Burnaford, 1994, 7). The wise mentor, however, knows from experience that the roles of teachers include more than just teaching the academic curriculum to the students. The successful teacher must interact daily with bus drivers, cafeteria staff, counselors, special education teachers, paraprofessionals, and parents. This section focuses on the many interactions protégés must establish in order to develop learning communities within the classroom and school that provide an enriching environment for all students. Mentors guide protégés in developing these relationships by sharing their own stories of past experiences, providing tools needed for communication, and modeling strategies to help novices learn how to build relationships within the classroom community.

Joseph-Bolotin and Burnaford (1994) explain the many different roads teachers take and the roles they play. Some roles include teacher as parent, advocate, companion, interpreter, storyteller, and, of course, mentor. Mentors guide protégés through their professional journey and help them establish relationships with others. Working well with others is a vital component of life; moreover, it becomes a critical skill when working all day with students, and sometimes adults, within the confines of a classroom.

In Selection 7, **Working with Paraprofessionals**, Sausen explains the impact of the Individuals with Disabilities Education Act Amendments of 1997 (IDEA '97) on educators. The act ultimately created the inclusion movement—an unanticipated turn for many teachers who were not trained to work with students with special needs (Masterpoli and Scruggs 2000). Inclusion sometimes requires administrators to assign an assistant or paraprofessional to work with one specific student who needs extra cognitive or physical help in the regular education classroom. Mentors can help protégés understand what a paraprofessional can and cannot do in the classroom. Sausen provides tools mentors can use with protégés to maximize the collaborative efforts between the protégé and paraprofessional and, most importantly, help the students who require alternative lessons or extra time. Included in the selection are strategies for collaborating, building relationships, and setting student goals with the help of a paraprofessional. Templates are provided for scheduling, keeping track of student achievement, and setting up meetings.

Paraprofessionals are only one part of the learning community. Parents and community members form another part of the community that exists both inside and outside of the classroom walls. Parents and community members are stakeholders who can provide invaluable resources, help with activities, and support the teacher by reinforcing learning and providing richer learning opportunities for students outside of school. In Selection 8, **Establishing the Learning Community**, Sausen reviews guidelines to help protégés build relationships with parents as well as other members of the school community. Mentors should discuss these guidelines with protégés and encourage them to set parameters for parent and community-member relationships in order to build trusting partnerships. Sausen stresses the importance of including parents and community members in classroom activities or lessons and keeping them updated with classroom news. Sausen also provides tools for mentors and protégés to use for setting up meetings, inviting parents and community members into the classroom, and initiating communications to and from the home.

Even though new teachers might be nervous about working with other adults in the classroom and interacting with parents both inside and outside the classroom, they must establish a positive working relationship with all the people who have roles in the educational program. Novice teachers who know how to utilize and manage the assistance of others create a community of learners working together toward the common goals of improving the classroom climate and students' academic achievement.

REFERENCES

Bolotin-Joseph, P., and G. E. Burnaford. 1994. *Images of school-teachers in twentieth-century America: Paragons, polarities, complexities.* Edited by Pamela Bolotin-Joseph, and Gail E. Burnaford. New York: St. Martin's Press.

Conzemius, A., and J. O'Neill. 2001. *Building shared responsibility for student learning.* Alexandria, VA: Association for Supervision and Curriculum Development.

Masterpoli, M. A., and T. E. Scruggs. 2000. *The inclusive classroom: Strategies for effective instruction.* Upper Saddle River, NJ: Merrill.

Sausen provides strategies to foster communication and cooperation between the teacher and the paraprofessional. These strategies ensure that the teacher and paraprofessional create a positive working relationship by working together to meet the needs of the students. Mentors can help facilitate this relationship.

Working with Paraprofessionals

by **Julie Sausen**

Understanding the Law

The Individuals with Disabilities Education Act Amendments of 1997 (IDEA '97) specifies "that all children—including those with disabilities formerly excluded from school—were entitled to a free, appropriate public education. This law went far beyond any previous legislation in specifying that, to the greatest extent possible, this 'special' education was to be provided in the least-restrictive environment" (Masterpoli and Scruggs 2000, 3)." IDEA '97 and other similar laws increased the number of paraprofessionals and educational assistants in schools and classrooms across the country because the "least restrictive environment" is usually the general education classroom.

The adoption of IDEA '97 started what Masterpoli and Scruggs (2000) call the "full inclusion" movement (21). School administrations across the country must abide by the inclusion laws and place students with special needs in classrooms that are considered to be the least restrictive learning environment. In many cases, the general education classroom is considered the least restrictive environment to learn content and to provide social interactions for students with special needs. When the least restrictive environment for a student is defined as the general education classroom, the student is placed in that class-room for the entire school day. The full inclusion movement allows for many students with different types of disabilities to be placed in the same general education classroom.

Placing students in the least restrictive environment creates challenges for the administration of school districts with limited classes, many novice teachers, and few resource services, such as reading and math specialists. In some districts, it is not always possible to place students with special needs with experienced teachers and paraprofessionals—someone who helps a certified educator in the general education classroom—because of scheduling conflicts or insufficient resources. Moreover, in school districts with high attrition rates, students with disabilities may be placed in classrooms of first- or second-year teachers who may have little or no training in special or gifted education. Working with special needs students and a paraprofessional in the classroom adds new challenges to a first- or second-year teacher's assignment. The new teacher is already unfamiliar with the school and curriculum. Adding paraprofessionals requires them to familiarize themselves with laws and strategies for working effectively with other adults in the classroom.

Exploring Classroom Situations

A mentor guides a protégé in establishing procedures for classroom management, teaching lessons, and conducting assessments, but he or she may be faced with another responsibility—helping the protégé establish and build an effective relationship with a paraprofessional. Since most beginning teachers work alone in the classroom, they may not be accustomed to coordinating the actions of another person as well as all the individual learning styles of each student.

"Students with disabilities bring a spectrum of expectations to the school experience. Each student possesses unique learning characteristics that will possibly challenge the instructor and can potentially cause the school experience to be one of devastation for the student" (Shelton and Pollingue 2000, 23). To meet the challenges of students with special needs and to avoid difficulty for the students, a paraprofessional can assist the teacher in guiding one or many students in the development of academic and social skills. The paraprofessional may work in any one of the following situations:

- **General**—The paraprofessional can be a generalist, who assists all students in a classroom.
- **Small Group of Students to One**—The paraprofessional may be specialized in a specific area such as reading, math, a specific learning disability, or gifted and talented. This paraprofessional is assigned to a small group of students with similar learning needs.
- **One to One**—The paraprofessional may be assigned to a specific student with special needs, usually with an individual education plan (IEP) in a general education classroom.

A mentor can start by guiding his or her protégé in defining the classroom and paraprofessional situations. Figures 7.1–7.2 are examples of classroom situations teachers and paraprofessionals may encounter. (See also Blackline 7.1 at the end of this selection. Mentors can discuss this blackline master with their protégés to use to determine their classroom situation and their paraprofessional needs.)

Elementary/Middle School Situation

My current classroom situation is…

> This year in my fifth grade classroom I have 30 students. I have 5 specific learning disability (SLD) students who have individual education plans (IEPs). Each student has a different set of goals and expectations. All 5 students are reading below grade level; math is a problem for 2 of the 5 students. I have a paraprofessional to assist me in the classroom, as well as having help from reading and math specialists.

My paraprofessional situation is…

> My paraprofessional assists me by working with a small group of students. She helps them to organize tasks and assignments, track their schedules when leaving the room for reading or math, and assist them in troublesome situations. The paraprofessional assists SLD students one-on-one when conducting an assessment, building vocabulary skills, or working on individual math problems.

> My paraprofessional is gone 40 minutes a day between 11:00 and 11:40 to assist with lunch and recess duty.

Figure 7.1

Middle/High School Situation

My current classroom situation is…

> This year, I have three 55-minute tenth-grade western history classes and two 55-minute ninth-grade American history classes. In my third period tenth grade class, I have one student with a traumatic brain injury who has an individualized educational plan (IEP). This student is guided to classes with the assistance of a one-to-one paraprofessional. She has a motorized wheelchair, so space must be provided for her when setting up the classroom.

My paraprofessional situation is…

> The paraprofessional assists me in situations that include working with this student one-to-one. The paraprofessional assists this student when participating in cooperative group activities, field trips, history simulations, and other projects. The paraprofessional also guides the student through activities that are designed to help her achieve her IEP goals and create a learning environment that is enriching for her.

Figure 7.2

Outlining the Working Relationship

"Teachers who work together as a team often will transfer the collaborative teamwork they are experiencing with one another into cooperative learning in their classes" (Schmuck and Schmuck 1997, 237). Mentors can help novice teachers define and outline the working relationship they will have with a paraprofessional who is placed in the classroom. By defining the relationship from the beginning, the protégé can establish trust and positive communication with the paraprofessional. The cooperative relationship the mentor, the new teacher, and the paraprofessional establish models for students the example of working together to achieve learning goals. The mentor can guide the new teacher to demonstrate cooperative skills and then help him or her transfer these skills into cooperative classroom lessons.

Paraprofessional Roles and Responsibilities

As Morgan and Ashbaker (2001) point out, "Some classroom responsibilities belong to the teacher alone, whereas others can be shared. Within the legal limits imposed by your state and district, you need to consider which responsibilities must remain yours as a teacher and which ones you may share with your paraeducator or other adult who works with you" (19). Whether dictated by law or classroom needs, there are specific tasks that a paraprofessional can and cannot perform in the classroom. "When a paraprofessional is assigned to a teacher or classroom to assist students with special needs it is crucial that they are viewed as a support for all students" (McVay 1998, 3). The major role of a paraprofessional in the classroom is to provide extra educational support to the teacher and students.

Guiding students who have Individualized Education Plans (IEPs) and supporting teachers are the roles of the paraprofessional, but he or she is not the sole responsible party in making sure students achieve their goals. It is the certified educator's responsibility to keep track of individual student achievements and create a learning environment that allows all students to achieve their highest potential. To avoid problems with specific tasks a paraprofessional can and cannot perform, it is good practice for teachers to review and keep current on specific laws that refer to particular situations involving paraprofessionals. If a new teacher is unsure if a task is appropriate for a paraprofessional, the teacher can ask a mentor or administrator. The paraprofessional should not be assigned tasks that put a student in danger.

Careful planning will help beginning teachers avoid problems when assigning tasks to paraprofessionals. Figure 7.3 is a sample paraprofessional task planner mentors can show to their protégés to demonstrate the benefits of planning. (A blackline master of the planner appears at the end of this selection.) After completing the paraprofessional task planner, a teacher can review the plan for potential problems. For example, if the plan has a paraprofessional alone without a certified staff member, the teacher can reassign the task to a certified task member or redesign the task so the paraprofessional will not be alone.

When developing the paraprofessional-to-teacher relationship and setting tasks and responsibilities, it is important that mentors and their protégés be familiar with current laws and know the needs of individual students. Clear assignments of paraprofessional responsibilities establishes trust early in the relationship and avoids miscommunications.

Establishing Collaboration

A large part of establishing a strong working relationship depends on communication and collaboration between the teacher and the paraprofessional. "Collaboration is the process of developing interdependent relationships where all are focused on a common purpose and set of goals and where people must rely on each other to achieve these goals. It is the synergy created when a group's effectiveness exceeds what individuals can accomplish on their own" (Conzemius and O'Neill 2001, 15–16). The difficult part of collaboration, however, is finding time to plan together. Educators' duties reach beyond the classroom walls before and after school.

Sample Paraprofessional Task Planner

1. Task: *Read a short story to 4 students with reading difficulties.*

2. Purpose of the task: *Read a chapter and ask questions at the end of the reading to check for comprehension skills.*

3. The task involves: records (paper)   one student   (multiple students)

4.

Steps for Completing the Task	Person Completing the Task
a. *Select the next chapter in the book.*	*Teacher*
b. *Create questions that encourage higher-order thinking.*	*Teacher*
c. *Explain the task to the paraprofessional.*	*Teacher*
d. *Four students will go to the school library to read.*	*Paraprofessional*
e. *Discuss reading with students and encourage conversation.*	*Paraprofessional*
f. *Students complete the comprehension questions with guidance.*	*Paraprofessional*
g. *Students' work reported back to the teacher.*	*Paraprofessional*
h. *Work is graded and recorded in the gradebook.*	*Teacher*

5. Does the task meet or complete a student's IEP goal?   (Yes)   No

6. Do any of the steps require the paraprofessional to be alone without a certified staff member in the classroom with a student or group of students?
   The library has two certified adults, so this will not be an issue.

7. Is the safety of any students put at risk anytime during the steps of the task?   *No*

8. Is there a step for the certified educator to monitor the task?   *Yes, in the library*

9. What is the role of the paraprofessional?   (assistant)   facilitator   teacher?

10. What steps will the paraprofessional take to report the activities of the task back to the teacher?
    a. *Paraprofessional will discuss with teacher the processes that took place from notes that are taken.*
    b. *Paraprofessional will give completed student work to teacher for recording.*

Figure 7.3

Working with Paraprofessionals

During the school day, teachers find little time to eat lunch, much less collaborate with their paraprofessionals who might have a different schedule. Educators may be able to find time for collaboration without sacrificing other duties. For example, when teachers at Monona Grove High School were challenged to find collaboration time without increasing the budget or taking time away from student learning, educators came up with a list within five minutes (see Figure 7.4).

Find Collaboration Time

- Combine individual planning time into collaborative time.
- Rearrange teachers' preparation time or class schedules so that each teacher's class attends physical education, art or music class at the same time allowing the teachers of the same grade to plan together while the students are away.
- Have previous grade teachers take back their classes every two weeks. In other words, fourth grade students may partner up with fifth grade students for a group science activity, reading buddies, or research project. During this time, the fourth grade teachers have an opportunity to plan together.
- Move the academic start time back one hour and plan meaningful student activities during that time. Activities may include environmental awareness, technology, reading, orchestra/band, choir, debate, math, or tutoring other students.
- Create sectionals or groups of classes with similar schedules and have certified support staff take charge of students and discuss issues such as safety and community service.
- Hold monthly career exploration days where community members present to the students in large assembly.
- Create an enrichment team of certified support teachers (physical education, music, art, school psychologist, reading teacher, math teacher, etc.) to work with classrooms of students on a rotating basis.

(Adapted from Conzemius and O'Neill 2001, 70. Used with permission.)

Figure 7.4

Many teachers do not have the authority to make decisions about the length of school day or when their classes attend physical education, art, music, or foreign language classes. However, teachers can brainstorm a list of ways to collaborate with others within the district's parameters. Defining the collaboration plan opens the discussion for ideas that could be incorporated into the district's strategic plan. Administrators could consider involving a group of teachers from different areas within the school building during the brainstorming session. Involving a wide range of staff members in the brainstorming session results in more ownership by the staff and promotes school-wide collaboration. School staff meetings are suitable for discussing and planning brainstorming sessions.

Preparing Before School Begins

If a paraprofessional will work in the classroom, there are a number of issues the teacher may want to consider before school begins. The teacher and paraprofessionals should discuss workspace issues, classroom rules and procedures, schedules, and roles and responsibilities of the adults and the students. By discussing these issues before school begins, the teacher avoids problems and miscommunications once classes start. It is important that the classroom teacher and the paraprofessional present a "united front" on the first day of classes.

The Welcome Meeting

A successful relationship between the teacher and a paraprofessional begins with an initial meeting. In this meeting, it is important to define the roles and responsibilities of both the teacher and the paraprofessional before the students enter the classroom. Even though the teacher assumes the role as primary person responsible for the classroom, the paraprofessional must feel a sense of partnership and assume some ownership of the responsibilities of the classroom community. The initial meeting can be an invitation to stop by or a formal meeting with an agenda of items to discuss. Since the paraprofessional may be nervous about his or her role, a meeting invitation from the teacher can serve as a preliminary step in establishing an ongoing collaborative relationship. The Welcome Meeting Checklist (Figure 7.5) provides guidance during an initial meeting with a paraprofessional. The checklist can be adapted to accommodate additional roles and responsibilities the district may require.

Workspace

A workspace should be set up for the paraprofessional so that he or she can work with one student or a group of students in the classroom. The paraprofessional needs a space to assist students or to fill out paperwork, but the workspace should not isolate the paraprofessional from the teacher. After the physical classroom space is set up, the teacher should invite the paraprofessional to the classroom to see it.

Exploring a Five-Step Process for Special Education

"The teaching of students with disabilities is a monumental task that requires a tremendous amount of preparation" (Shelton and Pollingue 2000, 81). Well-prepared teachers face a challenging situation more confidently if they have an action plan. Shelton and Pollingue (2000) have created a five-step process (see Figure 7.6) that simplifies preparation for teachers of special education.

Step One: Review Students' Needs and Goals

Teachers need to be familiar with the needs and goals of individual students. Before school begins, teachers should review students' IEPs or other educational plans in the students' files. For example, a 504 plan is created for students who do not meet the requirements to be served under IDEA but qualify for special needs services through Section 504, which provides equal opportunities for all students in education. A 504 plan would be created for students who have attention deficit disorder (ADD), attention deficit hyperactivity disorder (ADHD), severe allergies, or other medical conditions not served under IDEA (Masterpoli and Scruggs 2000, 13).

Welcome Meeting Checklist

_____ Introductions

_____ Tour of Classroom

_____ Tour of School

_____ Review the Situations sheet

Roles

Teacher	Paraprofessional	Students

Responsibilities

Teacher	Paraprofessional	Students

Next Meeting Time _____

Teacher: _____   Paraprofessional: _____

Figure 7.5

Five-Step Process for Special Education

Step One
Review each student's IEP and identify academic goals and objectives that need to be addressed throughout the year.

Step Two
Review and select appropriate instructional materials that support the curriculum and challenge the needs of the students with disabilities.

Step Three
Create a class schedule that is accommodating to all students.

Step Four
Create a classroom environment that is suitable for all students to learn.

Step Five
Develop lesson plans that help students to process, practice, and learn information in exciting and ways.

Adapted from C. F. Shelton and A. B. Pollingue. 2000. *The exceptional teacher's handbook: The first-year special education teacher's guide for success.* Thousand Oaks, CA: Corwin Press. A Sage Publications Company. Reprinted with permission.

Figure 7.6

Student plans are designed to meet the needs of the special education laws. "Students who have been referred to special education must have an individualized education plan (IEP), that details their special learning needs and mandates appropriate services. Short- and long-term goals and objectives are listed explicitly on IEPs" (Masterpoli and Scruggs 2000, 16). Before setting up a second meeting with the paraprofessional, the teacher should review these plans. When reviewing the plans, the teacher can note specific information for each student in a chart to keep goals and needs organized (see Figure 7.7 for a sample chart). Once the students' needs have been organized, the teacher can share them with the paraprofessional so both parties have the same information and share the same goals to help each student.

Sample Overview of Student Needs and Goals

Student Name	Need Identified by Educational Plan	Learning Strategies Identified by Educational Plan	Goals Identified by Educational Plan
John	Attention Deficit Disorder	• Extra time on written tests in reading • Written directions • Behavior Modification Contract	• Increase vocabulary word set by 75+ new words • Understand written directions • Be able to walk to classes without problems and arrive on time
Amy	Hearing loss	• Desk close to teacher • Small group work for redirections	• Work on sounds *ch, sh, th, k,* and hard/soft *c* • Read small passage aloud • Increase social skills in small group work
Katie	Gifted and Talented	• Enrichment problems in math • Gifted group meeting once a week	• Complete next grade-level math problems • Work well in cooperative groups (giving others a chance to complete work)
Suzanne	ESL	• Read written tests aloud • Small group work • Reading group for 60 minutes, 4 times a week	• Increase vocabulary • Increase comprehension skills through a variety of strategies

Figure 7.7

Step Two: Find Resources and Materials

After reviewing the IEPs, the next step is to find resources and materials that help students reach their goals. This task requires the assistance of a paraprofessional, because the classroom teacher has 20–30 other students who also need resources and materials. Using the Overview of Student Needs and Goals (a sample is shown in Figure 7.7 and a blackline master is provided at the end of this selection), teachers and paraprofessionals survey the classroom and create a list of books, supplemental materials, and supplies that will help students accomplish their goals. Figure 7.8 lists items that are normally found in classrooms. (Blackline 7.4 at the end of this selection can help record resources and materials that will help students accomplish their goals.) To use the list as an aid when planning, teachers can post the list in a place where paraprofessionals have easy access to it.

Classroom Resources and Materials

Elementary/Middle School
- Tape player/recorder with headphones
- Calculators
- Counting blocks
- Picture books
- Vocabulary cards
- Educational software
- Alphabet chart
- Number line
- Assignment board
- Dictionaries

Middle/High School
- Tape recorder with headphones
- Calculators/graphing calculators
- Dictionaries
- Educational software
- Writing charts (paragraphs, editorial)
- Assignment board

Figure 7.8

Step Three: Create Schedules

Once the teacher and paraprofessional determine their roles and responsibilities and students' needs, they should decide on a daily routine. Creating and posting a classroom schedule helps teachers and paraprofessionals stay focused on meeting the needs of their students. "The class schedule provides class structure, ensures that instruction time for the core academic areas is maximized, and integrates lower priority classes with other miscellaneous activities" (Shelton and Pollingue 2000, 86). Scheduling, however, can be very difficult. The paraprofessional may work with many students and some students may see other specialists throughout the school day. The district or school administrator may also have additional duties for the paraprofessional to do during the school day. Paraprofessionals are often assigned bus or lunchroom duty or asked to proctor a study hall. Creating a schedule as a collaborative team can help teachers and paraprofessionals set priorities and plan how the classroom will operate. It is best if the teacher and paraprofessional complete individual schedules first and then meet to create a combined schedule. Times for planning and communicating must also be included in the schedule. Teachers and paraprofessionals should regularly meet to review the schedule and keep it updated. There will always be schedule changes and emergencies, but it is important to begin the year with a mutually agreed upon schedule. (For schedules that are organized and easy to read, see Blacklines 7.5 and 7.6 at the end of this selection.)

Step Four: Create a Positive Learning Environment

When establishing a positive learning environment in the classroom, teachers begin by reflecting on their students' goals. "Students appear to pursue learning content most energetically if they are involved along with the teacher in establishing cognitive group agreements which deal with the processes of learning" (Schmuck and Schmuck 1997, 201). Students learn when they are excited about content that relates to their lives. If students are involved in the learning process they will be more interested in the content. Although students may not always be included in planning, it is important to include students in the teaching and learning process. As cited in Renck-Jalongo (1991), "Goodlad's (1984) study *A Place Called School* found that opportunities for interaction are regarded by adolescents as the major reason for being in school. Rather than fighting this need for affiliation, educators need to harness its energy to promote learning" (41). Teachers and paraprofessionals can implement the following strategies to harness student energy and engage students:

- Cooperative groups
- Graphic organizers
- Gardner's multiple intelligences
- Thematic instruction
- Experiential learning activities
- Guest speakers
- Cross-age tutoring (students teaching other students from different grade levels)

See Blackline 7.7 for a blackline master that teachers can use to plan positive learning environments for their students.

Step Five: Develop Lesson Plans and Monitor Student Progress

It is important for beginning teachers to know that the teacher has primary responsibility for the achievement and goals of the students, not the paraprofessional. Although they can assist a teacher in planning and carrying out activities that help students achieve goals, paraprofessionals are not responsible for the students' achievement. Mentors are valuable resources in this regard. New teachers can rely on mentors to help in the planning process. The mentor is the certified staff member with experience who can guide the new teacher in planning for student achievement. Often, paraprofessionals are uncertified parents or community members who want to be involved in the school.

By law, achievement goals must align with a student's IEP. If a student is not on a specific plan and needs help, then careful review of the student's file, past work, and input from others can be considered when setting goals. Planning achievement goals is very personal to each student. Teachers and paraprofessionals need to be sensitive to the student's feelings and keep the student's privacy in mind. "It is always helpful to know where your students need enrichment. However, you must remember not to share specific information that would be violating a confidence" (Rosenblum-Lowden 2000, 137).

When planning lessons geared to students' achievement goals, the teacher and paraprofessional can document students' progress with individual student goal sheets. Individual student goal sheets work well with students with IEPs or 504 plans. Goal sheets can be kept on a weekly basis. Recording student progress tracks what the student has accomplished during the week, and what needs to be accomplished during the upcoming weeks.

The paraprofessional can be assigned the task of recording student progress. The detailed records of individual student goal sheets facilitate communication of students' progress between a teacher and paraprofessional. At the end of the week, the teacher should review each student goal sheet and discuss the recorded information with the paraprofessional. Using the recorded information, the teacher and paraprofessional can create new sheets and plan students' goals for the next week. By reviewing individual student goal sheets, teachers assess the paraprofessional's accomplishments with students, stay current on students' progress, and make informed choices when planning lessons that meet students' needs and goals. By discussing the recorded information on individual student goal sheets with the paraprofessional, the teacher avoids misunderstanding and miscommunications with paraprofessionals and with students. These goal sheets can also be used at parent/teacher conferences to show a record of students' progress. See Figure 7.9 for a sample individual student goal sheet; see Blackline 7.8 at the end of this selection for a blackline master.

Sample Individual Student Goal Sheet

Student Name: _Susan_   Week of: ___3/22___

Date/Topic	Goal	Activity	Accomplished	Needs to Be Worked On
3/18 Math	Master multiplication facts—tens, elevens, and twelves Part of goal 2 on IEP	Multiplication software on the computer	Susan accomplished levels nine and ten on the software program. Level nine covered multiplying numbers by nines, tens, and elevens. Level ten covered multiplying by tens, elevens, and twelves.	Susan has mastered the tens. She needs to continue working on her multiplication facts for elevens and twelves.
3/19 Literacy	Understand the meaning of unknown words from the reading chapter Part of goal 1 on IEP	Read chapter 2 and create a list of words that are unknown from the reading chapter	Susan read through chapter 2 and we discussed what was in the chapter. She created her list of words.	Susan needs to understand the meaning of the words and how they are used in a sentence.
3/20 Math	Master division facts—tens, elevens, and twelves Part of goal 2 on IEP	Small group division flash card activity Part of goal 3 on IEP	Susan completed the tens and elevens and did really well. She has tens mastered.	Susan needs to continue working on elevens and twelves.
3/21 Social Studies	Work together with 2 other students on a small group project Part of goal 3 on IEP	Work on a research project with two other students in the class	Susan and her group created a task sheet for what the group would like to accomplish next in the research.	The group decided that next on the task list would be organizing their research into categories. Susan will participate in this task.
3/22 Literacy	Understand the meaning of unknown words from reading chapter book Part of goal 1 on IEP	Find the meanings of the unknown words in the electronic dictionary	Susan looked up 7 of her 7 words in the electronic dictionary.	Susan needs to put each of these words in new sentences that have meaning to her.

Figure 7.9

Teachers and paraprofessionals of special education students benefit from thorough planning. The five-step process Shelton and Pollingue (2000) created gives educators a framework for planning. "The completion of these steps should maximize student performance and teacher effectiveness" (Shelton and Pollingue 2000, 81). Mentors can review these steps with their protégés and then discuss preparation for the individual protégé's classroom.

Working Out Conflicts

Even in a well-planned, trusting teacher/paraprofessional relationship, conflicts will arise. The teacher and the paraprofessional bring different skills and experiences into the relationship, and it is important to remember that the contribution of each person is of value. "Your paraeducator, as an adult learner, has a wealth of experience and knowledge, even though that experience may not be in education or related to children" (Morgan and Ashbaker 2001, 51). The teacher and the paraprofessional may have different pedagogical views. The paraprofessional also may have a different discipline style from the teacher. Moreover, a miscommunication in student progress could spark a conflict.

Regardless of the conflict source, the conflict must be handled professionally and quickly. The focus of the teacher/paraprofessional relationship is, after all, the student. Since the teacher is primarily responsible for the students' progress, the teacher must be straightforward and clear with the paraprofessional when resolving a conflict. As discussed earlier, the teacher must establish a positive working relationship with the paraprofessional. Although a trusting relationship may be developed, communication is a process, and must be nurtured. Because miscommunication is often the cause of a conflict, it is important for the teacher to state what is expected from the paraprofessional at the beginning. Compromise will be more attainable if everyone has a clear understanding of expectations.

To resolve conflicts, educators need to be objective and work for a compromise. Meridith (2000) recommends a "win-win" approach. Adhering to an approach where one person "loses" will result in negative feelings and make future collaborations difficult. Maintaining a win-win approach will enable teachers and paraprofessionals to continue a positive relationship. See Figure 7.10 for steps to resolve conflict.

Steps for Resolving Conflict

1. **Assess the situation.**
   Is the situation something that can be addressed in a one-on-one conversation?
   Is there a bigger issue involved where a mediator may be of assistance?

2. **Talk to the paraprofessional.**
   The teacher and the paraprofessional are both individuals with their own ideas and methods. Misunderstandings can often be resolved by talking things out.

3. **Use a mediator.**
   If the situation cannot be resolved by talking, bring in another paraprofessional, teacher, or an outsider who can help resolve the issue. Another staff member may have a new, objective idea for resolving the issue.

4. **Talk to an administrator.**
   If a teacher has tried to resolve the issue in every way possible, or if the issue involves violating the law, the teacher should talk to the administrator who can address the problem immediately.

Figure 7.10

The teacher is responsible for the safety and learning of the students within the classroom. "You are the leader of your classroom instructional team, and you can be as creative as you wish in deciding how best to use your paraeducator's skills and strengths. There are no standard roles for paraeducators and no standard procedures for effective supervision" (Morgan and Ashbaker 2000, 87). A paraprofessional and a teacher can make a dynamic team that maximizes student achievement; however, the teacher is always the person leading the team.

BIBLIOGRAPHY

Association of Supervision and Curriculum Development. 1995. The inclusive school (Special Issue). *Educational Leadership*, 52(4).

Baker, J., and N. Zigmond. 1990. Are regular education classes equipped to accommodate students with learning disabilities? Exceptional Children 56, 515–526.

Banks, J.A., and C. A. Banks. Eds. 1997. *Multicultural education: Issues and perspectives.* Boston: Allyn and Bacon.

Carroll, D. 2001. Considering paraeducator training, roles, and responsibilities. In *Exceptional Children* 34(2):60–64.

Conzemius, A. and J. O'Neill. 2001. *Building shared responsibility for student learning.* Alexandria, VA: Association for Supervision and Curriculum Development.

Doyle, M. B. 1998. My child has a new shadow…and it doesn't resemble her! *Disability Solutions* 3(1):5–9.

Falvey, M. 1995. *Inclusive and heterogeneous schooling: Assessment, curriculum, and instruction.* Baltimore, MD: Paul H. Brookes.

French, N. 1999. Supervising paraeducators—What every teacher should know. *CEC Today Online* 6(2):1–2.

Friend, M., and W. D. Bursuck. Eds. (1999). *Including students with special needs: A practical guide for classroom teacher,* 2nd ed. Boston: Allyn & Bacon.

Giangreco, M. F., S. W. Edelman, S. M. Broer, and M. B. Doyle. 2001. Paraprofessional support of students with disablilities: Literature from the past decade. In *Council for Exceptional Children* 68(1):45–63.

Goodlad, J. I. 1984. *A place called school: Promise for the future.* New York: McGraw-Hill Professional Publishing.

Gordon, S. P. and S. Maxey. 2000. *How to help beginning teachers succeed,* 2nd ed. Alexandria, VA: Association for Curriculum and Supervision.

Jones, V. F. and L. S. Jones. 1998. *Comprehensive classroom management: Creating communities of support and solving problems.* Needham MA: Allyn and Bacon.

Jorgensen, C. M. 1998. *Restructuring high schools for all students: Taking inclusion to the next level.* Baltimore, MD: Paul H. Brookes Publishing.

La Brecque, R. J. 1998. *Effective department and team leaders: A practical guide.* Norwood, MA: Christopher-Gordon Publishers.

Lipsky, D. K., and A. Gartner. 1997. *Inclusion and school reform: Transforming America's classrooms.* Baltimore, MD: Paul H. Brookes Publishing.

Masterpoli, M. A. and T. E. Scruggs. 2000. *The inclusive classroom: Strategies for effective instruction.* Upper Saddle River, NJ: Merrill.

McVay, P. 1998. Paraprofessionals in the classroom: What role do they play? In *Disability Solutions* 3(1):1–4.

Merideth, E. M. 2000. Leadership strategies for teachers. Arlington Heights, IL: SkyLight Training and Publishing.

Morgan, J. and B. Y. Ashbaker. 2001. *A teacher's guide to working with paraeducators and other classroom aides.* Alexandria VA: Association for Supervision and Curriculum Development.

Power-deFur, L. S., and F. P. Orelove. 1997. *Inclusive education: Practical implementation of the least restrictive environment.* Gaithersburg, MD: Aspen Publishers.

Renck-Jalongo, M. 1991. *Creating learning communities: The role of the teacher in the 21st century.* Bloomington, IN: National Educational Service.

Riveria-Pedrotty, D., and D. Smith-Deutsch. 1997. *Teaching students with learning and behavior problems,* 3rd ed. Needham MA: Allyn and Bacon.

Rosenblum-Lowden, R. 2000. *You have to go to school—You're the teacher!* 2nd Ed. Thousand Oaks, CA: Corwin Press.

Schmuck, R. A., and P. A. Schmuck. 1997. *Group processes in the classroom.* Madison, WI: Brown & Benchmark.

Shelton, C. F. and A. B. Pollingue. 2000. *The exceptional teacher's handbook: The first-year special education teacher's guide for success.* Thousand Oaks, CA: Corwin Press.

Spear-Swerling, L., and R. J. Sternberg. 1998. Curing our 'epidemic' of learning disablilities. *Phi Delta Kappan* 81(5): 397–401.

Tateyama-Sniezek, K. 1990. Cooperative learning: Does it improve the academic achievement of student with handicaps? *Exceptional Children* 56(5): 426–437.

Vaughn, S., C. S. Bos, and J. S. Schumm. 2000. *Teaching exceptional, diverse and at-risk students in the general education classroom,* 2nd ed. Boston: Allyn & Bacon.

Zionts, P. Ed. 1997. *Inclusion strategies for students with learning and behavior problems: Perspectives, experiences, and best practices.* Austin, TX: Pro-Ed.

Mentors can review Blacklines 7.1–7.8 with their protégés as protégés learn to work with paraprofessionals in the classroom. Protégés can use the blacklines as needed. (Mentors may want to encourage protégés to complete Figure 7.5 before their initial meeting with their paraprofessionals.)

Classroom Situation

My current classroom situation is . . .

My paraprofessional will…

Teacher:_____ Date: _____

Paraprofessional Task Planner

1. Task: _____

2. Purpose of the task: _____
_____

3. The task involves: **records (paper)**   **one student**   **multiple students**

4.
Steps for Completing the Task	**Person Completing the Task**
a. _____	_____
b. _____	_____
c. _____	_____
d. _____	_____
e. _____	_____
f. _____	_____
g. _____	_____
h. _____	_____

5. Does the task meet or complete a student's IEP goal?   **Yes   No**

6. Do any of the steps require the paraprofessional to be alone without a certified staff member in the classroom with a student or group of students?
_____

7. Is the safety of any students put at risk anytime during the steps of the task?
_____

8. Is there a step for the certified educator to monitor the task? _____
_____

9. The role of the paraprofessional: **assistant   facilitator   teacher**

10. What steps will the paraprofessional take to report the activities of the task back to the teacher?
    a. _____
    b. _____
    c. _____

Overview of Student Needs and Goals

Teacher:_____ Class:_____ Date:_____

Student Name	Needs Identified by Educational Plan	Goals Identified by Educational Plan

Working with Paraprofessionals

MENTORING

List of Resources and Materials

Teacher:_____ Class/Grade:_____ Date:_____

Student Name	Student Goals	Available Books	Available Manipulatives

Paraprofessional Schedule

Teacher: _____

Paraprofessional: _____

Class/Grade: _____

Date: _____

Time	Monday	Tuesday	Wednesday	Thursday	Friday

Blackline 7.5

Student Daily Schedule

Name of Student: _____ Class/Grade: _____ Date: _____

Time	Monday	Tuesday	Wednesday	Thursday	Friday

Blackline 7.6

Strategies to Achieve Student Goals

Teacher: _____ Paraprofessional: _____ Course/Class: _____ Date: _____

Student Name	Student Need	Instructional Strategy or Tool

Blackline 7.7

Working with Paraprofessionals

Sample Individual Student Goal Sheet

Student Name: _____

Week of: _____

Date/Topic	Goal	Activity	Accomplished	Needs to Be Worked On

Blackline 7.8

> Mentors can help novice teachers learn how to use parents, support staff, administrators, and community members as resources to create a positive learning community that benefits all of the students.

Establishing the Learning Community

by **Julie Sausen**

The Learning Community

Teaching is an 'interdependent' profession. Without the help of parents, fellow teachers, administrators, and support staff, your job would be overwhelmingly complex. You need to develop strong relationships with these people to make a school work.
— Rosenblum-Lowden 2000

Parents, support staff, community members, and others can contribute many talents and personal experiences to students' learning. Teachers can take advantage of these skills and talents by seeking out adults to be involved—or by including those who are asking to be involved—in educational activities. Teachers can cultivate this group of volunteers and create a learning community that benefits students and everyone who participates in the teaching relationship.

Learning community members include educators, school staff, parents, senior citizens, and community members interested in giving back to the community's youth. Of course, the most invested members of the learning community are the students' parents or caregivers.

Establishing the Learning Community

"While educators may have expertise in content and pedagogy, parents have knowledge of their own children that can be extremely helpful to teachers in meeting the needs of students" (DuFour 2000, 60). It is important for teachers to establish relationships with parents at the start of the school year. Teachers should treat parents and caregivers not only as a child's guardian or support system, but a valuable resource in the learning community. "Parents in a learning community are

- well informed about their child's learning;
- invited to participate in a wide range of activities (but not judged harshly if they cannot);
- treated as collaborators; and
- respected for their commitment to the child, which is necessarily different from that of the school" (DuFour 2000, 59).

Mentors can help novice teachers establish relationships with parents at in the start of the school year in order to form partnerships to enhance the learning experiences of each student in the classroom.

Getting other adults involved in the learning environment can be rewarding but also challenging for beginning educators. As the primary educator responsible for students' achievement, teachers should lead and direct all learning community involvement and introduce learning community members to classroom procedures, expectations, and appropriate levels of involvement. An effective learning community should build trusting, positive relationships among teachers and learning community members and enrich students' learning. Beginning teachers who are receptive to partnering with other stakeholders will tap a valuable resource that will help them manage and enhance their classroom environment.

Setting Up an Effective Learning Community

Creating a learning community can be daunting. New relationships must be established, and it may be difficult for teachers to know where to begin. Beginning teachers need assistance from mentors in creating guidelines for parent and community member relationships that will ensure a positive learning experience for everyone. Mentors can introduce protégés to a five-step process (see Figure 8.1) for setting up an effective learning community.

Five Steps for an Effective Learning Community

1. **Establish collaborative relationships.** The teacher meets students' parents and community members early in the school year to facilitate future involvement in learning activities.

2. **Create an involvement plan.** Students' needs are reviewed before school begins, so the teacher is aware of what types of goals must be set for the school year. The teacher creates an involvement plan for parents and community members to assist in educational activities and in meeting needs and goals.

3. **Communicate with learning communities.** Teachers set up a plan to communicate the goals, procedures, and expectations of the classroom to learning community members who want to be involved in activities.

4. **Activate the plan.** The teacher activates the involvement and communication plans through activities, lessons, field trips, and other opportunities. Community members participate in these events and help create a positive learning environment for students.

5. **Reflect on the learning community.** The teacher reflects on the involvement of learning community members at the end of a specific activity or time period. The teacher assesses how the learning community strengthened the learning experience as well as plan future involvement.

Figure 8.1

Step One: Establish Collaborative Relationships

There are many telltale signs of a collaborative environment. Groupings are open, and borders between groups are easily crossed. Parents, students, teachers, support staff, administration, board members, and community members use a common vocabulary to describe what they are trying to achieve together. There is a sense of shared risk as well as a feeling that 'we're all in this together.' —Conzemius and O'Neill 2001

Teachers who meet with parents and community members, and take an active interest in their lives, roles, perspectives, and potential contributions can apply that information to classroom goals and student needs. To establish a learning community, teachers must make an effort to familiarize themselves with the community. Before school starts, many administrators invite new teachers to participate on a bus trip around the district to see the surrounding community. This trip provides teachers with opportunities to see the recreational areas, businesses, and neighborhoods where their students live.

Families

When establishing collaborative relationships with parents and community members, it is important for teachers to remember that the definition of family has expanded to include many different arrangements. The teacher must think about what types of families belong to the community surrounding the school district. The teacher will probably find that their students come from families with single parents, blended families (both parents remarried after divorce), families in which grandparents serve as primary caregivers, foster care families, and other families with different arrangements. Parents or caregivers may work full-time, one may work full-time while the other works part-time, or one may work full time while the other stays home. All of these arrangements create different family dynamics and different personal needs that influence student learning. For example, a single parent may not be able to devote much time in the classroom due to work or other responsibilities. The teacher can work with that parent to find ways he or she can still contribute, such as preparation for classroom activities at home (cutting, pasting, putting materials in bags, etc.), or tutoring students before and after school. A student whose parents are divorced may have one parent who lives far away yet still wishes to be involved in the classroom. The teacher can have this parent provide resources for student activities, arrange a field trip day, or coordinate classroom volunteers over the phone. If a parent works nights, the teacher can involve the parent during late afternoon or after school activities. Understanding students' family situations helps the teacher plan for all parents or caregivers to be involved in the learning community.

Communities

The same ideas apply to the community. Assessing who is part of the school's community is essential when planning an effective classroom learning community. The community may include a stay-at-home parent who wants to assist in the classroom, senior citizens who have life experiences to share, teenagers who are interested in volunteering, and professionals interested in career development. The community may be urban with industrial businesses and few open spaces, part of several suburbs with homes and small or corporate businesses, or rural with scattered businesses and several open spaces. "Teachers in urban and rural areas are likely to complain of parental indifference, while teachers in suburban areas tend to complain of parental overzealousness or undue influence" (DuFour 2000, 59).

Teacher planning and preparation can prevent any perception of unbalanced contributions. A teacher in an urban school district with industrial businesses can create a learning community with strong support from business members' involvement during the school day and parental support at night, guiding students through homework or working at evening school events. A teacher in an affluent suburban school district can create a learning community where the reverse may occur: stay-at-home parents can contribute during the school day or at night, and professional community members can be involved in after-school or evening programs. Each community requires a different learning involvement plan. It is important for teachers to be aware of their community setup and tap all available resources. See Blackline 8.1 for a chart mentors can use with their protégés when planning collaborative relationships with the learning community.

Step Two: Create an Involvement Plan

After reviewing the types of relationships that can be created for building a learning community—or at least learning what types of relationships can be initiated—educators and administrators need to create an involvement plan for including parents and community members in students' learning. Some school districts may already have guidelines in place for parental involvement; if this is the case, the teacher should incorporate these policies and procedures into his or her classroom involvement plan. "School districts need to establish and implement parent-involvement policies, with input from parents. As district policies are developed, schools need to encourage and support parent involvement in the schools. In addition, school policies and support are needed to show teachers how to involve parents in their classrooms" (Fuller and Olsen 1998, 128). These policies for parental involvement can be adapted to include other community members. The teacher can also investigate district policies for school visitors. It is helpful to record the policies for easy reference when planning learning community involvement.

Teachers can also review the curriculum and state standards for opportunities to include parent or community member involvement in educational activities. "Good volunteer programs must be carefully planned, and the planning must begin with a look at the goals and objectives" (Barclay and Boone 1996, 173). Early planning organizes class activities and helps learning community members plan their schedules to include educational activities. "The planning process is important for two reasons. First, planning helps you to become proactive, as you learn to anticipate information needs, analyze your varied audiences, and assess the vehicles for reaching them. Second, these elements of planning give you a big-picture framework to be sure you've covered all bases" (Meek 1999, 96). Opportunities to reach student goals and meet state standards include field trips, class speakers, research projects, and community service projects. Completing the plan before an open house, meet and greet the teacher, or back to school night is ideal for optimum participation. See Figure 8.2 for a sample involvement plan; see Blackline 8.2 for a chart mentors can give to protégés to use when planning learning community involvement.

Step Three: Communicate with Learning Communities

If teachers establish a positive parent and community member plan, but do not clearly communicate the plan to the learning community, the plan will unravel. To prevent this from happening, the teacher should not only effectively communicate classroom schedules, policies, procedures, but also provide feedback on the educational activity to the learning community members who participated. Learning community members want to know they have an effect on the students they are helping. Communication is an integral part of the learning community.

Teachers need to keep the audience in mind as well when choosing a form of communication. In this technologically advanced world, there are many methods of communication. Teachers should evaluate the parents' or community members' situations and select the best form of communication. For example, if a volunteer schedule must be communicated to parents only, the teacher can send paper copies home with students. The teacher can mail or e-mail schedules to community members. If the learning community includes members who do not have access to computers, however, e-mail is not the best option. Teachers need to adjust communication methods to fit with learning community members' busy lives. A professional who is giving a career lecture to the class may not want to be called at work, but may prefer to be called at home instead.

Sample Involvement Plan

District Policies

1. All volunteers must sign in at the office when reporting to a classroom.

2. All volunteers must sign out when finished with an activity.

3. If participating in a field trip, volunteers must follow teacher, school, and district policies in regard to student behavior and safety.

4. Rules that apply in school (e.g., No Smoking) are also applied to field trips and outdoor activities.

5. Parents who volunteer on a field trip or near the end of the school day, must inform the office if they would like to take their child home. Otherwise, the child must take the bus home. This is for the safety of all children.

Curriculum Topic, Subject, or Activity	Parent or Community	Approximate Time of Year
Nature Hike	Parents or Community Volunteers	September
Field Trip to Botanical Gardens	Parents	October
Trip to the Theater	Parents	January
Class Theatrical Event	Parents and Community Members	February, March, and April

Figure 8.2

A parent who is an on-call volunteer and is also on the go all day may need to provide the teacher with a cell phone number. See Figure 8.3 for a sample checklist.

Checklist for Communication

- ❑ Written procedures
- ❑ Written volunteer process
- ❑ Blank schedules
- ❑ List of volunteer opportunities
- ❑ List of other classroom activities (cutting, pasting, typing, calling others)

Figure 8.3

There are several considerations in contacting community members, but a process can be worked out with individual members through the teacher's leadership. The teacher may develop guidelines for communicating with learning community participants (see Figure 8.4 for sample guidelines).

Sample Communication Guidelines

1. Send e-mail updates weekly.
2. Make phone calls once a month or when needed.
3. Send class newsletter home the first day of each month; mail to Alexander Home for Seniors.
4. Update Web site weekly.

Figure 8.4

A communications log can also help avoid misunderstandings. If the teacher prefers to communicate by phone, for example, a log to record the date of the conversation and key points discussed can prevent misunderstandings. (See Figure 8.5 and Blackline 8.4 at the end of this selection.)

Sample Communications Log

Teacher: _Mrs. Long_   Grade/Course: _3_   Date: _9–12_

Name	Contact Number	Date	Discussion
Ms. Smith	555–2606 (work)	9–12	Ms. Smith called concerning Trent's spelling tests. He usually receives good scores, and on the last two tests he has not done well.
Mr. Smith	555–1010 (home)	9–15	Called home and talked to Mr. Smith. Explained a new method for helping Trent study for his next spelling tests. Mr. Smith was very pleased with the method and said he would work with Trent.
Ms. Smith	555–1010 (home)	10–28	Called home and shared the good news with Ms. Smith about Trent receiving an 85% on his spelling test. Encouraged parents to keep trying the new studying method. She agreed they would.

Figure 8.5

E-mail can be saved on the computer or printed and stored in a binder. Teachers can also keep copies of letters and notes that are sent home along with notes sent to the teacher. This record help situations in case there are questions later. It is a good idea to take good notes and save them for portfolios, conferences, or meetings.

Volunteer Impact

Communicating to parents and community members about volunteering in the classroom is important. Thank you notes written by students can let a group of senior citizens who helped out with a bake sale know their involvement was appreciated. The teacher can send a short note or e-mail to a business whose employees lectured on a career development day to let them know students are researching that profession further. Teachers may also use a bulletin board to show off student work related to a learning community member's involvement in a research project or science experiment. It takes little effort to show appreciation, yet these efforts can bring enjoyment to the learning community member who gave his or her time to volunteer.

Student Progress

Parents or caregivers appreciate knowing their impact on students' achievement and learning experiences, but are most interested in their child's progress. "Communicating with families is not always easy, but that communication is absolutely necessary for building a relationship of trust and cooperation between adults who have the greatest influence over students' success" (Merideth 2000, 88). Many school districts require formal progress reports, but a teacher can regularly send home informal notes stating how a child is doing. The stereotype of the "note from the teacher" may lead parents to expect a negative report every time something is sent home or needs a parent signature. Since parents do not often hear or see the positive contributions their children make in school, teachers should also send home notes or make phone calls to inform parents of important successes as well. The more often parents are updated on their child's progress, the less likely miscommunications will arise during conferences or at report card time.

Beyond progress reports, parent-teacher conferences are the typical venue for teachers to communicate with parents. Bradley, King-Sears, and Tessier-Switlick (1997) suggest that "A variety of methods are available for increasing positive communication with students' families including letters, phone calls, student recognition ceremonies, informal home visits, home visits by home-school liaison specialists, school visits by family members and parent participation in school activities" (330). Merideth (2000) suggests using formal opportunities to communicate—open houses, quarterly or monthly newsletters, formal reporting of assessment and student progress, and classroom presentations —in addition to using more informal opportunities to communicate—phone calls or extracurricular activities.

Teachers can also create classroom Web sites to communicate classroom information to parents and community members. Completed student assignments can be posted on a classroom Web site. Information about upcoming classroom events and school activities can also be mentioned. Several Web sites provide teachers with free access to post classroom information for the purpose of keeping parents and community members updated. The most popular of these Web sites is Schoolnotes at <http://www.schoolnotes.com>. If it isn't possible to create a Web site, the same information may be published in a classroom newsletter.

English Language Learners

A growing number of immigrant families are establishing their homes in the United States, and the number of English language learners (ELL) is on the rise. Contacting an immigrant parent about volunteering or to report on a child's progress can be challenging, but it is not impossible. Mentors can introduce beginning teachers to the variety of community and technology resources available to educators that will assist in communicating with ELL parents.

Teachers can invite a community member, family member, or staff member who speaks the same language as the parents to translate for the parents at parent-teacher conferences, open houses, or back-to-school nights. Teachers can also contact community centers for a list of bilingual volunteers. Often, support staff and colleagues can speak a second language. ELL teachers can develop forms in the appropriate languages for teachers to use to facilitate communication. A variety of user-friendly translations programs exist on the Internet or as software. The teacher can type a note, report, or comment into the language translator program or software and select the needed language. The translator program automatically completes a translation. The note, report, or comment prints in both English and the student's language. The more advanced translators can translate many different language dialects. Teachers can search the Internet for such software using a search engine and typing "translation software."

Communication is on ongoing process and must be treated as an important tool for successful relationships with all parents and community members. Mentors can share their own problems related to communication breakdowns with their protégés and discuss how those situations could have been avoided. Figure 8.6 is a list of communication tools and methods.

Step Four: Activate the Plan

When the teacher has completed the involvement plan and communicated important information to learning community members, the involvement plan can be implemented. Because learning community members are volunteers and not paid participants, the level of involvement will vary from member to member. The teacher may want to ask what level of involvement each member is interested in, using a number scale (1 representing the least amount of involvement and 5 representing the most amount of involvement). The teacher could also use a form that lists involvement activities and ask each member to circle activities that interest them. (See Blackline 8.5 at the end of this selection for a volunteer survey.) Classroom volunteer and speaker sign up sheets can be posted in

Tools and Methods of Communication

Tools	Venues	Methods
• Phone/Cell • Fax • E-mail • Internet • Photocopier • Translator Software or Internet Program	• Meet and Greet the Teacher Nights • Parent School Nights • Award Ceremonies • Teacher Conferences • Open House • Curriculum Night	• Paper Note or Form • Classroom Web site • Classroom Newpaper (Quarterly) • Classroom Newsletter (Weekly) • Classroom Bulletin Board

Figure 8.6

the classroom during back to school night, curriculum night, or open houses (see Figures 8.7 and 8.8 for samples; see Blacklines 8.6 and 8.7 at the end of this selection). Phone calls must be made to businesses and community centers for members who would like to volunteer for classroom activities. Parents are a natural volunteer choice because they have a vested interest in the classroom—their children! Parents' time, however, can be monopolized if they are expected to participate at a high level of involvement. "Parents must be the ones deciding on their level of involvement. This level of involvement will widely vary from parent to parent. When a parent makes the decision to have minimal involvement, the team must respect that right. When a parent decides to become highly involved, teams can capitalize on that participation rather than become threatened by it" (Bradley, King-Sears, and Tessier-Switlick 1997, 105). There are a variety of ways to involve volunteers in and out of the classroom. In whatever ways teachers choose to determine volunteers' commitment levels, it must be understood that any level of involvement is usually an act of selflessness by the volunteer and should be appreciated.

Sample Classroom Volunteer Sign-Up Sheet

Name	Contact Number	Area of Interest	Dates Available
Mrs. Antonia	555-1414	Field trip chaperone	Any time in Feb. and March
Jack Smithe	Jack.Smithe@ business.com	Career Day	Weeknights after 5:30, Saturdays in May and April
Judy Theron	Send notes home with Brian	Making healthy snacks	Anytime except Thursdays

Figure 8.7

Sample Classroom Speaker Sign-Up Sheet

Name	Contact Number	Area of Interest	Dates Available
Martin Gugen	Adult Care Center	Lecture on collecting insects	Any days but need to know to arrange a ride
Mrs. Grissom	555-2266	Creating Web pages	Weekdays after 1:30
Mike Hill	Hill & Sons	Starting your own company	Anytime is fine!

Figure 8.8

Depending on the classroom situation, teachers may organize the involvement plan weekly, monthly, by semester, by thematic unit, or for the whole school year. Recording volunteer time and classroom speaker dates on a calendar (see Figure 8.9) will help keep the teacher and volunteers organized. The calendar can be copied and sent home to parents or mailed to learning community members. Periodic updates and reminders may be useful, especially if times change or people are unavailable. The teacher should have a list of names and contact information for learning community members for easy reference.

Step Five: Reflect on the Learning Community

Reflection is the examination of one's teaching practice in a thoughtful and even critical way, learning from this process, and then using what has been learned to affect one's future action.—McEwan 2002

After the event, trip, or presentation has taken place, reflection helps define what and how future relationships and involvements will happen. A record of parent and community involvement can also be added to a teacher's professional portfolio to demonstrate the building of a collaborative community within the classroom. Reflection is an important part of growing professionally and learning from specific situations. Working with community members is often included in professional teaching standards that new teachers are required to meet as part of their formal evaluation by administration.

It is important to note these items in the reflection: the name of the activity, trip, or speaker; what went well; and what should be changed (if anything). See Figure 8.10 for a sample; see Blackline 8.8 at the end of selection for a blackline master.

Sample Calendar of Events

Sept.	**8** 10:00 Mr. Jackson Science Speaker	
Oct.	**31** Trip to Pumpkin Patch for carving Mr. Foster Ms. White Mr. Ju	
Nov.	**10** ALL DAY Field Trip to Planetarium Mrs. Peterson Mr. Swanson Ms. Coolidge	
Dec.	**15** CLASS PLAY	
Jan.		
Feb.	**24** 2:00 Ms. Marks Speaking about Impressionists	**28** ALL DAY Field Trip to Art Museum Mr. Paulson Ms. Davis Ms. Marks Ms. Johnson
Mar.		
Apr.	**5** Mexican-American presentation from local community group	**23** Environmental Clean-up Day— Playground, Plant flowers
May		
June		

Figure 8.9

Reflection Log

Name of Event, Activity, or Speaker

Mr. Fredrick's chemistry demonstration

What Went Well	What I Would Change
Students were well—behaved and interested.	Have materials delivered the day before to reduce the amount of setup time.
Student prepared great questions for Mr. Fredrick about his experiment.	Have students research chemicals involved and how they can react with other chemicals before the demonstration.
Mr. Fredrick kept the interest of the students and explained the steps as he demonstrated the chemical reactions.	

Figure 8.10

The teacher can use the reflection log to assess volunteer participation in educational activities. It is important that parents and community members abide by the policies set forth by the teacher and school district while they are volunteering in an educational activity. For example, if a volunteer did not follow stated policies and procedures and a child's safety was jeopardized by the volunteer's actions, the teacher should not feel obligated to invite the volunteer to another activity involving direct interaction with students. The volunteer may be more helpful cutting, pasting, or preparing other materials for activities while at home.

The completed, the reflection log can be filed in a portfolio, binder, or folder for future reference. This type of record keeping can be useful. Many parents continue to be involved in classrooms even though their child has moved on to the next grade level. This log can also be useful for restructuring future activities or field trips. A reflection log also provides information to future teachers about specific parents or learning community members as well as an assessment of their strengths and weaknesses.

Conclusion

Successful schools understand that the direct improvement of teaching and learning in every classroom comes via a constellation of individuals and groups who undertake a myriad of activities and initiatives.—Glickman 2002

The involvement of parents and community members is vital to the development of a learning community within the classroom. The experiences and resources that stakeholders of a learning community bring to a classroom are invaluable to the education of the children. Parents, caregivers, senior citizens, professionals, and other community members who give of their time energizes curriculum activities and help students meet or exceed curriculum goals and state standards. The opportunities for community members to be involved in the classroom are endless. Preparing educational materials, demonstrating science experiments, providing career information; participating in field trips, classroom celebrations, and research activities, and developing a classroom Web site are just a few ways to involve community members in the learning experiences of children.

Beginning teachers or teachers who are new to a district can utilize staff members, community centers, and parents as volunteers for their classroom. Moreover, a mentor can provide resources and information to help the beginning teacher establish these initial contacts. For quick reference, contacts should be kept in a file, folder, or binder that can be easily updated.

Using the five-step process, the teacher builds positive and flourishing relationships with stakeholders of the learning community. Mentors who have had experience involving parents and community members can help new teachers orchestrate the partnerships to benefit both the teacher and the students.

BIBLIOGRAPHY

Banks, J.A., and C. A. Banks, eds. 1997. *Multicultural education: Issues and perspectives.* Boston: Allyn and Bacon.

Barclay, K., and E. Boone. 1996. *The parent difference: Uniting school, family, and community.* Arlington Heights, IL: SkyLight Training and Publishing.

Bolotin-Joseph, P., and G.E. Burnaford. 1994. *Images of schoolteachers in twentieth-century America: Paragons, polarities, complexities.* Edited by Pamela Bolotin-Joseph and Gail E. Burnaford. New York: St. Martin's Press.

Bradley, D.F., M.E. King-Sears, and D. M. Tessier-Switlick. 1997. *Teaching students in inclusive settings: From theory to practice.* Needham Heights, MA: Allyn and Bacon.

Conzemius, A., and J. O'Neill. 2001. *Building shared responsibility for student learning.* Alexandria, VA: Association for Supervision and Curriculum Development.

DuFour, R. 2000. Clear connections: Everyone benenfits when schools work to involve parents. In *Journal of Staff Development* 21(2): 59–60.

Falvey, M. 1995. *Inclusive and heterogeneous schooling: Assessment, curriculum, and instruction.* Baltimore, MD: Paul H. Brookes.

Fuller, M.L., and G. Olsen. 1998. *Home-school relations: Working successfully with parents and families.* Needham Heights, MA: Allyn and Bacon.

Gersten, R. 1999. The changing face of bilingual education. *Educational Leadership* 56(7): 41–45.

Glickman, C. D. 2002. *Leadership for learning: How to help teachers succeed.* Alexandria, VA: Association for Supervision and Curriculum Development.

Gordon, S. P. and S. Maxey. 2000. *How to help beginning teachers succeed,* 2nd ed. Alexandria, VA: Association for Curriculum and Supervision Development.

Jones, V. F., and L. S. Jones. 1998. *Comprehensive classroom management: Creating communities of support and solving problems.* Needham Heights, MA: Allyn and Bacon.

La Brecque, R. J. 1998. *Effective department and team leaders: A practical guide.* Norwood, MA: Christopher-Gordon Publishers.

Leu, D. J., D. Diadiun, Jr., and K. R. Leu. 1999. *Teaching with the internet: Lessons from the classroom.* Norwood, MA: Christopher-Gordon Publishers.

Lindeman, B. 2001. Reaching out to immigrant parents. *Educational Leadership* 58(6): 62–66.

McEwan, B. 1999. *The art of classroom management: The effective practices for building equitable learning communities.* New Jersey: Prentice Hall.

Meek, A. 1999. *Communicating with the public: A guide for school leaders.* Alexandria VA: Association for Supervision and Curriculum Development.

Merideth, E. M. 2000. *Leadership strategies for teachers.* Arlington Heights, IL: SkyLight Training and Publishing.

Midwood, D., K. O'Connor, and M. Simpson. 1993. *Assess for success: Assessment, evaluation and reporting for successful learning.* Toronto, ON: Ontario Secondary School Teacher's Federation.

Portner, H. 2001. *Training mentors is not enough: Everything else schools and districts need to do.* Thousand Oaks, CA: Corwin Press.

Roberts-Presson, M. 2001. *Your mentor: A practical guide for first-year teachers in grades 1–3.* Thousand Oaks, CA: Corwin Press.

Rosenblum-Lowden, R. 2000. *You have to go to school—You're the teacher!*, 2nd ed. Thousand Oaks, CA: Corwin Press.

Smith, D.D., and R. Luckasson. 1995. *Introduction to special education—Teaching in an age of challenge,* 2nd ed. Boston: Allyn and Bacon.

Tomlinson, C. 1999. *The differentiated classroom.* Alexandria, VA: Association for Supervision and Curriculum Development.

Traub, J. 1999. The bilingual barrier. *The New York Times Magazine,* January, pp. 31, 32.

Vaughn, S., C.S. Bos, and J.S. Schumm. 2000. *Teaching exceptional, diverse, and at-risk students in the general education classroom,* 2nd ed. Boston: Allyn and Bacon.

Wolfgang, C. 1999. *Solving discipline problems.* Needham Heights, MA: Allyn and Bacon.

Mentors may guide protégés as they make plans to involve community members in the classroom. Protégés may use the following blacklines when implementing and managing the learning community:

- Collaborative Opportunities (Blackline 8.1)
- Involvement Plan (Blackline 8.2)
- Invitation to Participate in the Classroom (Blackline 8.3)
- Communications Log (Blackline 8.4)
- Volunteer Survey (Blackline 8.5)
- Classroom Volunteer Sign-Up Sheet (Blackline 8.6)
- Classroom Speaker Sign-Up Sheet (Blackline 8.7)
- Reflection Log (Blackline 8.8)

Collaborative Opportunities

Teacher:_____ Class/Grade:_____ Date:_____

School District Setting	
Community Businesses, Funds, and Establishments	
Families	

Involvement Plan

Teacher:_____ Class/Grade:_____ Date:_____

District Policies

Curriculum Topic, Subject, or Activity	Parent or Community	Approximate Time of Year

Blackline 8.2

Invitation to Participate in the Classroom

Teacher:_____ Grade:_____ Course:_____ Date:_____

This year we will be studying the following topics:

This year we will be taking the following field trips:

This year we will be having the following celebrations:

If you would like to volunteer for an event, please sign up on the volunteer sheets provided.

Communications Log

Teacher:_____ Grade/Course:_____ Date:_____

Name	Contact Number	Date	Discussion

Blackline 8.4

Volunteer Survey

Name: _____

Contact Preference: _____

    ❏ e-mail: _____

    ❏ phone: _____

    ❏ written letters home: _____

Best time to contact: _____

Check all activities that interest you

    ❏ Field trips

    ❏ Phone calls

    ❏ Classroom functions

    ❏ Small group activities

    ❏ Cutting and pasting

    ❏ Typing

    ❏ Classroom demonstration

    ❏ Reading stories

    ❏ Writing process help

    ❏ Math help

    ❏ Technology assistance

    ❏ Proofreading

    ❏ Layout of newsletter

    ❏ Making costumes

    ❏ Preparing healthy snacks

    ❏ Chaperoning dances/events

    ❏ Other:

Blackline 8.5

Classroom Volunteer Sign-Up Sheet

Teacher: _____   Class: _____   Month: _____

Name	Contact Number	Area of Interest	Dates Available

Blackline 8.6

Classroom Speaker Sign-Up Sheet

Teacher: _____ Class: _____ Month: _____

Name	Contact Number	Area of Interest	Dates Available

Blackline 8.7

Reflection Log

Teacher:_____   Class:_____   Month:_____

Name of Event, Activity, or Speaker

What Went Well	What I Would Change

Blackline 8.8

Level 2

MENTORING GUIDEBOOK

SECTION IV

Reflecting on Professional Growth

Reflection is essential to a fully lived professional life. Among teachers, the finest are those who consider their progress in the classroom, who ponder effective teaching strategies and devise creative classroom activities, who practice reflection to set personal and professional goals, who think on their feet as they teach. These educators are the exemplars and leaders and mentors in our schools.

—Boreen et al. 2000

Discussing the importance of a philosophy of teaching and the values of metacognition with the novice teacher during the first few weeks of school is probably not a good idea. In the beginning, the novice switches into survival mode and is mostly concerned with the day-to-day activities like classroom management and lesson planning. Staying one step ahead of the students and navigating the uncharted routines of teaching are two very pressing challenges for beginning teachers that require all of their time and most of their energy. Needless to say, finding time for "reflection" and developing professional goals may not be a priority.

The mentor who has established open communication and trust with the protégé, however, will know the appropriate time to introduce the importance of reflection, professional growth, and maybe professional portfolios. Phrases like "I'm too busy to reflect!" or "I'll have more time to reflect when I retire!" are not uncommon. Hectic school schedules do not offer much "downtime" for teachers to pause and make sense of what they are doing. Reflective thinking, however, clarifies or changes one's perspectives. Reflection, according to Boreen et al. (2000), is a critical function of successful teaching and learning. "Reflection can be defined as an analytical process of data-gathering and sense-making through which teachers deepen their understanding of teaching and learning" (69). Novice teachers who record their thoughts in journals, write comments on lesson plans about how to improve their teaching, discuss their classroom practices with peers or mentors, or collect artifacts for a portfolio enrich their understanding of the teaching and learning process.

Teaching is not a job; it is a profession. Although the novice teacher may not see the immediate value of professional development, the veteran teacher can carefully structure growth experiences for the protégé. Boreen et al. (2000) believe a mentor's support and guidance is essential to the beginning teacher's continued professional development. "With years of experience and knowledge as a guide, a mentor can provide information and direction that will lead the beginning teacher to new investigations and strategies, new professional sources and organizations, and new commitment and resolve to improve curriculum and instruction" (99).

In Selection 9, **Philosophy of Professional Growth for Teachers**, I review the importance of helping novice teachers develop a philosophy of teaching and learning. Schools usually have a mission statement that provides the stakeholders with a shared vision and goals. Novice teachers who reflect on the mission statement think about the characteristics and skills they need in order to meet that vision. All teachers should take time to reflect on the attributes of an effective teacher. To generate a list of attributes, mentors can ask protégés the following three questions:

- What one teacher do I remember as most successful?
- Why do I think that that teacher was successful?
- Does research on teaching support these elements of success? (Duck 2000, 42)

Duck explains that the elements of success teachers remember in their favorite teachers are usually supported by research: "The criteria for success you apply reveal your own temperament type and learning style preference" (42). Mentors can discuss their protégés' answers to the three questions and then create their own list of attributes. These lists of attributes help protégés develop their philosophy of teaching and learning and set the framework for their own professional goals as well as the goals for their students. The philosophy of teaching and learning can be part of a professional growth portfolio or can be used more informally to spark conversations and analysis of one's successes and challenges.

In Selection 10, **The Reflective Practitioner**, the "metacognitive mentor" utilizes stem questions to facilitate an examination of the protégés' practice with the goal of improving it. One new teacher wrote a reflection about a lesson she conducted that didn't go well: "The lesson bombed. The kids didn't know what to do. The computer crashed. I lost my cool. But, I know that right now, I am the worst that I will ever be as a teacher. I know I can only get better." Taking the time to describe lessons, write about ways to improve, review videotapes of one's teaching, reflect on challenges, and celebrate successes yields positive results, despite the extra time and effort required.

Fostnot (1989 as cited in Taggart and Wilson 1998) states "An empowered teacher is a reflective decision maker who finds joy in learning and in investigating the teaching/learning process" (1). The reflections can be attached to items in a portfolio or stapled or taped to an artifact as a reminder for later discussions. If reflection is essential to a fully lived professional life, then mentors must ask guided questions to elicit thoughtful insight from their protégés. These reflections not only help to celebrate successes, but they also place the challenges into proper perspective. It is important that beginning teachers who experience a horrendous day are still able to think positively and say with confidence, "I know that I can only get better!"

REFERENCES

Boreen, J., M. K. Johnson, D. Niday, and J. Potts. 2000. *Mentoring beginning teachers: Guiding, reflecting, coaching.* York, ME: Stenhouse Publishers

Duck, L. 2000. The ongoing professional journey. *Educational Leadership* 57(8): 42.

Taggart, G. L., and A. P. Wilson. 1998. *Promoting reflective thinking in teachers: 44 action strategies.* Thousand Oaks, CA: Corwin Press, Inc. A Sage Publications Company.

Taking time to formulate a philosophy of teaching and learning helps beginning teachers reflect on the attributes of effective teachers. Mentors can guide novice teachers in the development of their vision of quality teaching and help them focus on important goals for their professional growth plan or portfolio.

Philosophy of Professional Growth for Teachers

by **Kay Burke**

The development of professional skills and knowledge should span the entire career. Those who stop growing after receiving tenure or upon approaching retirement hurt themselves and those they teach and supervise.—Glatthorn 1996

Professional Status

Professionalism is a form of liberty that is not simply conferred; it is earned.—Delaney and Sykes, in Lieberman 1988

Teachers want to be valued and treated as professionals and gain the respect of the public in order to make autonomous decisions to help the students they teach. Delaney and Sykes (as cited in Lieberman 1988, 3) say the question of whether teachers should gain the status of "professionalism" has already been settled by many—"of course we must have teachers who are thoroughly schooled and helpfully inducted, who are autonomous and responsible, who are valued and

Adapted from *Designing Professional Portfolios for Change* by Kay Burke, pp. 11–19. © 1997 by IRI/SkyLight Training and Publishing, Inc.

Philosophy of Professional Growth for Teachers

treated as professionals!" They note, however, that "this view is not self-evident to all who participate in or observe teachers' work. If entertained at all, it is not clearly and firmly settled in the minds of citizens, law makers, bureaucrats, school board members, district administrators, school principals, or even all teachers."

Darling-Hammond (as cited in Lieberman 1988) argues that if teachers want to make decisions without external regulations, they must adhere to at least three prerequisites to professional claims for self-governance:

1. Knowledge of the principles, theories, and factors that undergird appropriate decisions about what procedures should be employed—and knowledge of the procedures themselves.
2. The ability to apply this knowledge in nonroutine circumstances, taking relevant considerations into account.
3. A commitment to do what is best for the client, not what is easiest or most expedient.

Definitions of Teaching

Eisner discusses two meanings of the word *teaching*. Teaching can be regarded as a "set of acts performed by people we call teachers as they attempt to foster learning" (Eisner 1985, 180). By this definition, when teachers engage in activities such as lecturing, asking questions, leading discussions, or demonstrating ideas, they are teaching.

Eisner also describes the view espoused by John Dewey, who felt that the term *teaching* was similar to the term *selling*. "That is, one could not teach unless someone learned, just as one could not sell unless someone bought. Teaching and learning were regarded as reciprocal concepts. . . . Thus, if a teacher attempts to teach but does not succeed in helping the students learn, then he or she may be said to have lectured, conducted a discussion, demonstrated, explained, but not to have taught. To teach, in this sense, is known by its effects" (Eisner 1985, 179).

Before educators begin the professional development process, then, they need to ask themselves some important questions about teaching:

1. What is my role as a teacher?
2. How can I best meet the needs of my students?
3. What methodologies are most effective?
4. Can I vary my instructional strategies to help my special needs students?
5. How much content or basic skills is enough? How much is too much?
6. How can I be a more effective teacher?

Theories of Learning

Before educators can plan their own professional development, they also need to clarify their roles as teachers and how they view the learning process. Some educators, reflecting on their own learning experiences, might feel that "skill and drill" exercises and memorization were and still are fundamental to learning. Others may feel that instead of the "pour and store" philosophy of attaining knowledge, students learn best when they construct their own understanding of the world. According to this latter view, students make sense of the world by integrating new experiences into what they already know and understand. Teachers holding this view would agree with Brooks and Brooks (1993, 5) that "educators must invite students to experience the world's richness, empower them to ask their own questions and seek their own answers, and challenge them to understand the world's complexities."

Other educators might follow Feuerstein's concept of mediated learning. Mediated learning occurs when teachers help learners "frame, filter, and schedule stimuli" that ultimately influence how the students transfer knowledge. "Mediation assumes that instruction is more concerned with going beyond the information given, with connecting the present with both the past and the anticipation of the future, than with mastering specific bits of here-and-now data" (Presseisen and Kozulin

Philosophy of Professional Growth for Teachers

1992, as cited in Ben-Hur 1994, 57). It is essential, therefore, that teachers form opinions and theories about how students learn before they develop their personal philosophies, pose essential questions, or set professional goals.

Before educators develop professional goals, they need to ask themselves how they feel about learning:

1. How do I learn best?
2. How do students learn best?
3. Can all students learn?
4. What can I do to mediate students' learning?
5. Which learning theories seem most effective for my students?

Purpose for Professional Portfolios

Educators about to embark on a professional enrichment journey, with the goal of helping their students learn, need first to reflect on their purpose for developing a professional portfolio. Dietz (1995, 41) recommends that participants begin the process by clarifying their purposes for the portfolio and formulating their credo—"their basic values and belief systems that drive their decisions and learning as teachers." Writing a "philosophy of education" is usually required for applications to graduate schools and for some job applications, but veteran teachers rarely take time to think about teaching and learning. More importantly, they seldom reflect on how their philosophy shapes their attitudes and performance. When asked what evidence or artifact in her portfolio best showed her growth and development as a professional, one student teacher enrolled in a professional development school, responded, "My philosophy of teaching, because before I wrote it, I had to really think about what I believe in about teaching. That's really the first step to becoming the kind of teacher I want to be."

GUIDEBOOK

Ownership of Professional Development

Educators also need to ask themselves if they are ready and willing to assume the autonomy and the responsibility of professionalism by assessing their needs, setting their goals, reflecting on their practices, and changing their practices to better meet the needs of students.

Educators must then continue to ask themselves key questions along the way: Who is ultimately responsible for my growth as a professional? What are my goals? What will I have to do to meet those goals? How will I measure my success?

Bernhardt (1994, 138) states, "A school culture ready for improvement consists of colleagues able to share their personal values, beliefs, and visions; able to communicate and collaborate with one another to build and implement a shared vision and mission; and able to trust each other to behave in a manner consistent with a new school mission and vision."

Covey (as cited in Bernhardt 1994, 138) believes that four basic needs must be recognized before individuals in an organization are willing to share a vision and collaborate: (1) the need for human growth and development; (2) the need to be treated well; (2) the need to contribute and have meaning; and (4) the need to be treated fairly. These needs must be met in professional development training because educators must believe that the investment they make in establishing goals and documenting their experience in portfolios will increase their students' overall performance.

The reculturing of the school will not be successful if only some of the educators assume responsibility for their professional development, while others welcome the demise of staff development days but neglect to embark on the journey to "earn" their professionalism. Darling-Hammond (1994, 10) warns that "major changes in the productivity of American schools rest on our ability to create and sustain a highly prepared teaching force for all, not just some, of our children." Similarly, the opportunity for educators to take charge of professional development must be explored by all, not just some, of our teachers.

SkyLight Professional Development

Section IV: Reflecting on Professional Growth | 233

Philosophy of Professional Growth for Teachers

The Power of Peer Interaction

Before educators can decide upon the course of professional development, they need to review their beliefs about teaching, learning, and professional development. Sharing ideas with peers helps clarify thinking processes; therefore, it is beneficial to include a friend, colleague, or mentor on the journey with whom to share ideas and encouragement. Working in cadres allows professionals to form a community of lifelong learners and to demonstrate to all concerned parties that "professionalism is a form of liberty that is not simply conferred; it is earned" (Delaney and Sykes, in Lieberman 1988, 3).

Conclusion

Dietz (1995) recommends that educators first clarify the basic values and belief systems that drive their decisions about teaching and learning. Teachers often reflect on their positive and negative teaching and learning experiences, formulate their own vision of teaching and learning, and develop or re-examine their philosophy of teaching and learning before they develop a professional development plan. The examples in Blackline 9.1 show how a teacher might start the process.

BIBLIOGRAPHY

Ben-Hur, M, ed. 1994. *On Feuerstein's Instrumental Enrichment.* Palatine, IL: IRI/Skylight Training and Publishing.

Bernhardt, V. L. 1994. *The school portfolio: A comprehensive framework for school improvement.* Princeton Junction, NJ: Eye on Education.

Brooks, J., and M. Brooks. 1993. *In search of understanding: The case for constructivist classrooms.* Alexandria, VA: Association for Supervision and Curriculum Development.

Darling-Hammond, L., ed. 1994. *Professional development schools: Schools for developing a profession.* New York: Teachers College Press.

Dietz, M. 1995. Using portfolios as a framework for professional development. *Journal of Staff Development* 16 (2): 40–43.

Eisner, E. W. 1985. *The educational imagination: On the design and evaluation of school programs,* 2nd ed. New York: Macmillan Publishing Co.

Glatthorn, A. A. 1996. *The teacher's portfolio: Fostering and documenting professional development.* Rockport, MA: ProActive Publishers.

Lieberman, A., ed. 1988. *Building a professional culture in school.* New York: Teachers College Press.

Mentors can discuss the examples in Blackline 9.1 with their protégés. Protégés may refer to these examples as they complete the corresponding blackline masters (9.2–9.5). Protégés should use these blacklines to develop their own philosophy of teaching and learning. Mentors should review protégés' responses.

Philosophy of Professional Growth for Teachers

Examples

Reflections on My Learning Experiences

Share your responses with a peer or mentor.

1. Describe how your favorite teacher influenced your teaching.

   One teacher read every Friday with the whole class for one hour. I usually finished the book over the weekend. I became a lifelong reader because of her.

2. Describe a positive or negative incident that has affected you.

   When I was in an algebra class, our teacher used the scores on a test to seat us—highest to lowest scores. I have never been so embarrassed and I grew to hate algebra.

   Kathy Brown
   August 26

Reflections on My Teaching Experiences

Share your responses with a peer or mentor.

1. Explain your greatest success as an educator.

   I've succeeded when students are reading other novels by the authors we have studied.

2. Explain your greatest challenge as an educator.

   Grading the performances of students quickly, fairly, and meaningfully. I hate the grading process.

   Kathy Brown
   August 26

My Vision of Teaching and Learning

Share your responses with a peer or mentor.

1. To create the "School of Best Practices," I would choose:

   —Cooperative learning
   —Team building
   —Block scheduling
   —Integrated curricula
   —Authentic assessment

2. What topics or problems in education would you like to explore to help your students?

   To know more about rubrics or scoring guides to help students assess their own work.

   Kathy Brown
   August 26

My Philosophy of Teaching and Learning

I believe that good teachers provide the framework for student learning. That framework includes:
   1. *A warm and caring classroom*
   2. *A knowledge base*
   3. *Opportunities for meaningful interaction with the content and their peers*
   4. *A fair and effective assessment process*

I believe students will learn best if I mediate their learning and then let them "fly on their own."

Signed: *Kathy Brown* Date: *8/22*

Peer/Mentor signature:
Patsy Angel Date: *8/28*

Reflections on My Learning Experiences

Share your responses with a peer or mentor.

1. Describe how your favorite teacher influenced your teaching.

2. Describe a positive or negative incident that has affected you.

Signed:_____ Date:_____

Peer/Mentor:_____ Date:_____

Reflections on My Teaching Experiences

Share your responses with a peer or mentor.

1. Explain your greatest success as an educator.

2. Explain your greatest challenge as an educator.

Signed:_____ Date:_____

Peer/Mentor:_____ Date:_____

My Vision of Teaching and Learning

Share your responses with a peer or mentor.

1. To create the "School of Best Practices," I would include the following teaching and learning experiences:

2. To help my students, I would like to explore these topics:

Signed:_____ Date:_____

Peer/Mentor:_____ Date:_____

Philosophy of Professional Growth for Teachers

My Philosophy of Teaching and Learning

Signed:_____ Date:_____

Peer/Mentor:_____ Date:_____

Even if beginning teachers are not required to use a formal professional portfolio to document their growth, mentors should encourage their protégés to collect, select, and reflect on key artifacts that demonstrate what has worked and what hasn't worked with their students. Reflection sparks growth.

The Reflective Practitioner

by **Kay Burke**

The process of looking at one's development through a portfolio process functions like a literal mirror—when one sees one's own image or performance—the literal reflection sparks internal reflection.

—Diez 1994

The Reflection Process

Reflection is a process of thinking systematically and insightfully about professional issues.—Glatthorn 1996

The reflection process is critical to developing the professional portfolio. Educators need to become reflective practitioners if they are to grow as professionals. Without written commentaries, explanations, and reflections, the portfolio is no more than a notebook of artifacts or a scrapbook of teaching mementos. Such a portfolio does not reveal the criteria for collecting the contents, the thoughts of why the items were selected, or what the teacher and the students learned. Even though many of these thoughts might surface in a conference, it cannot be assumed that the person who created the portfolio will always be present to discuss them. Sometimes the portfolio needs to be self-explanatory.

Adapted from *Designing Professional Portfolios for Change* by Kay Burke, pp. 90–104. © 1997 by SkyLight Training and Publishing, Inc. Used with permission.

The Reflective Practitioner

Wolf (1996, 36) believes that reflective commentaries are important parts of portfolios and do more than describe the portfolio contents: "They examine the teaching documented in the portfolio and reflect on what teacher and students learned." Glatthorn (1996) believes that the process of reflection begins with awareness—an awareness of teachers' feelings and thoughts; an awareness of their teaching decisions; and an awareness of their students' reactions.

Metacognition

An intellectual is someone whose mind watches itself.
—Albert Camus

Metacognition—thinking about thinking—is an essential component of professional growth. Fogarty (1994) uses the example of a person reading and getting to the bottom of the page, when a little voice inside his head says, "I don't know what I just read!" With the awareness of knowing that he doesn't know, he employs a recovery strategy of reading the last sentences of each paragraph, scanning the page, looking for key words, or rereading the entire page. After using one or more strategies, he captures the meaning and continues.

Teachers are generally aware of their thinking every time they teach a lesson. They start at the planning stage, where they stand outside the situation and imagine the actual lesson and the students' reactions. Once they begin the actual lesson, they monitor and adjust as needed. Sometimes they sense total confusion on the faces of students, so they stop and clarify or reteach. Teachers monitor students' reactions and adjust instruction on an ongoing basis. "Whenever we watch student behaviors and log the information for 'minor adjustments or repairs'—we act metacognitively—beyond the cognitive" (Fogarty 1994, ix). It is as if we "freeze frame" the teaching to take a second look at what is going on. This awareness level is metacognition.

Metacognition also entails evaluating what one knows, how one knows it, and why one knows it. Fogarty uses the example of remembering something memorized years ago—a poem, lines from Shakespeare, or a nursery rhyme. She asks people to think about how they learned the piece and why they are able to recite it accurately and instantly today. Did they write it many times? Did they visualize the words on the page? Did they recite it aloud over and over again? Metacognitive reflection is "thinking about how you learn and being able to generalize those skills and strategies for transfer and use into diverse situations" (Fogarty 1994, x). Costa (1991, 87) describes metacognition as "our ability to know what we know and what we don't know." Costa also describes metacognition as occurring when a person having an "inner dialogue" stops to evaluate her decision-making and problem-solving process. The Reflective Lesson Planner (Blackline 10.2 at the end of this selection) helps the teacher make adjustments during the lesson and plan for future lessons after reflecting on what worked and what did not work.

Metacognitive Reflections

The "inner dialogue" that Costa describes occurs in schools all the time. Principals experience it when they introduce a new report card format—"How will parents react? Will the teachers feel it's too time consuming?" Teachers experience the "inner dialogue" every time they teach a lesson or try a different classroom management technique—"How will Jimmy react to these consequences? How will my third period students manage their portfolios?" This "inner dialogue" is transferred to the portfolio in the form of a written commentary or reflective entry that captures on paper the thoughts running through an educator's head. The very act of writing the thoughts helps to clarify them. Additionally, sharing thoughts with peers provides a different perspective as well as constructive feedback.

Metacognitive reflections are key elements of professional portfolios and professional growth. Without such reflections, a portfolio is only a "notebook of stuff."

Other Metacognitive Tools

Metacognitive reflections come in many shapes and sizes. Written commentaries are not the only methods of exploring the "inner thoughts" of an educator. The following tools may add variety to the reflection process.

Reflective Stems

One method that encourages reflection is the reflective stem. The stem is a statement that triggers ideas and asks the practitioner to finish the thought about a particular piece in the portfolio.

Possible Stems

1. This piece represents a watershed moment for me because . . .
2. This piece did not work for me because . . .
3. This artifact taught me something insightful about myself (or a student) because . . .
4. This piece was a stretch for me because . . .

The questions stimulate thought. The stems also encourage practitioners to include ideas that did not work and tell why. Sometimes the "disasters" cause people to rethink ideas and reflect on current practices more than a series of successful pieces will. Additional stems are inclued in Blacklines 10.1 and 10.3 at the end of this selection.

Artifact Registry

Dietz (1993, Facilitator's Guide, IV-7) suggests using an artifacts and evidences registry to list any artifacts and evidences that cause people to reflect on their question. The page would contain the following:

Registry Item
Date
Description
Why It Belongs in the Portfolio
Removed from Portfolio Date
Reason for Removal and Outcomes

This registry provides ongoing documentation of what items are included in the portfolio, the rationale for how items meet the person's goals, and an explanation of why items no longer meet the goals and have been removed. The decision to include or exclude items in a portfolio is in itself a reflective process. What were the criteria for selection? Why did an item meet the criteria at one time, but then lose its status? What changed in the learner or the process?

The "X" Files—What's Hot, What's Not

Another idea for monitoring the collection/selection process would be to keep track of only those items that are excluded from the working portfolio. The items that are left in will be explained and reflected upon in the final portfolio, but it would be interesting to know what didn't make the final cut and why it wasn't deemed worthy of inclusion in the final portfolio. The rationale of why the item was excluded provides metacognitive insight into the "inner thinkings" of the portfolio owner (see Figures 10.1 and Blackline 10.4 at the end of this selection).

Portfolio Rejection Log

Name: _Kathy Brown_   Focus Topic: _Authentic Assessment_

Date	Rejected Item	Rejection Rationale
Sept. 16	Rubric to assess the visual aids used in speeches.	It was an early attempt. We used vague descriptors like "good visuals," "adequate design," "creative ideas" without knowing what the words meant. We couldn't grade the visual aids reliably.
Oct. 3	Abstract of "Why Authentic Assessment?" by Sid Smith.	I thought this was good because it defined assessment. After further reading, however, I found that it just talks about theory—others describe actual tools to use.

Figure 10.1

Biography of a Work

Another method for reflecting on one's selections is to review the steps in the process. When the final selections appear in the portfolio, someone looking at the selections has very little information about the steps the person took to arrive at the final products—unless that person is there to explain the process. Sometimes, even the portfolio owner cannot remember the steps because the selections were made at an earlier time or she did not monitor her actions metacognitively! The biography of a work delineates the steps a person or group went through to arrive at a final product or performance. This tool can also be used to chronicle the steps in the entire portfolio process (see Figure 10.2).

Biography of a Work Log

Name: _Kathy Brown_   Focus Topic: _Authentic Assessment_

Task: _Creating a Teacher-Made Test_

Date	Creating a Teacher-Made Test
Feb. 2	Asked students for 5 questions on 3" × 5" cards about _Red Badge of Courage_.
Feb. 3	Used student questions to develop ten matching items, ten fill-in-the-blanks, five true-false, and three essay questions.
Feb. 4	Added a Civil War mind-map question where students mapped major battles.
Feb. 5	Added point values; timed the test; added a bonus question; added instructions and choices for different learning styles.
Feb. 6	Gave the test. The students were excited to see some of their questions on the test.

Figure 10.2

Sticky Note Reflections

One of the easiest ways to reflect on a lesson or artifact quickly and succinctly is to use different sizes of sticky notes to attach thoughts. Some people use the 3" x 5" size; others prefer the 4" x 6" style with lines. The advantage of using the notes is that a person can record an immediate reaction to an artifact, lesson, or article and then go back later and expand or amend the ideas before writing the final reflection. Often, the initial reaction may be amended after the teacher gauges students' reactions or assesses the effectiveness of a lesson. Sometimes it is effective to attach two reflections to an artifact. The first dated entry describes how the educator felt the day a lesson or strategy was introduced; the second entry, dated days or weeks later, describes how the educator felt after reflecting on the results or after hearing student reactions.

Example

Feb. 7   Reflection
Gave the <u>Red Badge of Courage</u> test today. Students were excited to see some of the questions they had submitted.

Feb. 14   Reflection
Their scores on the <u>Red Badge</u> test were the best this year. The students said the test was fair and comprehensive. It's worth taking the time to write an authentic test.

Mirror Reflections

Often times a sticky note does not allow enough space for metacognitive reflection on an artifact. It may provide the initial thoughts, but upon further reflection, the author decides to elaborate on the entry. One of the most effective ways to "dig deeper" is to align the final portfolio so that the artifact is on the left page and the commentary, explanation, and/or reflection is on the right page (see Figure 10.3). This mirror image allows the reader to review the artifact and then immediately see the thoughts of the person who included the entry.

Mirror Reflections

<table>
<tr><td>

Artifact

CRITERIA
FOR A SPEECH

- Eye Contact
- Organization
- Content
- Creativity
- Appropriate Gestures
- Visual Aid
- Hook

</td><td>

Description

These are early criteria we created for our persuasive speeches. We watched three videos of speeches and then brainstormed the criteria for a good speech.

Reflections

We tried to cover too many criteria for the first speech. We should have selected about five criteria to evaluate. The students had too much to think about and it was hard to finish the grading in five minutes.

</td></tr>
</table>

Figure 10.3

Sometimes people prefer to separate the description of the entry from the reflection. The description section describes the entry (what it is, who developed it, why it is included, what the context of the piece was) and the reflection section features the reflections or reactions of the professional: "What have I learned from this piece? How can I connect it to other things? What do I still need to do?" Sometimes an entry is critical enough to warrant a whole page of description and reflection to document its importance.

Self-Evaluation

To see ourselves as others see us—Robert Burns

The reflective practitioner needs to conduct a self-assessment, a critical look at "how I am now" versus "how I would like to be." Even though few people enjoy hearing their own voices on tape or seeing themselves on video, these methods are valuable tools for identifying needed improvement (see Figure 10.4). A self-evaluation of a lesson can be found in Blacklines 10.1 and 10.5 at the end of this selection.

Evaluation of Video

Teacher: _Kathy Brown_   Date: _November 16_

Description of Class: This is a heterogeneous group of 35 eleventh-grade students enrolled in the American literature course.

Description of Lesson

Unit: _Red Badge of Courage_ (Civil War Unit)

Context: We had been discussing whether Henry, the protagonist, was a coward because he ran away his first time in battle

Objective: To have students reflect on the terms _hero_ and _coward_ and apply them to their own lives

Target Observation Area: I will observe how well I question students and elicit thoughtful responses. I want to probe for deeper understanding.

Hook: I asked for students' reactions to this quote: "Cowards die many times before their death; the valiant taste of death but once." Julius Caesar, Shakespeare

My Insights from Viewing the Tape: I would ask a question and then wait five to seven seconds before I called on a student. When Mike didn't have a response, I asked who his personal heroes were and then asked if he could name any "cowards." Once he answered these questions, he commented on the quote. I need to wait longer after the student answers to allow for additional answers or piggybacking from other students.

Signed: _Kathy Brown_

Figure 10.4

Administrators could tape their presentations at back-to-school night and analyze how well they explained ideas to parents. Did I talk too fast? Did I use educational jargon that confused parents? Was my speech too long? The administrator could include a copy of the video in the portfolio with an analysis of the speech and a reflection on what she could do to improve future presentations.

Counselors could use an audiocassette to record their facilitation of meetings in order to analyze their facilitation skills. Teachers could record on audiotape or videotape a lesson they teach and then review the tape and evaluate their effectiveness in meeting their objective. They could later include the video or cassette in their final portfolio with a critique of the experience, focusing on areas they want to improve. Educators could also include audiotapes or videotapes of students giving a performance or creating a project as evidence that students are learning and the educators are achieving their target goals.

Transfer

Ordinary learning contrasts with transfer. In ordinary learning, we just do more of the same thing in the same situation. . . . Transfer means learning something in one context and applying it in another.—Fogarty, Perkins, and Barell 1992

Eisner has said that if it's not worth teaching, it's not worth teaching well. Teachers must ask themselves the critical questions, "Why am I teaching this? Does it have transfer potential? How can students use it in other situations?" Costa (as cited in Fogarty, Perkins, and Barell 1992, xii) suggests that teachers "selectively abandon" everything without transfer potential and "judiciously include" those things that have transfer power.

Just as students need to be able to "automatize" knowledge and skills in order to transfer them to other situations, so too educational professionals need to become more thoughtful and reflective in reaching their target goals in order to transfer them to other teaching situations. They need to seek generalizations, look for opportunities to apply prior knowledge, monitor their thinking, and ponder their strategies for approaching problems and tasks (Fogarty, Perkins, and Barell 1992).

Making the Connection

Many people have described "transfer" as the most important outcome of education. If students are not able to transfer what they have learned in school to real-life situations, what have they really learned? So too, if professionals implement a strategy or program in their classroom or school that few students ever use, what have they accomplished? To meet their focus goals, educators must incorporate mediation strategies that bridge learning into their teaching. Fogarty and Bellanca (1993) have suggested a strategy that promotes transfer (see Figure 10.5). Teachers can select a bird that represents their self-assessment of their progress in attaining a goal on the "Transfer Journal" in Blackline 10.6 at the end of this selection. Novice teachers should understand that they may achieve different levels of transfer for different skill areas. For example, Kathy may be a "Catching the Carrier Pigeon" when it comes to rubrics, but she may rate herself as a "Dan the Drilling Woodpecker" when it comes to technology. Self-awareness is a prerequisite for self-assessment.

Metacognition and Transfer

The more practitioners take the time to reflect on their experiences, the more they will begin to make the connections between prior knowledge, current learnings, and future applications. Metacognitive reflection is a prerequisite to transfer. The more professionals think about their practices, share their insights with peers, and write about their reactions, the more they will clarify their thoughts and assess their ability to meet their target goals. Moreover, the reflection must be performed on a regular basis in order to be effective. Waiting until the last minute to write reflections for a whole year's worth of artifacts defeats the real purpose of the portfolio and weakens the link between metacognition and transfer.

The Reflective Practitioner

Transfer: The Creative Connection

Reflecting Metacognitively

Reflect on your transfer level by asking: Am I . . .

Ollie the Head-in-the-Sand Ostrich

Missing appropriate opportunities; overlooking; persisting in former ways?

Dan the Drilling Woodpecker

Performing the drill exactly as practiced; duplicating with no change; copying?

Laura the Look-Alike Penguin

Tailoring, but applying in similar situations; all looking alike; replicating?

Jonathan Livingston Seagull

More aware; integrating; subtly combining with other ideas and situations; using with raised consciousness?

Cathy the Carrier Pigeon

Carrying strategy to other content and into life situations; associating and mapping?

Samantha the Soaring Eagle

Innovating; taking ideas beyond the initial conception; risking; diverging?

(From *Patterns for Thinking, Patterns for Transfer* by R. Fogarty and J. Bellanca, p. 300. © 1993 by IRI/SkyLight Training and Publishing. Reprinted with permission.)

Figure 10.5

Journals

Posner (1996 as cited in Taggart and Wilson 1998) believes that more learning is derived from reflecting on an experience than is derived from the experience itself. Journals help protégés think reflectively by linking their classroom practice with their own understanding of how students learn. Mentors can read and respond to the journals their protégés write or the journals could be included in a portfolio. Sometimes the new teacher will choose to share journal entries with peers or keep them private. Figure 10.6 lists tools that can be used to help teachers reflect on their teaching practices in order to improve them.

Reflective Tools

- ❏ Reflective Stems
- ❏ Artifact Registry
- ❏ Portfolio Rejection Log
- ❏ Biography of a Work Log
- ❏ Sticky Note Reflections
- ❏ Mirror Reflections
- ❏ Self-Evaluation
- ❏ Journals
- ❏ Reflective Lesson Planner
- ❏ Portfolio

Figure 10.6

Teachers might want to start slowly by slapping a sticky note on a lesson plan to comment on its effectiveness. "Too complicated" or "students needed more time" conveys initial thoughts. The mentors, however, should work with the novice teachers to expand their thoughts and extend their responses as they become more reflective practitioners in their quest to become better teachers.

BIBLIOGRAPHY

Costa, A. L. 1991. *The school as a home for the mind.* Palatine, IL: IRI/Skylight Training and Publishing.

Diez, M. 1994. The portfolio: Sonnet, mirror, and map. Keynote presentation at Linking Liberal Arts and Teacher Education: Encouraging Reflection through Portfolios, 6 October. Mission Valley Hilton, San Diego, Calif.

Fogarty, R. 1994. *The mindful school: How to teach for metacognitive reflection.* Palatine, IL: IRI/Skylight Training and Publishing.

Fogarty, R., D. Perkins, and J. Barell. 1992. *The mindful school: How to teach for transfer.* Palatine, IL: IRI/Skylight Training and Publishing.

Fogarty, R., and J. Bellanca. 1993. *Patterns for thinking, Patterns for transfer.* Palatine, IL: IRI/Skylight Training and Publishing.

Glatthorn, A. 1996. *The teacher's portfolio: Fostering and documenting professional development.* Rockport, MA: Proactive Publications.

Taggart, G. L., and A. P. Wilson. 1998. *Promoting reflective thinking in teachers: 44 action strategies.* Thousand Oaks, CA: Corwin Press, Inc.

Wolf, K. 1996. Developing an effective teaching portfolio. *Educational Leadership* 53 (6): 34–36.

- Mentors can review the examples in Blackline 10.1 with their protégés. The examples correspond with Blacklines 10.2–10.5. Protégés can choose to use any of these blacklines (10.2–10.5) to reflect on their portfolio pieces.

- Mentors can also help protégés evaluate their progress in achieving their professional goals by asking them to complete and discuss their answers on Blackline 10.6.

GUIDEBOOK

Examples

Reflective Lesson Planner

Name: _Kathy Brown_   Grade: _11_   Date: _Sept. 25_
Topic: _Performance Rubric_
Lesson: _Introducing Students to Rubrics_

Describe what happened	Describe your feelings
Before the Lesson	Thoughts
I wrote a fun rubric assessing school lunches to model for the students.	_I wanted students to be comfortable with the process and have fun before we created a real rubric._
During the Lesson	Strategies that work; lessons learned
I assigned roles for the group work. Two groups couldn't think of a topic and one group struggled with criteria and indicators.	_Form groups to include a "creative" person in each group._
After the Lesson	Insights for future lessons
After each group shared their rubric, we talked about the process of developing rubrics. The fun rubric helped prepare them for the real rubric.	_Do one fun rubric with the class to model before assigning groups to do them._

Reflective Stems

Create stem questions that trigger responses and provoke insight into what a person is thinking.

This piece gave me new insight into one of my students because . . .

I will save this piece forever because . . .

People who knew me ten years ago would not believe this piece because . . .

This piece shows I have met my target goal because . . .

This piece shows I have a great deal to learn about my topic because . . .

Portfolio Rejection Log

Name: _Kathy Brown_
Focus Topic: _Authentic Assessment_

Explain why you rejected items from your working portfolio.

Date	Rejected Item	Rejection Rationale
Sept. 1	First speech rubric	We tried to include too many criteria for the first speech. Also, we used a three-point scale with no zero.
Nov. 6	My rubric for the American lit. research papers.	I realized that my "rubric" was really just point values for doing things with no regard for quality.
Dec. 9	The videotape of me teaching students how to create fun rubrics.	The camera was focused on me, but I wanted the students' reactions.

Self-Evaluation

Name: _Kathy Brown_
Focus Topic: _Authentic Assessment_

1. Describe the experience you are evaluating.
   I am introducing the fun rubric to my students.

2. Describe your method of self-evaluation.
   I had my peer videotape my lesson.

3. What do you feel you did well?
   I showed the students two fun rubrics for evaluating school lunches. They enjoyed them.

4. What would you do differently the next time?
   I would have modeled a fun rubric with the class before I assigned them to do one in groups. Some groups were really confused.

5. How can you improve?
   I need to practice creating more rubrics so I'll be confident leading my students through them.

Blackline 10.1

SkyLight Professional Development

Section IV: Reflecting Professional Growth | 255

The Reflective Practitioner

Reflective Lesson Planner

Name:_____ Grade:_____ Date:_____

Topic:_____ Lesson:_____

Describe what happened in the lesson	Describe your feelings
Before the Lesson	**Thoughts**
During the Lesson	**Strategies that work; lessons learned**
After the Lesson	**Insights for future lessons**

Reflective Stems

Create stem questions that trigger responses and provoke insight into what a person is thinking.

1. This piece shows my professional growth because . . .

2. This piece will surprise (my principal, peers, students) because . . .

3. If I could reteach this lesson I would change _____ because . . .

4. This piece shows I have met Professional Standard #_____ because . . .

5. This piece showed me that educational theory doesn't always translate into educational practice because . . .

Brainstorm additional stems:

6.

7.

8.

9.

10.

Portfolio Rejection Log

Name:_____ Focus Topic:_____

Explain why you rejected items from your working portfolio.

Date	Rejected Item	Rejection Rationale

Self-Evaluation

Name:_____ Focus Topic:_____

1. Describe the experience you are evaluating.

2. Describe your method of self-evaluation (videotape, cassette tape, photographs, script, other).

3. What do you feel you did well?

4. What would you do differently the next time?

5. How can you improve?

The Reflection Practitioner

 Transfer Journal

Reviewing the "Transfer Birds" on Figure 10.5. Which bird best represents your stage of development in achieving your professional goals?

I feel I am most like transfer bird _____ when it comes to

achieving my goal of _____ because . . .

Signed: _____ Date: _____

Conclusion

The idea that beginning teachers require a structural system to support their entry into the profession has moved from the fringes of the policy landscape to the center; it is now generally recognized as a critical component of a comprehensive approach to teacher development and is mandated in many states.—Villani 2002

Teacher quality is the single most important school-related factor in student achievement. Solmon and Firetag (2002) cite one large study where equally able fifth-grade students with the bad luck to have had weak teachers three years in a row scored at the 29th percentile, while those students who had three strong teachers scored at the 83rd percentile. Solmon and Firetag state, "The key to internal capacity is the talent and energy of veteran teachers who, along with the principal, provide essential coaching and leadership" (48).

In order to understand how novice teachers feel, mentors need to be aware of their feelings. Barry Sweeny and others have written about the focus of new teachers when they enter the profession. Many teachers face "reality shock" when they encounter the demands of teaching, and they concentrate mostly on trying to survive—or what Sweeny calls **Stage One: Focus on Self**. The first volume in this mentoring series, *Mentoring Guidebook Level 1: Starting the Journey,* deals with basic lesson-plan designs and the fundamental issues of classroom management teachers need to master in order to survive the first critical year. Establishing behavior expectations, procedures, rules and consequences forms the essentials of classroom management. Gordon and Maxey (2000) have identified "managing the classroom" as the number one challenge for beginning teachers. Teachers need to know how to manage their classrooms and establish clear expectations for behavior in order to move to **Stage Two: Focus on the Whole Class**. Villani (2002) says "Teachers cannot be thinking about the nuances of curriculum design and instruction until they know the protocols of their school and have established that their students are engaged and ready to learn" (5).

This volume, *Mentoring Guidebook Level 2: Exploring Teaching Strategies*, examines techniques to help teachers implement instruction, curriculum, and assessment models to address the needs of the whole class. Utilizing brain-compatible strategies, integrating lesson designs, using cooperative groups, and assessing student work become more important to the beginning teacher who has moved beyond the survival stage to a higher level of concern for the students. The more confident teacher is better able to deal with members of the learning community like paraprofessionals and parents during Stage Two. Moreover, as the novice develops confidence, he or she begins to focus on reflecting on professional growth and a more in-depth analysis of his or her practices.

Sweeny says that in **Stage Three: Focus on the Individual Student** new teachers switch their attention to the needs of the individual students. It is challenging enough to meet the needs of an entire class of students, but it is even more difficult to attempt to meet the social and academic needs of each individual student. The next book in this series, *Mentoring Guidebook Level 3: Meeting the Needs of the Learner*, will explore differentiated learning strategies, problem-based learning, dealing with at-risk students and bullies, and other instructional strategies geared toward meeting the emotional, behavior, and academic needs of each learner. These strategies require a more in-depth knowledge of pedagogy and an ability to adapt curriculum, instruction, and assessment strategies or models to serve the diverse needs of learners in today's inclusive classroom.

Martin-Kniep (2000) believes that many beginning and veteran teachers lack the training and administrative support to meet the social, emotional, and cognitive needs of their students. Moreover, many teachers in the United States do not have access to ongoing professional development.

"Their induction into schools and subsequent survival depend greatly on the people they work with, the conditions that surround them, and the more experienced peers who mentor them" (Martin-Kniep 2000, vii).

Hopefully, the instructional strategies reviewed in this guidebook will pave the way for a fulfilling professional journey for mentors and the new teachers they support. The novice teacher may enter the profession alone, afraid, and dependent upon the kindness of strangers. If the mentor has been successful, however, the teacher will gain the confidence, skills, and insights to become an independent decision maker and problem solver who designs, delivers, and assesses quality learning experiences for the students he or she teaches.

—KAY BURKE
May, 2002

REFERENCES

Gordon, S. P., and S. Maxey. 2000. *How to help beginning teachers succeed.* Alexandria, VA: Association for Supervision and Curriculum Development.

Martin-Kniep, G. O. 2000. *Becoming a better teacher: Eight innovations that work.* Alexandria, VA: Association for Supervision and Curriculum Development.

Solmon, L. C., and K. Firetag. 2002, March. The road to teacher quality. *Education Week* 21(27): 48.

Sweeny, B. 2001. *Leading the teacher induction and mentoring program.* Arlington Heights, IL: SkyLight Training and Publishing.

Villani, S. 2002. *Mentoring programs for new teachers: Models of induction and support.* Thousand Oaks, CA: Corwin Press. A Sage Publications Company.

Resources

by **Barry Sweeny**

The following section offers lists of online as well as audio and video resources that provide further information and support for many of the strategies and ideas discussed in this book.

Induction and Mentoring Web Sites

Best Practice Resources, Inc. (BPR)

http://www.teachermentors.com

This is my own Web site. It has over 300 web pages, 1,100 links, and it is continually growing! The Web site is dedicated to promoting powerful induction and mentoring programs. The research-based materials and assistance are very practical and based on expert information. The information on this site is offered in four ways:

1. Forty-seven categories contain a mix of resources, books, research reports, and Web site links. This section includes links to other organizations that are interested in or support mentoring, as well as a section with Web pages on any of the state-level beginning teacher programs in any of the fifty states.

2. A listing of over 100 BPR staff development publications is provided, most of which are on induction and mentoring. Some of these publications are free and can be accessed right from the Web site. Others are for sale at very reasonable prices. The publications include mentor training manuals, overheads, a training script, mentoring calendars and check-lists, information on how to develop an induction program, a summary of the research on mentoring and induction, and information on improving the impact of the mentoring and mentor program.

Adapted from *Leading the Teacher Induction and Mentoring Program* by Barry Sweeny, pp. 159–174. © 2001 SkyLight Training and Publishing Inc. Used with permission.

In addition to mentoring and induction, BPR provides resources for:

- Effective staff development
- School improvement planning
- Peer coaching
- Authentic performance assessment

Each of these sections offers links, information on current events, written materials, and other resources.

3. Free limited assistance and guidance to induction and mentoring programs is offered with leaders through the role of Mentor of Mentors carried out over e-mail and via telephone.

4. Consulting, training, and presentations in induction and mentoring are included. There is a section of the Web site that includes information about the services BPR provides, a client list, and client comments about the work of BPR.

Mentoring Leadership and Resource Network (MLRN)
http://www.mentors.net

Another great mentoring Web site worth visiting and exploring is MLRN. This group is an affiliate of the ASCD. MLRN was started in 1991 by a group of mentoring experts who wanted to help others access the knowledge base about mentoring of teachers. In January 1998, MLRN stopped its paper-based approach to publishing and put all their materials on their Web site. The members of this group (membership fee is $15 a year) can now access all the newsletter articles, papers, and journal articles MLRN has published since 1991. There are currently about seventy-five resources available.

A newer section of the site is designed specifically for mentor program coordinators and there is a membership listing to help coordinators locate and access educators who are interested in mentoring in their area. Most of the resources are in a Member's Only section of the Web site. Non-members can access parts of the site to learn about MLRN and to see a listing of the materials that are available to members to help them decide if they want to join. Program leaders can submit mentoring articles or studies to MLRN for web publication.

SkyLight Professional Development

Links to Other Mentoring and Induction Resources on the Internet

On my Web site, which is described above (BPR), there are over 1,100 links to mentoring and induction Web sites. The following listing of links are mentoring and induction Web sites that are in addition to those on my Web site. These are arranged by category.

Please keep in mind when checking out the Web sites listed here that some of these links may have changed or become inactive by the time you try them.

Advice for and About Beginning Teachers

Helpful Hints for Beginning Teachers
http://www.positiveparenting.com/jane4.html

Information on School-to-Work
http://www.ncrel.org/sdrs/areas/issues/envrnmnt/stw/sw5camp.htm

Kappa Delta Pi New Teacher Advocate
http://www.kdp.org/

New Math Teacher Advice
http://ncrtl.msu.edu/

I Love Teaching
http://www.iloveteaching.com/

New Teacher Seminars
http://www.rochester.k12.mn.us/gip/calendar.htm

Been There Done That Seminar
http://www.utofd.com/Teachers/NewTeach/beenther.htm

Dade County New Teacher Web Page
http://www.utofd.com/Teachers/NewTeach/newtchsc.html

Realistic Assignments for New Teachers
http://www.columbiagroup.org/retention3.htm

Survival Kit for New Teachers
http://www.inspiringteachers.com/

The Substitute/Student Teacher's Survival Handbook
http://www.teachergroup.com/

What to Expect Your First Year of Teaching
http://www.ed.gov/pubs/FirstYear/

Web-Based Books and Publications on Mentoring and Induction

Beginning Teacher Handbook
http://www.ccthomas.com/catalog/esped/more/
0-398-05833-4.html

Kappa Delta Pi New Teacher Advocate
http://www.kdp.org/

Mentoring and Peer Coaching Resources
http://www.teachermentors.com/

Characteristics of Effective Mentors

Mentor Characteristics
http://education.lanl.gov/resources/Mentors/character.html

Teacher as Caregiver, Model, and Mentor
http://www.cortland.edu/www/c4n5rs/wheel/12.htm

Descriptions of Mentoring Programs

North Platt, Nebraska
http://www.esu16.k12.ne.us/brochures/entry.html

SmokeyHill
http://www.smokyhill.org/BTMT.htm

Mentoring Program for Science Teachers
http://www.imsa.edu/team/spi/impact2/catalogs.html

University of Dayton: Mentors Help New Teachers Adjust
http://www.udayton.edu/news/nr/012397a.html

Montana
http://www.nsf.gov/od/lpa/news/publicat/frontier/2-97/
2montana.htm

One Year Internship (United States Department of Education) *Education Week* **on the Web**
http://www.edweek.org/ew/vol-16/30cincy.h16

Indiana Beginning Teacher Internship
http://ideanet.doe.state.in.us/super/083096/do1.html

Internship Training Plan
http://ideanet.doe.state.in.us/super/083096/safe2.html

Peer Resources Mentor Programs
http://www.peer.ca/mentorprograms.html

Mentors Forum—Mentoring Guidance and Information
http://www.mentorsforum.co.uk/

The Mentoring Group
http://www.mentoringgroup.com/

Evaluating a Mentoring Program

Evaluation of Professional Development
http://www.ncrel.org/sdrs/areas/issues/educatrs/profdevl/pd500.htm

Program Evaluation
http://www.mentorsforum.co.uk/cOL1/tools/Evaluating.htm

Evaluation of or by Mentors

Evaluating the Relationship by the Protégé
http://www.vcu.edu/teaching/oldteaching/medicine/mgevaluating.html

X-Change for a Day—Program Evaluation
http://www.nnlm.nlm.nih.gov/train/xchange/mentor.html

Grants and Funding for Mentoring

Public Funding and Professional Development
http://www.columbiagroup.org/public.htm

Cost Neutral Induction Program
http://www.rochester.k12.mn.us/gip/isgip.htm

Help for Mentors

The Mentor Teacher Casebook
http://darkwing.uoregon.edu/~ericcem/mentor.html

The National Board of Professional Teaching Standards
http://www.nbpts.org/

Mentoring, Coaching, and Staff Development Resources
http://www.teachermentors.com/

Preparing New Teachers for Bilingual Education
http://www.ed.gov/pubs/ModStrat/pt2d.html

Mentoring the Mentor
http://www.nsdc.org/library/mentoring.html

Mentors and Mentoring
http://www.erlbaum.com/Books/searchintro/BookDetailscvr.cfm
? ISBN=0-8058-9932-4

Incentives and Recognition

Incentives in a Graduate Induction Program
http://www.rochester.k12.mn.us/gip/clinical.htm

Quality Standards and Incentives for Teachers
http://www.columbiagroup.org/quality.htm

International Mentoring

International Mentor Program
http://www.iteachnet.com/teachnet.html

The European Mentoring Centre
http://www.mentoringcentre.org/

How Are Other Countries Preparing Teachers?
http://www.columbiagroup.org/howare.htm

Teacher Induction in Countries Around the Pacific Rim
http://www.ed.gov/pubs/APEC

Mentor Program Coordination

Mentoring the Mentor
http://www.nsdc.org/library/mentoring.html

Induction Program Governance Committee
http://www.rochester.k12.mn.us/gip/coord.htm

Consultants in Mentoring and Induction
http://www.teachermentors.com

National Reforms and Standards

The National Board of Professional Teaching Standards
http://www.nbpts.org/

Organizations that Support Teachers and Technology

Association for the Advancement of Computing Education (AACE)
http://www.aace.org/

Association for Educational Communications and Technology (AECT)
http://www.aect.org/

International Society for Technology in Education (ISTE)
http://www.iste.org/

ASCD Professional Development Online
www.ascd.org/pdi/pd.html

AT& T Learning Network
www.att.com/learningnetwork

The Community Learning Network
www.cln.org

Ed's Oasis
www.edsoasis.org

The Global Schoolhouse
www.globalschoolhouse.org

International Education and Research Network (I*EARN)
www.iearn.org

PBS Mathline
www.pbs.org/teachersource/math

Tapped-In
www.tappedin.org

U.S. Department of Education
www.ed.gov/inits/teachers/teach.html

The Well Connected Educator
www.gsh.org/wce

Orientation of New Teachers

Orientation Schedule
http://www.rochester.k12.mn.us/gip/calendar.htm

Fairfax County, Virginia—New Teacher Orientation
http://www.fcps.k12.va.us/DIS/OSDT/nto.htm

Portfolios/Professional Development Plans

Teacher Portfolio Assessment
http://www.ed.gov/databases/ERIC_Digests/ed385608.html

Preservice Teacher Mentoring

Answers to Student Teacher Problems
http://www.lll.hawaii.edu/esl/crookes/Narita.html

Mentoring Student Teachers
http://www.udayton.edu/news/nr/050696.html

Recruiting and Retaining New Teachers

Preparing New Teachers for Bilingual Education
http://www.ed.gov/pubs/ModStrat/pt2d.html

Recruitment for Induction Program
http://www.rochester.k12.mn.us/gip/app.htm

The Job Market—Teacher Recruitment Agencies
http://www.2teach.govt.nz

South Carolina Center for Teacher Recruitment
http://www.scctr.org/minority.htm

Office of Teacher Recruitment
http://www.firn.edu/doe/bin00023/teachin.htm

About Recruiting New Teachers
http://www.rnt.org/about/index.html

Teacher Recruiting and Retention via Mentoring
http://www.columbiagroup.org/retention2.htm

Recruiting and Retention: Rewarding Teachers
http://www.columbiagroup.org/recruiting6.htm

Recruitment Partner Network Information
http://www.rnt.org/collaborations/index.html

Recruitment of Mentors

Effort To Recruit Mentor Teachers Fails
http://www.edweek.org/ew/vol-16/37guff.h16

Research in Mentoring

Teacher Mentoring: A Critical Review
http://www.ed.gov/databaes/ERIC_Digests/ed397060.html

Research Activities in Europe
http://www.mentoringcentre.org/frames/researchframe.htm

Empowering the Faculty
http://www.ed.gov/databases/ERIC_Digests/ed399888.html

Resources for Mentor Programs

Mentor Teacher Forms
http://www.khsd.k12.ca.us/MENTOR/mentor9798/forms/
index.htm

**American Federation of Teachers Mentor Contract
Language**
http://www.aft.org/research/models/language/tquality/
mentor.htm

Roles, Tasks, and Strategies for Mentors

A Quiver Full: Mentoring Strategies Book
http://home.earthlink.net/~drdelliott/quiverful.html

Components—Induction Programs
http://www.ed.gov/databases/ERIC_Digests/ed269407.html

State Induction Programs

A Survey of State-Mandated Induction Programs in the Fifty States
http://www.teachermentors.com/

Indiana's Beginning Teacher Internship
http://ideanet.doe.state.in.us/super/083096/do1.html

Indiana I-CAN Update
http://www.indianacc.org/tables/3news3.html

Indiana New Teacher Training
http://ideanet.doe.state.in.us/super/083096/safe2.html

Indiana—Requirements
http://www.tc.columbia.edu/~teachcomm/POL-INFO/
Indi-ah.htm

Nebraska Entry Year Assistance Program
http://www.esu16.k12.ne.us/brochures/entry.html

North Carolina Web Book—Mentoring New Teachers
http://www.dpi.state.nc.us/mentoring_novice_teachers/

SouthEast USA State Standards for Teachers
http://www.columbiagroup.org/state.htm

Wyoming Mentoring House Bills
http://legisweb.state.wy.us/97sessin/HBILLS/HB0047.htm

Support for Teachers

Designing Internet Projects
http://www.ncsa.uiuc.edu/edu/RSE/RSEviolet/RSEviolet.html

Internet for Girls: World Wide Web Resource List
http://www.sdsc.edu/~woodka/resources.html

SkyLight Professional Development

Lesson Plan Design and Other Issues
http://www.su.edu/faculty/jcombs/

Technology in Mentoring

Technology in Mentoring—Abstract
http://archives.math.utk.edu/ICTCM/abs/7-FC13.html

The Role of Computers in Mentoring
http://mbhs.bergtraum.k12.ny.us/mentor/what.html#5

Telementoring

Teleapprenticeships in Teaching
http://www.ed.uiuc.edu/projects/tta/design.sup.html

Lessons in Telementoring
http://curry.edschool.virginia.edu/go/mining/96/oct/

Online Innovation Institute for Teacher Development
http://oii.org/

Telementoring Web
http://mbhs.bergtraum.k12.ny.us/mentor/

Examples of Telementoring
http://mbhs.bergtraum.k12.ny.us/mentor/exam.html

Telementoring Guidelines
http://mbhs.bergtraum.k12.ny.us/mentor/guide.html

Hewlett-Packard Mentors for Students
http://www.sfusd.k12.ca.us/resources/hpmentor.html

Telementoring Resources and WWW Links
http://nsn.bbn.com/telementor_wrkshp/tmlink.html

Mighty Mentors—E-mail Mentoring for Teachers
http://www.mightymedia.com/mentors/

EDC/CCT Telementoring Project
http://www.edc.org/CCT/telementoring/docs/pmentoring.html

Bemidji State Virtual Mentorship Program
http://cel.bemidji.msus.edu/virtual/mentor.html

Training and Staff Development for Mentors

Montana State University Mentor Training for Cooperating Teachers
http://www.msubillings.edu/opp/

Mentoring and Peer Coaching Training Materials
http://www.teachermentors.com/

SkyLight Consulting Services—Mentoring
Click on the In-district Training link at
http://www.skylightedu.com.

Audio and Video Resources

Videotape Programs

• *High Performance Mentoring: A Multimedia Program for Training Mentors* (1999) by Dr. James Rowley and Dr. Patricia Hart. Includes a Facilitator's Guide, four videotapes, a CD-ROM with visuals, and a participant's notebook. The series provides twenty-five training modules, including two for administrators on confidentiality and how to support a teacher mentor program. $795.00. Published by Corwin Press, 2455 Teller Road, Thousand Oaks, CA 91320-2218, (805) 499-9774.

• *Mentoring to Improve Schools* (1999). Includes a Facilitator's Guide with eight workshops and two videotapes: "Successful Mentoring Programs," and "Effective Mentoring Practices" by Barry Sweeny and Todd Johnson. # 498325H09, $228 (ASCD members), $298 (nonmembers). Association for Supervision and Curriculum Development, 1703 N. Beauregard St., Alexandria, VA 22311-1714. 800-933-2723.

• *Mentoring the New Teacher* (1994) by Dr. James Rowley and Dr. Patricia Hart. Includes nine videotapes, a Facilitator's Guide, and two other ASCD books on mentoring. Focused primarily on the needs of beginning teachers, such as dealing with parents, classroom management, etc. Association for Supervision and Curriculum Development, 1703 N. Beauregard St., Alexandria, VA 22311-1714, 800-933-2723.

• *The New Teacher: Meeting the Challenges* (1999) featuring Linda Darling-Hammond. Order # VTNT-WEB. $99.95. National Professional Resources, Inc., 25 South Regent Street, Port Chester, NY 10573, 800-453-7461.

• *Teacher Induction, Mentoring, and Renewal* (1996) featuring Harry Wong. Order # 505. $355.00. Tape 1 is thirty-five minutes and is on new teacher preparedness through effective induction. Tape 2 is thirty minutes and includes mentoring and teacher renewal. Also includes a guidebook and an audiotape. Published by Video Journal of Education, 8686 South 1300 East, Sandy, UT 84094, 800-572-1153.

• *Mentoring Case Studies* (2002): The Inclusive Classroom, Standards and Assessment, Classroom Management, and Instructional Planning. SkyLight Professional Development. For more information visit the Web site at http://skylightedu. com.

Audiotape Programs

• *How to Mentor in the Midst of Change* (1998). Two audiotapes (# 298181H09) are $24.95 for ASCD members and $29.95 for nonmembers, and the book (# 61192015H09) is $6.95 for ASCD members and $8.95 for nonmembers. Association for Supervision and Curriculum Development, 1703 N. Beauregard St., Alexandria, VA, 22311-1714, 800-933-2723.

Bibliography

Ashton-Warner, S. 1993. *Teacher*. New York: Simon and Schuster.

Association of Supervision and Curriculum Development. 1995. The inclusive school (Special Issue). *Educational Leadership* 52(4).

Baker, J., and Zigmond, N. 1990. Are regular education classes equipped to accommodate students with learning disabilities? *Exceptional Children* 56, 515–526.

Banks, J.A., and Banks, C.A. (Eds). 1997. *Multicultural education: Issues and perspectives*. Boston: Allyn and Bacon.

Barclay, K. and E. Boone. 1996. *The parent difference: Uniting school, family, and community*. Arlington Heights, IL: SkyLight Training and Publishing.

Beane, J. A. 1993. Problems and possibilities for an integrative curriculum. In *Integrating the Curricula*, ed. R. Fogarty, 69–83. Arlington Heights, IL: IRI/SkyLight Publishing, Inc.

———. 1993, September. Problems and possibilities for an integrative curriculum. *Middle School Journal* pp. 18–23.

———. ed. 1995. *Toward a coherent curriculum: 1995 yearbook of the ASCD*. Alexandria, VA: Association for Supervision and Curriculum Development.

Bellanca, J. A. and R. Fogarty. 1991. *Blueprints for thinking in the cooperative classroom*. Palatine, IL: IRI/Skylight Publishing, Inc.

———. 2002. *Blueprints for achievement in the cooperative classroom*, 3rd ed. Arlington Heights, IL: SkyLight Professional Development.

Ben-Hur, M, ed. 1994. *On Feuerstein's instrumental enrichment*. Palatine, IL: IRI/Skylight Training and Publishing.

Bloom, B. S. 1981. *All our children learning: A primer for parents, teachers, and educators*. New York: McGraw-Hill.

Board of Education for the City of Etobicoke. 1987. *Making the grade: Evaluating student progress*. Scarborough, Ontario, Canada: Prentice-Hall Canada.

Bolotin-Joesph, P. and G. E. Burnaford. 1994. *Images of schoolteachers in twentieth-century America: Paragons, polarities, complexities*. Edited by Pamela Bolotin Joseph and Gail E. Burnaford. New York: St. Martin's Press.

Bradley, D.F., M.E. King-Sears, and D. M. Tessier-Switlick. 1997. *Teaching students in inclusive settings: From theory to practice*. Needham Heights, MA: Allyn and Bacon.

Brandt, R. 1988. On teaching thinking: A conversation with Arthur Costa. *Educational Leadership* 45(7): 10–13.

Brooks, J. G., and M. G. Brooks. 1993. *In search of understanding: The case for the constructivist classroom*. Alexandria, VA: Association for Supervision and Curriculum Development.

Brophy, J., and J. Alleman. 1991. A caveat: Curriculum integration isn't always a good idea. *Educational Leadership* 49(2): 66–70.

Brown, R. 1989, April. Testing and thoughtfulness. *Educational Leadership* pp. 113–115.

Bruner, J. S. 1973. *Readiness for learning. In Beyond the information given: Studies in the psychology of knowing*, edited by J. Anglin. New York: Norton.

Burke, K. 1993. *The mindful school: How to assess authentic learning*. Palatine, IL: IRI/Skylight Publishing.

———. 1999. *How to assess authentic learning,* 3rd ed. Arlington Heights, IL: SkyLight Training and Publishing, Inc.

Burke, K., R. Fogarty, and S. Belgrad. 2002. *The portfolio connection: Student work linked to standards*, 2nd ed. Arlington Heights, IL: SkyLight Professional Development.

Caine, R. N., and G. Caine. 1991. *Making connections: Teaching and the human brain*. New York: Innovative Learning Publications/Addison-Wesley Publications.

———. 1993. *Making connections: Teaching and the human brain*, 2nd Edition. New York: Innovative Learning Publications/ Addison-Wesley Publications.

Canady, R., and M. Rettig. 1996. Models of block scheduling. In *Block scheduling: Time to learn*. Arlington Heights, IL: SkyLight Training and Publishing.

Carroll, D. 2001. Considering paraeducator training, roles, and responsibilities. In *Council for Exceptional Children* 34, 2, 60–64.

Coles, R. 1997. *The moral intelligence of children: How to raise a moral child*. New York: Random House.

Conzemius, A. and J. O'Neill. 2001. *Building shared responsibility for student learning*. Alexandria, VA: Association for Supervision and Curriculum Development.

Costa, A. 1991. *The school as a home for the mind*. Palatine, IL: IRI/SkyLight Training and Publishing.

Costa, A., and B. Kallick. 2000. *Discovering and exploring: Habits of mind*. Alexandria, VA: Association for Supervision and Curriculum Development.

Darling-Hammond, L. 1994. What matters most: A competent teacher for every child. *Phi Delta Kappan* 78 (3): 193–200.

Dell'Olio, J. M. 1998. Hearing myself: reflection-in-action in experienced teachers peer-assistance behaviors. *Journal of Curriculum and Supervision* 13, 184–204.

Dewey, J. 1913. *Interest and effort in education*. Boston: Houghton Mifflin.

————. 1938. *Experience and education*. New York: Collier.

Diamond, M. 1988. *Enriching heredity: The impact of the environment on the anatomy of the brain*. New York: Free Press.

Dietz, M. 1995. Using portfolios as a framework for professional development. *Journal of Staff Development* 16 (2): 40–43.

Diez, M. 1994. The portfolio: Sonnet, mirror, and map. Keynote presentation at Linking Liberal Arts and Teacher Education: Encouraging Reflection through Portfolios, 6 October. Mission Valley Hilton, San Diego, Calif.

Doyle, M.B. 1998. My child has a new shadow…and it doesn't resemble her! In *Disability Solutions* 3, 1, 5–9.

Drake, S. M. 1993. *Planning integrated curriculum*. Alexandria, VA: Association for Supervision and Curriculum Development.

DuFour, R. 2000. Clear connections: Everyone benenfits when schools work to involve parents. In *Journal of Staff Development* 21, 2, 59–60.

Eisner, E. W. 1985. *The educational imagination: On the design and evaluation of school programs*. Second edition. New York: Macmillan Publishing Co.

Ellis, A. K. and J. T. Fouts. 1997. *Research on educational innovations*. Larchmont, NY: Eye on Education.

Epstein, H. 1978. *Education and the brain: The 77th yearbook of the National Society for the Study of Education*. Chicago: The Yearbook Committee and Associated Contributors, University of Chicago Press.

Falvey, M. 1995. *Inclusive and heterogeneous schooling: Assessment, curriculum, and instruction*. Baltimore, MD: Paul H. Brookes.

Feuerstein, R. 1980. *Instrumental Enrichment: An intervention program for cognitive modifiability*. Glenview, IL: Scott-Foresman Lifelong Learning Division.

Flavell, J. H. 1979. Metacognition and cognitive monitoring: A new area of cognitive-development inquiry. *American Psychologist* 34: 906–911.

Fogarty, R. 1991. *The mindful school: How to integrate the curricula*. Palatine, IL: IRI/Skylight Publishing.

————. 2002. *How to integrate the curricula,* 2nd ed. Arlington Heights, IL: SkyLight Professional Development.

————. 1994. *The mindful school: How to teach for metacognitive reflection*. Palatine, IL: IRI/Skylight Training and Publishing.

————. 1996. *Block scheduling: A collection of articles*. Arlington Heights, IL: SkyLight Training and Publishing.

————. 2002. *Brain-compatible classrooms,* 2nd ed. Arlington Heights, IL: SkyLight Training and Publishing, Inc.

Fogarty, R., and J. Bellanca. 1993. *Patterns for thinking, patterns for transfer*. Palatine, IL: IRI/SkyLight Training and Publishing.

Fogarty, R., D. Perkins, and J. Barell. 1992. *The mindful school: How to teach for transfer*. Palatine, IL: IRI/Skylight Training and Publishing.

French, N. 1999. Supervising paraeducators—What every teacher should know. In *CEC Today Online* 6, 2, 1–2.

Frender, G. 1990. *Learning to learn: Strengthening study skills and brain power.* Nashville, TN: Incentive Publications.

Friend, M., and W. D. Bursuck. (Ed). 1999. *Including students with special needs: A practical guide for classroom teacher* (2nd ed.). Boston, MA: Allyn and Bacon.

Fuller, M. L. and G. Olsen. 1998. *Home-school relations: Working successfully with parents and families.* Needham Heights, MA: Allyn and Bacon.

Gardner, H. 1983. *Frames of mind: The theory of multiple intelligences.* New York: Basic Books.

———. 1993. *Multiple intelligences: The theory in practice.* New York: HarperCollins.

Gehrke, N. J. 1993. Explorations of teachers' development of integrative curriculums. In *Integrating the curricula,* ed. R. Fogarty. Arlington Heights, IL: IRI/SkyLight Publishing, Inc.

Gersten, R. 1999. The changing face of bilingual education. *Educational Leadership* 56(7), 41–45.

Giangreco, M.F., Edelman, S.W., Broer, S.M., and Doyle, M.B. 2001. Paraprofessional support of students with disablilities: Literature from the past decade. In *Council for Exceptional Children* 68,1,45–63.

Gibbs, N. 1995. The EQ factor. *Time,* October. 146(14): 60–68.

Glatthorn, A. 1996. *The teacher's portfolio: Fostering and documenting professional development.* Rockport, MA: Proactive Publications.

Glazer, S. M. and C. S. Brown. 1993. *Portfolios and beyond: Collaborative assessment in reading and writing.* Norwood, MA: Christopher-Gordon Publishers.

Glickman, C. D. 2002. *Leadership for learning: How to help teachers succeed.* Alexandria, VA: Association for Supervision and Curriculum Development.

Goleman, D. 1995. *Emotional intelligence: Why it can matter more than IQ.* New York: Bantam Books.

Goodlad, J. I. 1980. How laboratory schools go awry. *UCLA Educator* winter. 21 (2).

———. 1984. *A place called school: Prospects for the future.* New York: McGraw-Hill.

Gordon, S. P., and S. Maxey. 2000. *How to help beginning teachers succeed,* 2nd ed. Alexandria VA: Association for Curriculum and Supervision.

Gould, S. J. 1981. *The mismeasure of man.* New York: Norton.

Guthrie, J., and A. McCann. 1997. Characteristics of classrooms that promote motivations and strategies for learning. In *Reading engagement: Motivating readers through integrated instruction,* ed. J. Guthrie and A. Wigfield, 128–148. Newark, DE: International Reading Association.

Hansen, J. 1992, May. Literacy portfolios: Helping students know themselves. *Educational Leadership* 66–68.

Harmin, M. 1994. *Inspiring active learning: A handbook for teachers.* Alexandria, VA: Association for Supervision and Curriculum Development.

Hart, L. 1983. *Human brain, human learning.* Kent, WA: Books for Educators.

Healy, J. M. 1987. *Your child's growing mind: A guide to learning and brain development from birth to adolescence* (A Main Street Book). New York: Doubleday.

———. 1990. *Endangered minds.* New York: Touchstone/Simon and Schuster.

Hills, J. R. 1991, March. Apathy concerning grading and testing. *Phi Delta Kappan* pp. 540–545.

Isaacson, R. L. 1982. *Limbic system,* 2nd ed. New York: Plenum Press.

Jacobs, H. H. (Ed.). 1990. *Interdisciplinary curriculum: Design and implementation.* Alexandria, VA: Association for Supervision and Curriculum Development.

———. 1991a. On interdisciplinary curriculum: A conversation with Heidi Hayes Jacobs. *Educational Leadership* 49(2): 24–26.

———. 1991b. Planning for curriculum integration. *Educational Leadership* 49(2): 27–28.

———. 1997. *Mapping the big picture.* Alexandria, VA: Association for Supervision and Curriculum Development.

Jensen, E. 1996. *Completing the puzzle: A brain-based approach to learning.* Del Mar, CA: Turning Point Publishing.

———. 2000. *Brain based learning.* Del Mar, CA: Turning Point Publishing.

Johnson, R., and D. Johnson. 1982. Cooperation in learning: Ignored but powerful. *Lyceum,* October.

Johnson, D. W., and R. Johnson. 1974. Instructional goal structure: Cooperative, competitive, or individualistic. *Review of Educational Research* 44, 213-240.

Johnson, N. J., and L. M. Rose. 1997. *Portfolios: Clarifying, classifying, and enhancing.* Lancaster: Basil Technomic Publishing Company.

Jones, V.F., and L.S. Jones. 1998. Comprehensive classroom management: Creating communities of support and solving problems. Needham, MA: Allyn and Bacon.

Jorgensen, C. M. 1998. Restructuring high schools for all students: Taking inclusion to the next level. Baltimore, MD: Paul H. Brookes Publishing.

Joyce, B. R., M. Weil, and E. Calhoun. 2001. *Models of teaching,* 6th ed. Boston: Allyn and Bacon.

Kovalik, S. 1993. *ITI: The model: Integrated thematic instruction.* Oak Creek, AZ: Books for Educators.

Krogness, M. M. 1991. A question of values. *English Journal* 80(6), 28–33.

La Brecque, R.J. 1998. *Effective department and team leaders: A practical guide.* Norwood, MA: Christopher-Gordon Publishers.

Lazear, D. 1991. *Seven ways of teaching: The artistry of teaching with multiple intelligences*. Palatine, IL: IRI/Skylight Publishing, Inc.

———. 1999. *Eight ways of teaching: The artistry of teaching with multiple intelligences*. Arlington Heights, IL: SkyLight Training and Publishing, Inc.

Lieberman, A., ed. 1988. *Building a professional culture in school*. New York: Teachers College Press.

Leu, D. J., D. Diadiun Jr., and K. R. Leu. 1999. *Teaching with the internet: Lessons from the classroom*. Norwood, MA: Christopher- Gordon Publishers.

Lewis, A. 1993. Getting unstuck: Curriculum as a tool of reform. In *Integrating the Curricula*, ed. R. Fogarty, 49–60. Arlington Heights, IL: IRI/SkyLight Publishing, Inc.

Lindeman, B. 2001. Reaching out to immigrant parents. In *Educational Leadership* 58,6, 62–66.

Lipsky, D. K., and A. Gartner. 1997. *Inclusion and school reform: Transforming America's classrooms*. Baltimore, MD: Paul H. Brookes Publishing.

Lounsbury, J. H. (Ed.). 1992. *Connecting curriculum through inter-disciplinary instruction*. Columbus, OH: National Middle School Association.

Lozanov, G. 1978. *Suggestology and outlines of suggestology*. New York: Gordon and Breach.

Luria, A. 1976. *Working brain: An introduction to neuro-psychology*. New York: Gordon and Breach.

MacLean, P. D. 1969. New trends in man's evolution. In A triune concept of the brain and behavior. Paper presented at Queen's University, Ontario, Canada. Ann Arbor, MI: Books on Demand, University Microfilms International.

———. 1978. A mind of three minds: Educating the triune brain. In *Education and the brain*, edited by Jeanne Chall and Allan Mirsky. Chicago: University of Chicago Press.

Marcus, S. A., and P. McDonald. 1990. *Tools for the cooperative classroom*. Palatine, IL: Skylight.

Masterpoli, M.A., and T. E. Scruggs. 2000. *The inclusive classroom: Strategies for effective instruction*. Upper Saddle River, NJ: Merrill.

Mayer, J. D., and P. Salovey. 1993. The intelligence of emotional intelligence. *Intelligence*. 17(4): 422–433.

McVay, P. 1998. Paraprofessionals in the classroom: What role do they play? In *Disability Solutions* 3, 1, 1–4.

Meek, A. 1999. *Communicating with the public: A guide for school leaders*. Alexandria VA: Association for Supervision and Curriculum Development.

Merideth, E. M. 2000. *Leadership strategies for teachers*. Arlington Heights, IL: SkyLight Professional Development.

Midwood, D., K. O'Connor, and M. Simpson. 1993. *Assess for success: Assessment, evaluation and reporting for successful learning*. Toronto, ON: Ontario Secondary School Teacher's Federation.

Mills-Courts, K., and M. R. Amiran. 1991. Metacognition and the use of portfolios. In P. Belanoff and M. Dickson, eds. *Portfolios: Process and product* (pp. 101–111). Portsmouth, NH: Boynton and Cook Publishers.

Morgan, J. and Ashbaker, B.Y. 2001. *A teacher's guide to working with paraeducators and other classroom aides*. Alexandria, VA: Association for Supervision and Curriculum Development.

Moye, V. 1997. *Conditions that support transfer for change*. Arlington Heights, IL: IRI/SkyLight Training and Publishing.

O'Keefe, J., and L. Nadel. 1973. The hippocampal syndrome: Persistence or something more? Conference on Partial Reinforcement and Persistence Phenomena. Sussex, United Kingdom.

———. 1974. Maps in the brain. *New Scientist*, June 27.

———. 1975. The psychology of space. Invited address to the Canadian Psychological Association, Quebec City, Canada.

———. 1978. *The hippocampus as a cognitive map*. Oxford, England: Clarendon Press.

———. 1979. Precís of O'Keefe and Nadel's The hippocampus as a cognitive map, and author's response to commentaries. *The Behavioral and Brain Sciences*. 2: 487–534.

Ornstein, R., and D. Sobel. 1987. *The healing brain: Breakthrough discoveries about how the brain keeps us healthy*. New York: Simon and Schuster.

Palincsar, A. S., and A. Brown. 1984. Reciprocal teaching of comprehension-fostering and comprehension-monitoring activities. *Cognition and Instruction*. 1 (2): 117–175.

Paulson, F. L., P. R. Paulson, and C. A. Meyer. 1991, February. What makes a portfolio a portfolio? *Educational Leadership* 60–63.

Perkins, D. N. 1986. *Knowledge as design*. Hillsdale, NJ: Lawrence Erlbaum Associates.

———. ed. 1995. *Outsmarting IQ: The emerging science of learnable intelligence*. New York: Free Press.

Perkins, D. N., and G. Salomon. 1988. Teaching for transfer. *Educational Leadership* 46(1): 22–32.

———. 1989. Are cognitive skills context bound? *Educational Researcher* 18(1): 16–25.

Piaget, J. 1970. Piaget's theory. In *Carmichael's manual of child psychology*, edited by P. Mussen. New York: Wiley.

Popham, W. J. 1999. *Classroom assessment: What teachers need to know*, 2nd ed. Boston: Allyn and Bacon.

Portner, H. 2001. *Training mentors is not enough: Everything else schools and districts need to do*. Thousand Oaks, CA: Corwin Press.

Power-deFur, L. S., and Orelove, F. P. 1997. *Inclusive education: Practical implementation of the least restrictive environment*. Gaithersburg, MD: Aspen Publishers.

Purves, A. C., J. A. Quattrini, and C. I. Sullivan. 1995. *Creating the writing portfolio: A guide to students*. Lincolnwood, IL: NTC Publishing Group.

Relan, A., and R. Kimpston. 1993. Curriculum integration: A critical analysis of practical and conceptual issues. In *Integrating the Curricula*, ed. R. Fogarty, 31–47. Arlington Heights, IL: IRI/SkyLight Publishing, Inc.

Renck-Jalongo, M. 1991. *Creating learning communities: The role of the teacher in the 21st century*. Bloomington IN: National Educational Service.

Rippa, S. A. 1988. *Education in a free society*. New York: Longman.

Riveria-Pedrotty, D., and Smith-Deutsch, D. 1997. *Teaching students with learning and behavior problems*, 3rd ed. Needham, MA: Allyn and Bacon.

Roberts-Presson, M. 2001. *Your mentor: A practical guide for first-year teachers in grades 1–3*. Thousand Oaks, CA: Corwin Press.

Rolheiser, C., B. Bower, and L. Stevahn. 2000. *The portfolio organizer: Succeeding with portfolios in your classroom*. Alexandria, VA: Association for Supervision and Curriculum Development.

Rosenblum-Lowden, R. 2000. *You have to go to school—You're the teacher!*, 2nd ed. Thousand Oaks, CA: Corwin Press.

Sapon-Shevin, M. 1991. Cooperative learning in inclusive classrooms: Learning to become a community. *Cooperative Learning* 12(1), 8–9.

Shaklee, B. D., N. E. Barbour, R. Ambrose, and S. J. Hansford. 1997. *Designing and using portfolios*. Boston: Allyn and Bacon.

Shanahan, T. 1997. Reading-writing relationships, thematic units, inquiry learning. . . In pursuit of effective integrated literacy instruction. *Reading Teacher*. 51(1): 12–19.

Shelton, C.F., and A. B. Pollingue. 2000. *The exceptional teacher's handbook: The first-year special education teacher's guide for success*. Thousand Oaks, CA: Corwin Press.

Slavin, R. E. 1977. Classroom reward structure: An analytic and practical review. *Review of Educational Research* 47:4.

Smith, D.D., and Luckasson, R. 1995. *Introduction to special education—Teaching in an age of challenge*, 2nd ed. Boston: Allyn and Bacon.

Solmon, L. C., and K. Firetag. 2002, March. The road to teacher quality. *Education Week* 21(27): 48.

Sousa, D. 1995. *How the brain learns: A classroom teacher's guide*. Reston, VA: National Association of Secondary Schools.

Spear-Swerling, L., and R. J. Sternberg. 1998. Curing our 'epidemic' of learning disablilities. *Phi Delta Kappan* 81(5), 397–401.

Sprenger, M. 1999. *Learning and memory: The brain in action*. Alexandria, VA: Association for Supervision and Curriculum Development.

Sternberg, R. J. 1986. *Intelligence applied: Understanding and increasing your intellectual skills*. New York: Harcourt Brace Jovanovich.

Stiggins, R. J. 1985, October. Improving assessment where it means the most: In the classroom. *Educational Leadership* pp. 69–74.

———. 1994. *Student-centered classroom assessment*. New York: MacMillan College Publishing Co.

Swartz, R. J., and D. N. Perkins. 1989. *Teaching thinking: Issues and approaches*. Pacific Grove, CA: Midwest Publications.

Sylwester, R. 1995. *A celebration of neurons: An educator's guide to the human brain*. Alexandria, VA: Association for Supervision and Curriculum Development.

Tateyama-Sniezek, K. 1990. Cooperative learning: Does it improve the academic achievement of student with handicaps? *Exceptional Children* 56(5), 426–437.

Tomlinson, C. 1999. *The differentiated classroom*. Alexandria, VA: Association for Supervision and Curriculum Development.

Traub, J. 1999. The bilingual barrier. *The New York Times Magazine* 31, 32.

Vars, G. F. 1993. *Interdisciplinary teaching: Why and how*. Columbus, OH: National Middle School Association.

Vaughn, S., C. S. Bos, and J. S. Schumm. 2000. *Teaching exceptional, diverse and at-risk students in the general education classroom*, 2nd ed. Boston: Allyn and Bacon.

Vavrus, L. 1990, August. Put portfolios to the test. *Instructor* 48–53.

Vygotsky, L. S. 1978. *Mind in society: The development of higher psychological process*. Cambridge, MA: Harvard University Press.

Wiggins, G. 1989, April. Teaching to the (authentic) test. *Educational Leadership* pp. 121–127.

Withrow, F., H. Long, and G. Marx. 1999. *Preparing schools and school systems for the 21st century*. Arlington, VA: American Association of School Administrators.

Wolf, D. 1989, April. Portfolio assessment: Sampling student work. *Educational Leadership* 35–39.

Wolf, K. 1996. Developing an effective teaching portfolio. *Educational Leadership* 53 (6): 34–34.

Wolfe, P. 1996. A staff developer's guide to the brain (2 audiotapes). Front Royal, VA: National Cassette Services.

———. 2001. *Brain matters: Translating brain research into classroom practice*. Alexandria, VA: Association for Supervision and Curriculum Development.

Wolfgang, C. 1999. *Solving discipline problems*. Needham Heights, MA: Allyn and Bacon.

Zemelman, S., H. Daniels, and A. Hyde. 1993. *Best practice: New standards for teaching and learning in America's schools*. Portsmouth, NH: Heinemann.

Zionts, P. (Ed.). 1997. *Inclusion strategies for students with learning and behavior problems: Perspectives, experiences, and best practices*. Austin, TX: Pro-Ed.

Index

lesson planning and monitoring student
progress, 180–183
positive learning environment creation,
179–180
review needs and goals in, 174–178
schedules (routines) for, 179
Special needs students. *See also* Paraprofessionals;
Special education
inclusion movement and, 162–163
modifications of teacher-made tests for, 128
Splinter questions. *See* Research questions, related
Staff development. *See* Professional development
Stakeholders
in learning community, 213
parents and community members as, 163
Standardized tests, compared to teacher-made tests,
124
Standards
assessments and, 119–120
in calendar curriculum map (integrated
instruction), 40
in integrated instruction, 36
parent/community member involvement with
state, 200–201
Standards portfolios, 143, 181
Starting Process of Professional
Development–Examples (Blackline), 238
State induction programs, Web sites, 274
State level, portfolio assessment at, 181
State standards, parent/community member involve-
ment with, 200–201
Stem questions, in student portfolio reflection
process, 152
Stems, reflective, 246
Sticky note reflections, professional development
and, 249
Strategies to Achieve Student Goals (Blackline), 193
Structuring interaction, teaching WITH thinking
and, 16–19
Student Daily Schedule (Blackline), 191
Student goal sheets, 177, 181, 182, 193, 194
Student Needs and Goals
Blackline, 189
Sample Overview, 177
Student portfolios. *See* Portfolios (student)
Student progress
monitoring and recording, 180–181
reports, 205–206
Students
reflection by, 154
selection process for portfolios and, 148
signals to gain attention of, 4

teaching other students from other grade levels,
180
Suburban school district, creating collaborative
community relationships in, 199–200
Support staff, in learning community, 195
Survival mode, of novice teachers, 226

Task groups, in cooperative learning, 97–98
Teacher(s). *See also* Beginning teachers; Mentor(s);
New teachers
attributes of effective, 227
relationships with parents, 196
responsibility in inclusive classroom, 169–170
role in cooperative learning, 105
student portfolio selection process and, 148
support for, Web sites, 275
and technology, Web sites for, 269–270
Teacher-centered classroom, xi
Teacher development. *See* Professional development
entries; Professional growth entries
Teacher-made tests, 119, 123–139
adjustments in, 126
Big Ten Teacher-Made Test Checklist, The
(Blackline), 137
compared to standardized tests, 125
described, 123
designing better tests, 128–129
Examples (Blackline), 135
formats for, 123
Gardner's theory of multiple intelligences and,
126
guidelines for, 129, 130
learning modalities and, 127–128
learning styles and, 127
misconceptions about objective tests, 131–133
need for, 125–126
objective evaluation and, 130–131
objective-style questions for, 130, 132
as part of assessment, 126
problems with, 124–125
questioning techniques and Three-Story
Intellect, 133, 134
Teacher-Made Tests Reflection Page
(Blackline), 139
Three-Story Intellect Verbs Review (Blackline),
138
Teacher-Made Tests–Example (Blackline), 135
Teacher-Made Tests Reflection Page (Blackline),
139
Teaching
definitions of, 232–233
developing philosophy of, 227

Excerpts included in
Mentoring Guidebook Level 2: Exploring Teaching Strategies are taken from the following SkyLight titles.

Robin Fogarty

Brain-Compatible Classrooms
SECOND EDITION

Janice Skowron

Powerful Lesson Planning Models: The Art of 1,000 Decisions

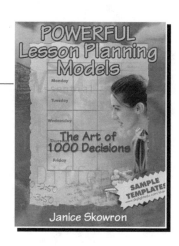

Robin Fogarty and Judy Stoehr

Integrating Curricula with Mutliple Intelligences: Teams, Themes & Threads

James Bellanca
and Robin Fogarty

**Blueprints for Achievement in
the Cooperative Classroom,**
THIRD EDITION

Kay Burke

**How to Assess
Authentic Learning,**
THIRD EDITION

Kay Burke

**Designing Professional
Portfolios for Change**

Barry Sweeny

**Leading the Teacher Induction
and Mentoring Program**

**For more information on these titles, videotapes, and conferences
please visit SkyLight's Web site at**

www.skylightedu.com